Fathering
Your School-Age
Child

A Dad's Guide to
the Wonder Years:
3 to 9

For Father's Day, I'm giving my dad an hour of free tech support.

Fathering Your School-Age Child

A Dad's Guide to
the Wonder Years:
3 to 9

Armin A. Brott

Abbeville Press Publishers
New York • London

Editor: Susan Costello
Copyeditor: Miranda Ottewell
Production Editor: Erin Dress
Production Manager: Louise Kurtz
Designer: Misha Beletsky, based on design by Celia Fuller

First edition
10 9 8 7 6 5 4 3 2 1

For cartoon credits, see page 248.

Paperback:
ISBN-13: 978-0-7892-0924-5
ISBN-10: 0-7892-0924-1
Hardcover:
ISBN-13: 978-0-7892-0923-8
ISBN-10: 0-7892-0923-3

Library of Congress Cataloging-in-Publication Data

Brott, Armin A.
   Fathering your school-age child : a dad's guide to the wonder years: 3-9 /
by Armin A. Brott.—1st ed.
      p. cm.
   Includes bibliographical references and index.
   ISBN 978-0-7892-0924-5 (pbk. : alk. paper)—ISBN 978-0-7892-0923-8
(hardcover)
1. Child development. 2. Father and child. I. Title.

   HQ767.9.B76 2007
   649'.123—dc22
                                        2007004986

For bulk and premium sales and for text adoption procedures, write to Customer Service Manager, Abbeville Press, 137 Varick Street, New York, NY 10013, or call 1-800-ARTBOOK.

Visit Abbeville Press online at www.abbeville.com.

Contents

For the Goose, Roo Pie, and the Pokester, who never let me forget that there are no easy answers and there's always more to learn. And to Liz, who makes the second time around more fun than the first.

Acknowledgments

As Isaac Newton once wrote, "If I have seen further it is by standing upon the shoulders of giants." For me, there are two groups of Goliaths who knowingly and unknowingly made this book and much of my other fatherhood work possible. First, the pioneering researchers who opened my eyes: Henry Biller, Phil and Carolyn Cowan, Pamela Jordan, Michael Lamb, Rob Palkovitz, Glen Palm, Ross Parke, Kyle Pruett, Norma Radin, and John Snarey. Then there are the hundreds and hundreds of dads I've interviewed over the years, who bravely and openly shared their insights, thoughts, fears, worries, advice, and wisdom.

But all that information and inspiration wouldn't have meant much if weren't for the amazing number of people who helped transform it into a book. Bob Abrams, Susan Costello, and Jackie Decter have been the godparents to the New Father series since it was in its infancy; Celia Fuller and Misha Beletsky created the design; Miranda Ottewell copyedited the text; Erin Dress was the production editor; and Louise Kurtz shepherded the production. Jim Levine brought us all together; Sally Ann Berk helped with the research; Kenny Shea Dinkin shared his wisdom on all things tech; Susan Raab made some terrific book suggestions; my parents, Gene and June Brott, read some of the early drafts, babysat, forgave me for the blueberry muffins, and have been a constant source of support. And speaking of support, no one could possibly have been more supportive and understanding than my wonderful wife, Liz, who keeps me focused on what's really important.

It's just a correction. The fundamentals are still good.

Introduction

The preschool and school years are a time of tremendous change—for your child and for you. Over the course of just a few years she'll go from having a vocabulary of a few hundred words to knowing more than you do; from sitting quietly on your lap while you read stories to reading by herself; from being completely dependent on you to scheduling her own play dates and managing her own social life; from being the center of the universe to being just another star. Along the way, you'll catch glimpses—some wonderful, others frightening— of the adult your child is on her way to becoming. All in all, it's a wonderful time, which is why we're referring to the years from three to nine as The Wonder Years.

Those years are full of change for you too. During your child's preschool years the most significant interactions you'll have with her are going to be physical, through play. At the same time, though, this is the stage of both of your lives when your relationship with each other will take shape and solidify. It's also a time when you'll be figuring out exactly what your priorities are, what kind of dad you want to be, and how on earth you're going to accomplish your life goals.

As your child moves into the school years, you'll continue to evolve. You may find yourself reevaluating your work-family balance, doing whatever you can to spend more time with your child because you know that the days of her cuddling up on your lap for a story are numbered. At the same time you'll probably devote a lot of time thinking about the world your child is entering and looking for ways to change it, to make it safer and healthier.

You'll also spend some time pondering about how being a father has shaped your life . . . the bad back you have from spending years as a living piece of playground equipment, the lack of sex, having less disposable income because it's all been spent on tuition, the minivan you'd have never, ever set foot into a few years ago. And let's not forget about the good stuff: the incredible joy at watching your child grow, the pride you feel at her accomplishments, and the inspiration your child gives you to take better care of yourself. Being a father has made you the man you are today and forever altered your behavior, your priorities, your choices, your attitudes about the world and your place in it, and even where and how you live. In short, being a father has changed *everything*.

Fathering Your School-Age Child is the fourth book in the New Father series, which is devoted to exploring parenthood from the father's perspective, under-standing his experiences, examining the ways fathers and children affect each other's growth and development, and giving men the tools they need to become the fathers they want to be. The first book, *The Expectant Father*, covered preg-nancy and childbirth. The next two volumes, *The New Father: A Dad's Guide to the First Year* and *Fathering Your Toddler: A Dad's Guide to the Second and Third Years*, went from birth through your child's third birthday. *Fathering Your School-Age Child* picks up right there, and continues up until her tenth birthday.

Like the other books in the series, *Fathering Your School-Age Child* is the product of years of ongoing research. I've talked extensively with dozens of leading experts and studied the research and writings of many more. I've inter-viewed literally thousands of fathers—and received e-mails and letters from hundreds more—about their experiences, feelings, and in-the-trenches knowl-edge of what works and what doesn't. And from time to time I've thrown in some of my own experiences as the father of three. It's my hope that giving you access to all this wisdom and experience will leave you far better prepared to meet the challenges of being—and staying—an active, involved father.

How This Book Is Organized

Although your child probably seems like a very big kid—and she is—her rate of growth is way, way down from her early days as an infant. And that's a good thing. Infants put on about a pound and a half and an inch in length every month. By her first birthday, the average baby has tripled her weight and increased her length by 50 percent. If she kept up that pace, by age four she'd weigh in at about 650 pounds and be over eight feet tall. Fortunately, between ages three and ten, your child will get only a couple of inches taller and gain four or five pounds every *year.*

Because of this decreased growth and development, changes in your child's skills and abilities take place over longer periods of time. For that reason, I've divided this book into seven chapters, one for each of the years we cover here. Each of these chapters contains the following sections:

What's Going On with Your Child

In this section I'll briefly explain how your child is developing physically, intellectually, emotionally, and socially. This isn't meant to be a comprehensive look at child development. Instead, I just want you to know what your child is and isn't capable of at any given age. Where your child is developmentally will have a tremendous impact on how you interact with each other. Having reasonable expectations will make it much easier and much more fun to build and maintain a strong relationship.

At this point you're a pretty seasoned dad, and you already know that children develop on very different schedules, and that the range of "normal" development is quite broad. For that reason, I suggest that you consider the time period covered in each chapter as an estimate. Read a chapter ahead of wherever your child is, and one behind. As I wrote in the introduction to *Fathering Your Toddler*, if your child is two chapters ahead of her age, call Oprah. If she's two behind, read the occasional "Developmental Red Flags" sections. And of course, if you're genuinely worried for any reason, don't be shy about calling your pediatrician.

What's Going On with You

There isn't a lot of social support out there for fathers who want to be actively involved, which means that most dads don't have very many people to talk to about parenting feelings and concerns. As a result, far too many fathers end up thinking not only that they're absolutely alone in what they're experiencing but that they're abnormal as well. Chances are, however, that with very few exceptions what you're going through at any particular moment of your fatherhood is fairly similar to what millions of fathers before you have felt and millions more after you will. Just as your children will develop along a more or less predictable path, so will you. And in this section of each chapter, I'll examine what fathers typically go through at that particular time, so you'll be able to monitor your own physical and emotional development. I'll discuss the emotional ups and downs, the joys, the frustrations, the anger, the confusion, the incredible pride, and the confidence that fatherhood brings to all of us. If what you're reading in one chapter doesn't sound like it applies to you, or there are specific issues you want to hear about, feel free to skip around and use the index to find what you're looking for.

AND AS AN EXTRA, ADDED BONUS . . .
Sprinkled throughout the book you'll find sections that deal with the special concerns of older and younger dads, stepfathers, divorced dads, adoptive dads, stay-at-home dads, and military dads, as well as with the traits I believe separate truly strong, involved dads from average dads.

You and Your Child

It always surprises me that so many people—men as well as women—have no idea how much fathers contribute to their children and to their families. So here is the summary. Dads are not just nice-to-haves, they're essential players.

Each of the "You and Your Child" sections is divided into several parts. In the first, "Why Be Involved?" I'll give you age-specific examples of the fantastic benefits of being actively involved in your children's life—benefits to your children, your partner, and yourself. Once you know how critical your role is, I'll move on to the second part of the chapter: the specific tools you'll need to develop and deepen your relationships with your children—even if you can't be there as much as you'd like to.

Besides being very important, these sections are undoubtedly the most fun. I'll talk about age-appropriate ways to play with your child, when and how to use computers and other tech gadgets, online safety, the importance of music, teaching good manners, helping your child make friends, getting kids to do chores, dental hygiene, finding books and films with positive father role models, obesity, learning disabilities, puberty, and much more. Throughout I talk about the differences between boys and girls (and there are plenty of them) and the difference between *fathering* boys or girls. Every one of these sections is completely different and covers age-appropriate material.

Because your child is going to be spending an increasing amount of time in school, I've included a section on education in almost every chapter. This is where I'll talk about why and how you should get involved at your child's school, the dangers of pushing your child too hard, understanding your child's unique learning style, homeschooling, and single-sex schools, among other subjects.

You and Your Partner

Although the focus of this book is mostly on you and your wonder-years-age child, the two of you are still very much part of a family, which includes your partner and any other children you might have. For that reason, I've included separate sections that cover a number of topics that can have a major impact on everyone in your house. We'll talk about your relationship with your partner and how to keep it strong as you face new challenges together, your sex life and how to keep it alive as you get older, the ups and downs of being a stepfather and how to support a stepmother, and even staying involved with your children in case of divorce.

A Note on Terminology

He, She, Girl, Boy, Your Partner, Your Wife

As with the other books in the New Father series, I alternate between "he" and "she" when referring to your child, a chapter at a time. Even-numbered chapters are female, odd chapters are male (largely because with a wife, three daughters, and three female cats in my house, boys are a little odd around here). Except in very specific circumstances whatever's being said about "him" applies equally to "her" and vice versa.

As a general rule, I'll refer to the mother of your children as "your partner." This is *not* any kind of political statement. While I believe that in a perfect world, a marriage would be the best setting in which to raise children, we don't live in a perfect world. And the reality is that not every mother is a wife. Many are girlfriends, lovers, fiancées, domestic partners, and so on. Lots of married parents raise completely screwed-up kids, and many unmarried parents raise delightful, well-adjusted kids. I'll talk about this more in the book, but suffice it to say here that my main concern in writing this book is to help you build a strong relationship with your child and the child's mother. This is not the forum to tell you how to live your life or to debate the sanctity (or lack of sanctity, depending on your perspective) of marriage.

If You're Just Joining Us . . .

Some of the major themes in this book are revisited from time to time, and that's only natural. Issues such as reading, computer technology, education, adapting to changing relationships, learning to let go, and independence crop up again and again over our lifetimes, often with varying degrees of intensity. Each time, though, they're a little different.

. . . And If You're Not . . .

If this is your first New Father book, all of this will be new to you. But if you're a New Father vet, a few very small sections of this book may sound familiar. The reason is that people with children of different ages face these issues (such as selecting the right preschool). And for the sake of readers tuning in, it would have been remiss of me to leave those sections out here just because they've been visited in previous volumes.

Finally, a Note from Our Lawyers

I'm not a pediatrician, financial planner, accountant, or lawyer, nor do I play one on TV (although I do host a radio show). This means that even though all the medical, financial, and legal advice in this book has been reviewed by experts and proven to work by real people (including me, in most cases), you should still check with an appropriate professional before trying it out on yourself and your family.

When trying out any of the recommended games or other activities in this book, safety should always be your number-one concern. Activities—especially any that involve water or small objects—are meant to be done *with* your child, so don't leave her alone. Finally, know your child's limitations and don't push her to do anything she's not developmentally ready for. I've made every effort to ensure that the activities in this book are safe when you or another trusted adult are there to supervise them. However, neither Abbeville Press nor I can be responsible for any unforeseen consequences.

Bye, Bye, Baby

What's Going On with Your Child

Physically

♦ Your child is getting bigger, but not nearly at the same pace as he was as a toddler, so kiss that baby belly good-bye now, because it's not going to be around much longer. Over the course of this year, your three-year-old will grow just two or three inches and put on only five or six pounds. By the time he turns four, he'll have a full set of baby teeth.

♦ By now, your child will be getting an uninterrupted 10–12 hours of sleep at night, except, of course, those nights when you've planned a romantic evening at home. He often wakes up dry, but accidents are still common. By the end of this year, a lot of girls will be toilet-trained. Boys usually take a little longer to get completely out of diapers, but they're on their way too.

♦ He walks and runs like a champ—usually without having to hold his arms out for balance. In fact, he's so good that he can even take corners at full speed. Once he does slow down, you might catch him practicing walking on tiptoe.

♦ He's a good climber and runner, and should be able to jump up and down, as well as hop on one leg. He can kick a ball forward, catch one if it lands on his outstretched arms, and walk up (but not down) stairs alternating feet.

♦ And how 'bout those fine motor skills. Somebody's feeding himself with a spoon, and most of the food is actually getting inside. He brushes his teeth, holds a crayon sort of like we do, traces some (very basic) shapes, and may even take a crack at drawing people—most of whom will bear an uncanny

We've done a lot of important playing here today.

resemblance to Mr. Potato Head. He can build a tower nine or ten blocks high; he's figured out how to screw open jars and bottles (although he has no interest in closing them), and how to turn the pages of a book one at a time.

♦ Sometime around the middle of this year, your child may backslide a little physically. He'll fall down and bump into things more often than he did a few months ago, and those block towers won't be nearly as steady or as high as they were. Not to worry, this will pass as he nears his fourth birthday.

Intellectually

♦ Your child will not stop talking, and you can understand about three-quarters of what he says. He's got an active vocabulary of over 600 words and likes to arrange them in three-to-five-word sentences.

♦ Even with the nonstop chatter, he's still not much of a conversationalist and prefers announcements and demands to give and take.

♦ He loves stories and rhymes, preferably over and over and over and over. The good news is that if you get laryngitis, he's perfectly able to "read" you the book in his own words, using the pictures as a guide.

♦ He's got "now," "soon," and "in a minute" down pretty well, but he's a little fuzzy on more abstract time words such as "tomorrow," "yesterday," and "today." He also understands simple sequences much better than before and can handle two or three steps in a row: we went to the park, then we came home, and then we watched a video.

♦ He associates people with places, which means he may not recognize his favorite pediatrician if you bump into him in line at the grocery store.

♦ He can identify the primary colors and maybe a few others, and counts "one, two, a lot."

♦ He can put together six-piece puzzles and loves the relationship between whole objects and the parts that make them up. But he thinks like Yogi Berra, the famous New York Yankees catcher. When ordering a pizza, Berra was asked how many pieces he wanted it cut into. He replied, "You better cut it into four pieces, because I'm not hungry enough to eat six." If you pour a cup of water into a bowl, and another cup into a tall glass, your child will insist that the glass has more in it. And if you cut one cookie in half and another into four pieces, he'll take the one with four pieces every time.

♦ His imagination is soaring, and his active fantasy life includes dress-up and role-playing. Cross-dressing is still common at this age, as are imaginary friends. These characters serve a very important purpose, helping him try out different behaviors and emotions, and giving him someone to blame if things don't work.

Emotionally/Socially

♦ Whew, those terrible twos are pretty much over. There's a good chance that your three-year-old will do what you ask him to the first or second time instead of the seventeenth or twenty-ninth. He says yes more often than no, and, craving your approval, he's ready and eager to help you with household chores. When he does ignore you or misbehave, he may express some guilt or embarrassment later.

♦ But about halfway through this year, your compliant, cooperative, cheerful little angel may become possessed. He'll be obstinate, ornery, insecure, anxious, and will completely refuse to go along with anything you ask. Fortunately, there's no need to call in an exorcist, as this phase will begin to fade by the end of this year.

♦ He may also spend some time testing your limits, pushing you just to see what kind of reaction he'll get. Luckily, he's got a fairly short attention span, and you can easily distract him, which makes it easier to avoid a crisis.

♦ He's becoming a little less self-centered, changing from "I want" demands to "Let's do" requests.

♦ He's becoming very aware of differences in race and gender, and understands that certain activities are "boy" things and others are "girl" things. Most of the kids he plays with will be of the same sex. Interestingly, though, he may start expressing a preference for the opposite-sex parent.

♦ He enjoys playing *near* other children his own age, but not necessarily with them. And although he'll occasionally give one of his toys to another child, he's still a ways away from mastering the fine art of sharing.

♦ He's discovered the joy of making other people laugh, and can be quite silly at times.

♦ He is learning that other people are real and have real feelings. The tiny seeds of compassion have begun to sprout, and on occasion, he may comfort you if you hurt yourself.

What's Going On with You

Experiencing More Empathy

Over the past decade, I've interviewed several thousand fathers. And one theme that comes up again and again is that fatherhood seems to open all sorts of emotional doors. Many men say that after having children, they were all of a sudden able (or forced) to experience feelings they didn't even know they were capable of, everything from joy and pride and intense love to blinding fury, disgust, and jealousy. And there was one more feeling, which may or may not qualify as an emotion: empathy. Call it the ability to understand and imagine what other people are feeling without them having to tell you.

During the preschool and early school years, most children can't really express their emotions verbally as well as they'd like to, which makes it hard for parents to understand what's going on inside their kids' hearts and minds. Fortunately, you have some conscious or subconscious memories of what *you* felt like when you were a kid, and that makes it possible for you to empathize with your child at least a little bit. For example, if your child is still wetting his bed at night or having accidents during the day, you may be reminded of the shame you felt when you did the same thing at the same age. That kind of empathy can make you a lot more tolerant and patient—not only of your child but of others as well. "To be able to feel what the child feels enlarges the parents' capacity for empathy in other interpersonal relationships," writes the Group for the Advancement of Psychiatry. Doctors who are parents, for example, are better able to empathize with their patients, which is something a lot of parents instinctively feel. Think about when you take your child to the pediatrician. You probably never asked whether he has kids of his own, but don't you really want to know? This isn't to say that childless people shouldn't be allowed to be pediatricians or that pediatricians who have kids are naturally better. That's not true at all. What *is* true, though, is that as we become more empathetic with our children, we naturally want people to be more empathetic with us. (I actually know a pediatric emergency medicine doctor who had to change specialties after becoming a father. He simply couldn't deal emotionally with all the injured children.)

As your child gets older and his vocabulary increases, he'll begin using words to express many of his innermost feelings. To be truly empathetic, you need to really listen to him—not just to the words, but to the emotions behind them. Connecting with your child on that kind of level leads to a far deeper kind of empathy than you experienced before—again, toward both your child and others.

Confronting Your Demons—
and Putting Them to Work for You

Like it or not, who you are as a dad right now has a lot to do with the kind of childhood you had. "To brew up an adult," wrote psychologist Roger Gould, "it seems that some leftover childhood must be mixed in; a little unfinished business from the past periodically intrudes on our adult life, confusing our relationships and disturbing our sense of self."

But your own often-zany childhood doesn't necessarily have to have a negative impact on your fathering. In fact, for most men, it's just the opposite. Most fathers try hard to give their children the positive things they experienced during their own childhood, to spare their children the pain they themselves suffered, and to make sure their children never lack what they did.

Harvard researcher John Snarey found that that men with positive memories of being fathered use their fathers as models. In other words, if a boy's father gave him a good education, was warm and nurturing, and supported his emotional and physical growth, he tends to do the same with his own kids when he becomes a father himself. At the same time, when men have negative memories of their fathers (for example, their dads didn't provide a good education or a stable economic situation, or relied too much on physical punishment), they tend to use their father's shortcomings as an example of exactly what *not* to do and as motivation to do better.

Were you an only child? If you loved being one, you might want only one kid. If you hated it, you might want to have a large family. Similarly, if you're one of nine kids and were continually getting lost in the shuffle, you might want a small family. If your brothers and sisters put together a championship baseball team, you might want to have nine or ten kids of your own. If you never graduated from high school, you might do everything you can do to ensure that your children get the best education possible. If you grew up in a rich family, you might want your kids to learn what it's like to have to earn their own money. And if you grew up in a poor family, you might want to make sure they never have to go without the things that money can buy. Ultimately, having kids isn't exactly a second chance to live your own life. You can, though, boost the odds that the next generation will have it better than you did.

One big question here is whether (and if so, how much) you should talk to your children about these things. If the decision is about how large a family to have, your children probably won't be invited into the discussion. If the issues have to do with education or money, you may talk about them over a number of years. But what about events or experiences that were decidedly negative, or at least murky? When—if ever—would you tell your child that you spent time in jail, whether it was the result of a silly college prank gone wrong or something more serious? Do you tell him about a previous marriage? What about if you killed someone in a car accident? And what if something awful happened to you?

I faced this last dilemma (and I'm still facing it now) with regard to an experience of abuse at the hands of a trusted friend who worked at the YMCA where I spent a lot of time after school lifting weights. It happened more than thirty years ago, but I still sometimes feel a twinge of shame when I think about it. Should I tell my children? If so, when and how? Do I write my experience off as something so rare and unpredictable that there's no possible way to guard against it, or do I teach my children to be wary of everyone—even the people they think are friends? After all, just one error in judgment could forever change—or even end—a life.

At this point in your child's life, the answer is pretty black-and-white: Keep your past to yourself. We'll be talking about this in great detail in the next book in this series. But for now value your child's innocence and help him stay that way.

You and Your Child

Why Be Involved with Your Three-Year-Old?
Simple. Because the more involved you are in raising your children, the better a father you'll be. Being an involved dad is good for everyone: your kids, your partner, and even yourself. Of course, what exactly "being involved" means to you will probably be different from what it means to anyone else. But however you define it, remember that it's a function of both quality time *and* quantity time. Kids whose dads are around but don't spend much time with them end up

doing about as poorly as kids whose fathers aren't around at all. Here are some of the specific benefits to being actively involved with your three-year-old:

♦ The closer and more positive your relationship with your child, the better his friendships with his peers will be.

♦ You're helping your child separate from his mother. "Healthy though dependency on their mother is for children at the beginning of their life," writes fatherhood researcher Kyle Pruett, "they will not experience, let alone practice, their own competence and mastery skills if they do not strike off in search of their own physical and emotional autonomy."

♦ As amazing as it sounds, the quality of your relationship with your three-year-old is a good predictor of his capacity for empathy toward others when he grows up, according to researchers at McGill University in Canada.

♦ Your child will be more curious and a better, more confident problem-solver.

♦ Seeing you participate in child care and other home-related tasks will make your child less likely to have traditional, stereotyped ideas of what women and men are supposed to do. Your involvement at this age is also a good predictor of how involved your children—especially boys—will be when they become parents.

♦ By playing physically with your child, you're giving him a great way to burn off some of his aggression that might otherwise get directed at others.

♦ You'll be a more effective parent. Researcher Mary De Luccie did a study of 177 firstborn boys and girls in an attempt to figure out what made dads get involved and feel satisfied. She found that it was a kind of loop: fathers who were warm and firm with their kids felt they were doing a good job and thought they had good relationships with their kids. That, in turn, made them want to get even more involved. It just keeps getting better and better.

Education

Looking for Preschools—The Pressure's On

By the time their children hit three, most parents have already started thinking about moving their child into a more formal preschool or pre-kindergarten situation. In fact, over 60 percent of children under five are in some kind of non-parental child-care situation. Could be a nanny, a babysitter, your parents or in-laws, a company-sponsored day-care center, or some other arrangement, or even a combination of several of these alternatives.

Unfortunately, getting a child into preschool isn't as simple as it was when we were kids. In a lot of places it's easier to get into an Ivy League college, and

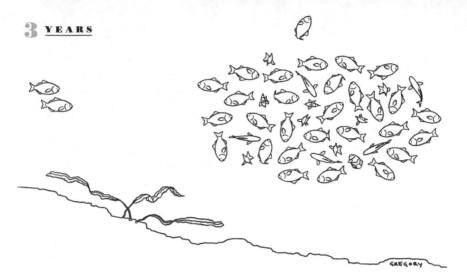

I believe that's a Montessori school.

the application process sometimes starts before the babies are even born. Parents may have to write essays profiling their children, and they hire high-priced consultants to coach the kids for their interviews (including beefing up their scissors-handling and coloring-between-the-lines skills). Favors are called in, bribes are made.

Hopefully you won't need to resort to underhanded tactics. But if you're planning to put your child in preschool and haven't finalized the arrangements, you'd better get started now. On the pages that follow, you'll find some guidelines that will help you narrow your search and find the best program for your child. Because many parents start thinking about preschools when their children are one or two, I covered a lot of this material in the previous book in this series, *Fathering Your Toddler*. If you read that book, feel free to skip ahead to page 30. If not, stick with me.

The Choices

There are literally dozens of preschool opportunities in your community, most of which fall into one of the following categories:

- ♦ **Cooperative**. The parents help out a lot, volunteering in the classroom, organizing activities, creating the curriculum.
- ♦ **Play-based**. Exactly what it sounds like.
- ♦ **Orthodox**. The teachers are trained in a specific method or philosophy of educating young children. This may involve using certain equipment or teaching methods. Montessori is the most common.
- ♦ **Free-form**. The school may include the best (or the worst) of a variety of educational philosophies.

Compared to other child-care options, preschools have some distinct advantages and disadvantages. Here are just a few:

ADVANTAGES	DISADVANTAGES
♦ Most teachers have some experience in early childhood education and development.	♦ Your child may have to be potty-trained before being accepted.
♦ Children learn to socialize and get along with people who aren't in their family.	♦ Your child may not be able to go to school if he is sick or may be sent home if he gets sick at school.
♦ State or local licensing ensures that the school will meet at least minimum health and safety standards.	♦ You may need to make a year-long commitment to a minimum number of days per week.
♦ Usually less expensive than a nanny or other in-home care option.	♦ The child-teacher ratio may be higher than you'd like. This may mean that your child could get less individual attention than with a nanny or other caregiver.
♦ Schools probably have more equipment and a larger play area than you do. They also have a structured program that should expose your child to a wide variety of activities.	
♦ You might meet some other parents who have similarly aged children.	♦ Schools may be closed on holidays or for training days (often called "teacher in-service" days), which could leave you scrambling to find a caregiver.
♦ You don't have to worry about a nanny or sitter getting sick and leaving you without care.	♦ The school's scheduled operating hours may not work well for you, or there could be extra charges for early drop-off or late pickup.

♦ **Academic**. Structured classes in traditional subjects (math, language). Many early childhood development experts think this may be too much, too soon. See the sidebar on page 24 for more on academic pressure on preschoolers.

♦ **Homeschooling**. See pages 32–34 for more.

As with anything to do with education, preschools have become the subject of a lot of controversy. One side cites research that "proves" that preschools are mediocre at best and that too many hours there can lead to behavior problems, jeopardizing children's attachment to their parents and setting them on a path toward a life of delinquency and crime. The other side cites equally respectable research that comes to the opposite conclusion—that kids who

THE END OF CHILDHOOD?

It seems to me that too many people have completely lost track of what preschool is supposed to be about. Consider the following:

- ◆ Sylvan Learning, a major private tutoring company, now has special programs for four-year-olds.
- ◆ Kumon, another leader in the private tutoring biz, created a new division, Junior Kumon, which takes kids as young as two.
- ◆ In Alabama, Arizona, Maryland, and other states, some preschools have eliminated nap time and recess so preschoolers have more time to prepare for tests.
- ◆ In Atlanta, Georgia, and several other cities, new schools are being built without playgrounds. Apparently all that mindless fooling around during recess was getting in the way of the kids' academic performance.

According to some studies, pushing three- and four-year-olds in this way may have some academic benefits. But they come at a pretty high cost in terms of emotional development. Kathy Hirsh-Pasek and a number of other researchers have found that children in highly academic preschools exhibited more stress and anxiety and had more behavior problems than kids in "child-initiated" (a.k.a. more play-oriented) programs. They also scored lower on tests of creative thinking and originality, and had lower verbal skills than those in child-initiated programs. So as you're considering preschool options for your child, try to put yourself into his size one shoes. There's definitely a place for academics, but make sure he's got plenty of opportunity to play and be a kid for a while longer.

enter preschool as toddlers are more self-reliant and confident and do better in school. The contradictions are enough to drive you nuts.

Having looked at dozens of studies on the short- and long-term effects of preschool, I've reached a few conclusions:

- ◆ There's a big difference between causation and correlation. And family problems such as stress and insufficient income cause at least as many difficulties as full-time day care does. In other words, if you and your partner really need to work full time, reducing your (or her) hours at work so one of you can take on more child care could cause financial strain and tension at home that would have a negative impact on your child.
- ◆ Your child will do best in a preschool that is safe and stimulating, that meshes well with his learning style, where child-adult ratios are low, and

where the staff is experienced and educated. Yes, some preschools out there are bad. But you don't have to send your child there. If you know what to look for and what questions to ask, you can ensure a loving, caring learning environment for your child.

WHAT TO CONSIDER WHEN CONSIDERING PRESCHOOLS

Perhaps the most important factor is your child's temperament and how it meshes with what the school has to offer (see the chart on pages 26–27). Another important factor is stability—particularly that of the children. "In child-care settings, the availability of a stable group of age-mates results in more complex, coordinated play," say researchers Barbara and Philip Newman. "Children who have had many changes in their child-care arrangements are less likely to engage in complex social pretend play."

General Guidelines

Because finding the right preschool is the first big decision you'll have to make about your child's education, it may take a while, but don't give up until you've got exactly what you were looking for or have come as close as you possibly can. At a minimum, the day-care center you choose for your child should comply with your state's rules and regulations. But standards vary wildly from state to state, so licensing and accreditation are not necessarily the guarantees of quality that they ought to be. On the national level, however, the National Association for the Education of Young Children (NAEYC) accredits programs that meet their extremely high standards, and you can get referrals to accredited providers in your area at their Web site, www.naeyc.org. Another great source of high-quality referrals is Child Care Aware (www.childcareaware.org or 800-424-2246).

But accreditation and assurances of quality aren't all there is. You should also keep the following general guidelines in mind (some of which were suggested by the NAEYC, Child Care Aware, and the American Academy of Pediatrics):

RATIOS

♦ The younger the kids allowed in the preschool, the lower the child-teacher ratio should be. In a typical preschool, kids' ages range from two and a half to five. Overall, there should be no more than seven kids to each adult caregiver, and the total size of the group (not including the teachers) shouldn't exceed twenty.

TEMPERAMENT AND YOUR PRESCHOOLER

TRAIT	SPECIAL CONSIDERATIONS
If your child's energy level is high . . .	♦ He'll need lots of room to run around, plenty of indoor activities for rainy days, various ways to burn off excess energy. He will, however, need some moderately structured activities. Look for a program that has many kids his age or older: he'll admire their skills and want to emulate them. And make sure the teachers' energy level is at least as high as your child's.
If your child tends to be low-energy . . .	♦ He needs a quieter, smaller setting, and small groups.
If your child is in the middle energy-level-wise (and especially if he takes a little extra time to warm up to new situations) . . .	♦ He'll probably stick to the sidelines for a few days, watching and learning. He'll jump in after about a week. He likes more structure and predictability, and doesn't do well in large preschools, especially if there are a lot of more active kids his age—they can be frightening.
If your child is very sensitive to light, noise, and activity . . .	♦ Look for a fairly calm, subdued, relaxed environment. Lots of noise, colors, and activity can frighten your child.

NUTRITION AND HEALTH

♦ No smoking on the premises.

♦ Proof of immunization required for each child.

♦ If the school provides meals and/or snacks, they should be varied, wholesome, and nutritious. Menus should be available in advance.

♦ Rest and nap times should be scheduled, and each child should have a clean, individual place to sleep. There should also be special quiet activities for kids who don't nap.

♦ Teachers should wear disposable gloves and clean their hands with soap and water or alcohol gel whenever changing diapers. They should also

TRAIT	SPECIAL CONSIDERATIONS
If your child is highly distractible and has a short attention span . . .	♦ He'll need a constantly changing array of things to do and play with. Look for a staff that is large enough so that a teacher can spend extra time with your child to expose him to new things.
If your child craves routines and does everything at the same time every day . . .	♦ He'll need a regular schedule, regular meal and nap times, and so forth.
If your child's routines are all over the place . . .	♦ He doesn't need much in the way of scheduling, but should have some anyway.
If your child takes a long time to adapt to new situations . . .	♦ Avoid schools with rigid schedules and highly structured activities. Also avoid unstructured schools. Look for teachers who will make a special effort to involve your child and introduce him to new materials slowly. Make sure you can stay with your child for a few minutes each morning (for at least the first week or so) to help ease his transition.
If your child tends to be loud, intense, theatrical . . .	♦ He may occasionally bite or hit other children. This will fade as he becomes more articulate. He may be upset when you drop him off at school and just as upset when you come to pick him up.

wash their hands after helping a child go to the bathroom and before touching food.

♦ Parents should be notified immediately of any accident or contagious illness, and there should be a clear policy for what to do (isolation, for starters) with kids who get sick while at school.

♦ Teachers should give medication to children only with a parent's written permission.

♦ Emergency numbers should be clearly posted near a phone.

♦ At least one teacher (but all would be better) should have up-to-date first aid and CPR certifications.

GENERAL CLEANLINESS

♦ Hot running water, soap, alcohol gel, and paper towels should be available—at kid level—and should be used after going to the bathroom and before all meals and snacks.

♦ The entire area—kitchen, tabletops, floors, sleep areas—should be clean. All garbage cans, diaper pails, and bathrooms should be cleaned thoroughly and disinfected regularly.

SAFETY

♦ The facility should be licensed by your state.

♦ Outlets, heaters, and radiators should be covered.

♦ Equipment should be up-to-date and meet current safety codes.

♦ Cleaning fluids, medicines, and any other potentially dangerous substances should be kept in places inaccessible to the children.

♦ There should be an emergency plan, including regular fire drills. Fire extinguishers should be available as required.

♦ The school should have a plan for dealing with violent children. While some hitting, pushing, and biting is pretty normal for kids this age, anything more serious (stabbing, hitting with large objects, or repeated, unprovoked attacks) is not.

♦ Children should not be allowed to ride in any moving vehicle without a properly installed car seat.

♦ Children should be adequately supervised on all field trips—even if it's only a nature walk around the block.

♦ Children should not be released to any adult whose name is not on a written list provided by you and your partner.

♦ Outdoor play areas should be carefully supervised.

♦ Outdoor areas should be safe from animal contamination (for example, the sandbox should be tightly covered).

PROGRAM

♦ The school's program and philosophy should be a good match to what you want and what your child needs. If you have a child with special needs that can't be accommodated at a mainstream preschool, contact the National Dissemination Center for Children with Disabilities, a wonderful source of referrals and resources, at 800-695-0285 or www.nichcy.org.

♦ To the extent possible, substitute teachers should be familiar to the kids.

♦ Children should have daily opportunities to participate in a variety of active

He goes to a real party preschool.

and quiet activities, including free play, age-appropriate academics, art, music, and group and individual play.

♦ Children should have adequate time to play outside every day, weather permitting. There should be plenty of space for active, physical play, such as climbing, running, and jumping.

♦ Indoor areas must be large enough to accommodate all the kids at one time. The area should be well organized so kids know where things go and what happens where. There should be a wide variety of age-appropriate toys, books, and materials. And there should be more than one of each toy so that the kids don't have to wait in long lines to play.

♦ Parents should be welcome at any time, without advance notice. When you visit, pay attention to how the children behave. If they basically ignore you, that's good news: it means that they're involved and interested in what

A FEW PRESCHOOL RED FLAGS

As far as I'm concerned, any school that doesn't satisfy all the qualifications listed on these pages should be viewed with suspicion. Beyond that, though, here are a few things that should make you take a prospective preschool off your list completely and run the other way.

◆ Parents are not allowed to drop in unannounced. You need to call before visiting or coming to pick up your child.

◆ Your child is unhappy or scared after more than a few months.

◆ The staff seems to change every day.

◆ The staff ignores any of your concerns.

◆ Your child reports being hit or mistreated, or you hear similar reports from other parents. Check this one out thoroughly, though. Kids have been known to fabricate stories. And others may jump on board if they see that it's a good way to attract attention.

they're doing. If they come running over, that could mean that they aren't being given activities that are stimulating enough.

◆ Overall, the preschool should be a place you wish you could have gone to when you were a kid.

◆ If you need child care but can't afford it, check out Head Start (www.headstartinfo.org) or Even Start (www.evenstart.org).

STAFF

◆ Ideally, should have completed some college-level work in early childhood education and child development.

◆ Should seem to genuinely care for the children.

◆ Should be available to answer the children's questions and get down to their level when speaking with them.

◆ Should give you regular reports on how and what your child is doing.

ACING THE INTERVIEW

Many preschools—especially ones that are tough to get into—insist on doing pre-admissions interviews with prospective students. In most cases, these interviews are designed to get a rough idea of the child's physical, social, and emotional development and his ability to get along with others. Unfortunately, far too many parents turn what should essentially be a relaxed playdate into a traumatic ordeal for everyone concerned.

It's important to understand that even though your child is the one being

B. Smaller

He doesn't have to worry about his preschool placement—
he interviews well.

"interviewed," you're being evaluated as well. Hopefully, whoever's doing the interview has enough experience to know that your normally brilliant, well-behaved, articulate, outgoing child probably won't be at his best. That's normal. Getting down on your hands and knees and helping ease your child into a new situation is fine. But if you stand over his shoulder and tell him what to say and do and think and what not to, or you chastise him for not sharing or saying "thank you" or covering his mouth when he sneezes, or you continually act angry or embarrassed and tell the interviewer that "he's not usually this way," you're the one who's going to look bad, not your child.

So what can you do to help? Two things:

♦ **Relax.** If you find yourself prepping your child for the interview by trying to get him to memorize algebraic equations and four syllable words, stop now. He'll know something's up and will be even more nervous on the big day than he would have been otherwise.

♦ **Consider leaving mom at home.** One of the interesting differences between fathers and mothers is that dads are constantly preparing our children for the outside world. We generally encourage and support their independence more than moms, and we tend to be less tolerant of clinginess than moms are. As a result, there's a good chance that your child will feel more comfortable running off and playing with other kids, participating in activities, and even playing by himself if you bring him to the interview than if his mother does.

Homeschooling: Not for the Faint of Heart

Over two million children in the United States are being taught at home, and that number is growing every year. But watch out for the politics: the radical pro-homeschool crowd will tell you that homeschooled kids are smarter, faster, taller, and more beautiful than non-homeschooled kids. And the equally radical anti-homeschool people insist that homeschooled kids grow up to be antisocial nut cases, unable to function in polite society. The reality is that many homeschooled kids do very well on standardized tests, and many of them get into top colleges. But homeschooling isn't for everyone. Here are some of the pros and cons you should consider before making your decision.

ADVANTAGES

- **You're in charge**. You know exactly what your child is learning and when. You set the pace, the schedule, and the content. Nobody else's agendas to worry about. If you want to study geography, hop in the car and take a camping trip. Oceanography? Go to the beach and explore the tide-pools. Do you want your child to have sex ed classes? The decision is 100 percent yours. Are there certain values you want to instill? Do you want to take family vacations sometime other than the summer? It's all up to you.
- **Individualized instruction**. You can tailor your lessons to meet your child's exact needs and learning style. Some kids learn best by listening to lectures, others by picking up things up and handling them. If your child's a budding math genius, go ahead and teach him calculus. If he needs a little extra time on something, take as much as you need.
- **Cost**. Homeschooling can be as cheap or expensive as you'd like. Overall, though, it'll be more expensive than public school but less than private.
- **Fewer worries**. You don't have to worry about the quality of the schools, the teachers, or the programs. And you don't have to worry about your child getting bullied or falling in with the wrong crowd.
- **Less wasted time**. Kids in preschool and elementary school spend a huge percentage of their day standing in line, waiting for other kids to finish up,

waiting while the teacher explains something, waiting while the teacher deals with discipline problems. You'll be able to fit a whole day's worth of learning into just a few hours.

♦ **Better-rested children**. No more dragging kids out of bed before the sun comes up. No rushing around trying to get the kids dressed, pack their lunches, and bustle them out the door to the car or school bus.

DISADVANTAGES

♦ **Social life**. Homeschooling isn't nearly as isolating as some might make it out to be. You can join a co-op or other network of homeschoolers, or sometimes parents who are experts in certain areas organize workshops or seminars. But there's a difference between going on field trips and getting together with other kids once or twice a week and having to interact *every day* with cliques, bullies, best friends, enemies, peer pressure, and more. Similarly, homeschooled children have fewer opportunities to deal with a variety of authority figures (teachers, principals, bus drivers, janitors, other parents, and so on) than they would if they attended a "real" school.

♦ **Sports**. While there are often city sports teams that aren't affiliated with the local public or private schools, sometimes there aren't. Homeschooled kids often find it harder to get exposure to the variety of sports experiences, teams, leagues, tournaments, and so on that most schools offer.

♦ **Responsibility**. Do you feel confident that you have enough training or knowledge or access to resources to teach your child? Better make sure, because if things don't go the way you'd like them, there's no one to blame but yourself.

♦ **Commitment**. It's a big one in terms of time, money, and energy. If you go this route and you want to do it right, you or your partner will most likely have to quit work or cut back to a part-time schedule.

♦ **Kid overload**. Of course you love your child. But sometimes you just need some time to yourself. If you're homeschooling, it's all kids all the time, and those breaks will be few and far between.

♦ **Personal development**. While educating your child may be a noble occupation, you may get bored out of your mind and crave a little adult learning matter.

Finally—and this is neither an advantage nor a disadvantage—consider the match between your personality and your child's. Do you have the patience of a saint? You're going to need it. Be honest. Some kids take direction marvelously, while others know everything better than you do and won't listen to a word you say. You know your child better than anyone. Can the two of you really work together?

At the end of the day, there's no right or wrong answer. You'll need to make the choice that works best for you, your family, and your child. If you're interested in finding out more about homeschooling or are looking for some resources, check out www.homeschool.com or www.americanhomeschoolassociation.org.

Reading to Your Three- and Four-Year-Old

If you've read the previous books in this series, you know that in my view, reading aloud to children is one of the best things you can do with them (if you're just joining us, you're about to find out). In fact—I know this is going to sound a little grandiose, but it's true—hands down, the most important thing you can do to help your child succeed in life is read to him.

Children who are regularly read to have larger vocabularies, can focus for longer periods of time, are more empathetic, have better communication skills, have a more active imagination, and have fewer reading problems than those who don't have the same exposure. Reading instills a love of literature, teaches complex sentence and plot structure, helps you get to know your child's tastes and preferences, provides an important alternative to television, and gives you and your child a wonderful chance to snuggle up together under a blanket.

Hopefully you've been reading to your child for a couple of years now, and you've got a good home library going. If not, there are several lists in this book that will help get you up to speed. If you happen to have a copy of *Fathering Your Toddler* around, check out the books on pages 151–53 and 205–7. Here are a few ideas to make your reading experience more enjoyable and more fun for you and your preschooler.

- ♦ **Make reading a part of your child's daily routine.** If you can, do it at the same time every day.
- ♦ **Make your reading interactive.** Ask your child questions about what characters are doing and why.
- ♦ **Do more than just look at the pictures.** Many artists give clues of things to come, have involved subplots that exist only in the illustrations, or have hidden objects that appear on every page. If you're about to crack open a new book, let your child look through it for a few minutes first and ask him to tell you what he thinks it's about.
- ♦ **Don't be afraid to be theatrical.** Try out those accents, funny voices, and sound effects. Or act out the parts. One time you can be Goldilocks, then next time you're Baby Bear. And have your child pick a part too.

- **Don't worry about interruptions.** If your child asks you a question, go ahead and answer, even if it takes you on a detour.
- **Make mistakes.** This is especially good when you've read the same story twelve hundred times. Skip a page, leave out a word, or throw in a couple of extras, replace a character's name with your child's, pause in the middle of a sentence and wait for your child to fill in the blank, insist that there are three little wolves and a big, bad pig. The opportunities for error are endless—and, in your child's eyes, endlessly funny.
- **Don't read books you don't like.** Your child will hear your disdain in your voice. Instead, take the book off the shelf and donate it to charity.
- **Don't use books as weapons.** If you take away stories for not brushing teeth, mouthing off, or lollygagging around, your child will associate books with punishment and could end up hating to read.
- **Don't read too quickly.** If you find yourself whipping through books, putting your child in charge of turning the pages will slow you way down.
- **Create a kid-friendly reading environment.** A shelf that's just the right height for your child is a great way to subtly encourage him to read. If you've got the space, put a few books (especially new ones) face out. If you don't, just sit back and be amazed when your child picks out his favorites from a crowded shelf, when all he can see is the spine.

Below are some of my favorite books for three- and four-year-olds. In the Resources section you'll find a list of age-appropriate books for a number of specific issues, such as moving to a new home, losing a pet, divorce, and more.

GENERAL

Aunt LuLu, Daniel Pinkwater
Bear Dreams, Elisha Cooper
Blueberries for Sal, Robert McCloskey
Click, Clack, Moo: Cows That Type, Doreen Cronin
Daddies, Adele Greenspun
Danny and the Dinosaur, Syd Hoff
Days with Frog and Toad, Arnold Lobel
DW's Guide to Preschool, Marc Brown
Grizzly Riddles, Katy Hall and Lisa Eisenberg
Half of an Elephant, Gusti
Harry and the Lady Next Store, Gene Zion
The Hello, Goodbye Window, Norton Juster and Chris Raschka
How Are You Peeling? Foods with Moods, Saxton Freymann and Joost Elffers
How Do Dinosaurs Say Good Night? Jane Yolen

I Love Messes! Robie H. Harris
The Little House, Virginia Burton
Madeleine, Ludwig Bemelmans
Mama Don't Allow, Thacher Hurd
A Particular Cow, Mem Fox
A Play's the Thing, Aliki
Snapshot from the Wedding, Gary Soto
Sylvester and the Magic Pebble, William Steig
The Stinky Cheese Man and Other Fairly Stupid Tales, John Scieszka
The *Stupids* series, Harry Allard
Tooth Tales from Around the World, Marlene Brill
Uno's Garden, Graeme Base
A Tree Is Nice, Janice Udry
When I Was Little: A Four-Year-Old's Memoir of Her Youth, Jamie Lee
    Curtis
Where the Wild Things Are, Maurice Sendak
You're Just What I Needed, Ruth Kraus

STARTING PRESCHOOL
Don't Go! Jane Breskin Zalben
DW Goes to Preschool, Marc Brown
Going to Day Care, Fred Rogers
I Am Not Going to School Today! Robie H. Harris

Even if you haven't read to your child very much until now, it's not too late to start, so jump in. But be patient: it may take a while before your child gets into the new rhythm.

Big-Kid Beds, Nocturnal Wanderings, and Other Sleep Problems

One of the most important steps you can take to improve your child's physical, emotional, social, and intellectual development is to make sure he gets enough sleep. For the next six or seven years, that means ten to twelve hours of shut-eye every night.

Unfortunately, your child won't always do what's best for him, and as he moves into the preschool years, he may flat-out refuse to get into bed in the first place. Or, he might object to staying in his "big-kid bed" and could start getting up in the middle of the night to go play with his trains in the living room. Oh, yes, and because it's so much more fun to play with someone else, he'll wake you up and insist that you come with him. Obviously, these little nighttime expeditions are not something you want to cultivate.

If your child has infrequent sleep troubles, say once or twice a month, the next morning will be hell for you and your partner, your child, and anyone else who comes in contact with him. But if he's up later or earlier (or both) every night, it's a whole different ball game. For you, being sleep-deprived may leave you feeling tense, stressed out, and short-tempered, and you may have trouble focusing at work. For your child, sleep deprivation can cause behavioral problems, trouble concentrating, and poor academic performance. It has also been linked with an increase in ADD/ADHD symptoms and unintended injuries.

Here are a few steps you can take to start breaking the nighttime wakeup habit:

- **Talk to your child.** Tell him what a special thing it is to have a big-kid bed (I'm assuming you've already made the leap from crib to bed). Talk it up as much as you possibly can. Also, ask him to tell you why he's getting up. Is he scared of something? If so, you may be able to take some steps to reduce his fear.
- **Sleep hygiene.** Ideally, your child's bedroom should be a place where he sleeps and gets ready to sleep. That's it. So take out those tempting toys, remove any brightly colored murals or furniture, and keep the room dark.
- **Calm down.** Cut back on physical activity starting about thirty minutes before bedtime.
- **No nighttime, after-dinner snacks.**
- **Create a consistent bedtime routine.** Could be something like bath, brush teeth, story, backrub, bedtime song, and lights-out. Of course you can make up your own, but make it the same every night.
- **Anticipate his objections.** Preschoolers are masters at concocting excuses for why they shouldn't go to sleep: I need a drink of water, I left my luvvie in the car, the crickets are chirping too loud, one more hug, one more story, and so on. If he always asks for a glass of water, leave one for him in the bathroom in a place he can reach. And make sure that all his stuffed animals are nearby so he won't have to get up in the middle of the night for a teddy-bear hunt. You may also want to create a middle-of-the-night activity box, which could include a couple of books or a puzzle. There's no way to force someone to sleep. But if your child has something to keep him busy at 2:00 a.m., he might not feel the need to get you involved.
- **Cut back on or eliminate daytime naps.**
- **Get tough.** If you've done everything listed above and your child still gets up in the middle of the night, pick him up and take him back to his own

bed. When you get there, just rub his back or hum a song to help him get back to sleep. Keep the conversation to a minimum. Repeat this process as many times as it takes.

♦ **Try a little aromatherapy.** I know, I know, it sounds so Berkeley, but there may be something to it. Psychologist Namni Goel and her colleagues at Wesleyan University found that being exposed to the scent of jasmine helped subjects sleep better and more restfully. Another researcher, Bryan Raudenbush, conducted similar experiments and found that the scent of jasmine was even more effective in helping people sleep restfully and remain alert throughout the next day. If you want to try this, pick up a bottle of lavender or jasmine oil at a health food store. Pour two or three drops on a washcloth or tissue and put it near your child's bed. Be sure to take the bottle with you when you leave. And as long as you haven't turned up your nose at this, keep your child away from the scent of peppermint before bedtime; it's been shown to inhibit sleep.

Children with Disabilities and Chronic Conditions

It's nearly impossible to get accurate data on disabilities, but conservatively speaking, around 15 percent of preschool and school-age children in the United States have one or more "chronic conditions." These could be anything from asthma and autism to cancer and cerebral palsy.

Having a child with a chronic condition—whether it's a physical or mental one—puts a lot of stress on the entire family. Fathers and mothers have very different ways of reacting to this stress. Mothers typically worry more about the emotional strain of caring for a child and how the child will do socially. Fathers are concerned with more practical things, such as how to talk about the issue with family and friends, how the child will function in school, whether he'll eventually become self-sufficient. Many dads also experience a heightened sense of responsibility and protectiveness.

Although mothers are generally more involved in day-to-day caring for kids with chronic conditions, fathers are affected just as deeply by the emotional strain and often have an especially hard time coping. Part of the problem is a series of vicious circles:

Some of dads' biggest worries have to do with finances—whether they can afford to pay for treatments, tutors, and special medical attention, whether their insurance coverage is adequate, and so on. To combat those worries, dads may spend more time at work. That makes them feel better because they're easing their financial concerns. Plus, for many men, their jobs are a source of satisfaction, a place where they feel in control. But the more time they spend at work, the less they have available for their children, and the less they're able to be involved in treatment plans and meetings with professionals. As a result, they don't get information firsthand and feel out of the loop. It's a tough merry-go-round to get off.

Not surprisingly, conflict, tension, and even divorce are more common in families with a disabled child. But fortunately, there are some ways of reducing the strain.

♦ **Join a support group.** Men who get involved with other fathers who are facing the same issues (in a guy-only environment) feel less sadness, fatigue, pessimism, guilt, and stress, and have more feelings of satisfaction and success, fewer problems, and better decision-making abilities than dads who don't join groups, according to researchers Patricia Vadasy and her colleagues. These benefits will rub off on your relationship with your partner as well.

♦ **Explore every possible source for support.** If your friends are able to step in, that'll help. But also check with your local school district to see what kinds of resources they have. About.com (specialchildren.about.com) has a good collection of resources, and *Exceptional Parent* magazine (eparent.com) provides info, support, and resources for parents and families of children with disabilities. Also, be sure to check out the Fathers Network (fathersnetwork.org), a site specifically devoted to helping fathers of children with disabilities.

♦ **Play and communicate with your child.** Researchers at the University of Florida did a study where they taught dads to use everyday activities like building blocks, puppets, cars and trucks, and bubbles to connect with their autistic children. But there was a twist. The fathers were specifically instructed to follow the child's lead, wait for the child's response before continuing, and not give in to the temptation to direct the play. The results were wonderful. "Fathers were more likely to initiate play in an animated way and responded more to their children during playtime," said Jennifer Elder, the lead researcher. "Children also became more vocal and were more than twice as likely to initiate play with their fathers. . . . With the proper training at an early age, we feel that these techniques can help autistic children be more socially interactive and pick up language more easily."

One particularly interesting result that the researchers hadn't expected was that a lot of the fathers trained the mothers and siblings to do the same thing. Elder and her colleagues had done similar studies training mothers, with very much the same successes. The only difference was that mothers weren't as likely to teach the dads what they'd learned.

Uh-oh, Justin Legoed himself into his room again.

Playing with Your Three- to Four-Year-Old

A child's job is to play, and nowhere is this more evident than at ages three and four. Playtime is one of the most important times of day for children of this age. Here are some activities you and your child can enjoy together:

- **Air painting.** A great indoor activity for a rainy day. Drop small spoonfuls of paint in different colors (watercolor or watered-down tempera works best) onto a plain white piece of paper. Give your child a straw and show him how he can use air to move the paint around the paper and make interesting designs.
- **It's all about balls.** Try balls of all different sizes and types—soccer, basketball, football, golf ball, or baseball (if you're brave). Catch 'em, kick 'em, bounce 'em. One especially fun ball-related activity is bowling. Most alleys these days have super-light balls and bumpers that keep even the most wildly thrown balls from landing in the gutter.
- **Don't pack up those blocks just yet.** Blocks, including Lego and Mega Bloks, are not only terrific for honing fine motor skills, they can be the start of anything from a racing car to a magic castle to a spaceship. By building

towers and other structures, you can also slip in a few lessons about weight and balance. A recent study by researcher Dimitri Christakis found that children who engage in block play have better language skills and watch less TV than kids who don't play with blocks. Of course none of that educational stuff will matter when you're sneaking back into the living room after your child is asleep to build a few cities of your own.

♦ **Puzzles.** Quiet-time play can involve puzzles with four to six pieces. Get sturdy wooden ones; the cardboard kind tends to shred or get soggy when your little one decides to chew on it.

♦ **Oh, those long family car trips!** One surefire antidote to the are-we-there-yets? is the I See Something game. Each passenger takes a turn saying, "I see something blue!" (or some other color). It's up to the other passengers to guess what it is. In a moving car, this can be just the kind of tricky guessing game kids this age love. A more advanced version of the game replaces colors with letters of the alphabet; the first person starts with A, the next B, and so on.

♦ **Pretend play.** What could be more fun for a three- or four-year-old (or his dad) than pretending to be an animal? So make a zoo tour of your house: hop through the living room like a kangaroo, waddle into the bathroom like a duck, leap into the backyard like a gazelle, then into the kitchen to scratch like a gorilla. . . . If you're looking for something a little calmer, jump into a cardboard box and go for a ride.

♦ **Don't toss that old suit and tie or your partner's old prom dress.** Preschoolers *love* dress-up play. You'll be amazed at the dramas these mini-minds come up with, given the right cast-off clothing. Actually, the kids don't even have to get dressed up. My youngest would sometimes run through the house gathering up shoes (from her two older sisters, me, and my wife), which she'd use to act out elaborate scenes. You can participate, or just watch. It's better than television, but then again, when you've got a preschooler, what isn't?

♦ **Be a scientist.** Try some simple, safe experiments where your child can be a participant rather than an observer. One favorite is making ice. Very young children are amazed when the liquid they've poured into a jar gets hard after being in the freezer. Try dropping some colorful beans or small plastic figures in the jar when the water has reached the slush stage. Growing potatoes by sticking toothpicks in the potato and placing it in a glass of water on the windowsill is an oldie but goodie. You can also go to your local nursery and let your child pick out seeds to be planted in a small terra-cotta pot. Many a giant pumpkin had its start this way.

Your little scientist also likes to take things apart and, occasionally, put them back together. The two of you can dismantle anything from a videotape to a broken truck to last year's Barbie. Whatever you end up dissecting, make sure the parts aren't dangerous in any way.

Don't think you have to confine yourself to the kitchen—or even to overly simple activities. If you're patient, you can even explain some pretty sophisticated concepts. For example, you can talk with your child about how we need light to see by taking him into a pitch-black closet, then turning on a flashlight. Or, while you've got the lights off, shine the flashlight into a mirror and watch how the light bounces.

♦ **Wheels, wheels, wheels.** He can pedal a tricycle by now, and by his fourth birthday he may be ready for a two-wheeler with training wheels. So strap on your helmets and knee pads and take a spin around the neighborhood.

♦ **Work, work, work.** As Mary Poppins said, "For every job that must be done there is an element of fun; you find the fun and, snap!, the job's a game." How true that is. Simple chores like sorting socks, putting silverware away (no knives please), helping make dinner, and dusting bookshelves are all more fun for your child when you do them together. They also give your child the feeling that he's doing something important as well as that that oh-so-important sense of mastery.

♦ **Build an obstacle course.** You don't have to spend much money on this at all—some of the greatest home courses are made of cardboard boxes, blankets, toys, pillows, chairs, and all sorts of things you already have lying around the house. Besides over, under, through, and around, backwards, and forwards, be sure to integrate rolling, climbing, jumping, and maybe even a few push-ups or sit-ups. If you think your child would enjoy it, use a stopwatch so he can compare times.

♦ **The music man.** Musical play at this age can mean anything from singing along with a favorite CD, seeing how long you and your child can sing your sentences instead of talking, or making animal sounds to the games that go with classic songs like "London Bridge," "Ring Around the Rosie," and "Farmer in the Dell." And don't forget about the Freeze Dance game. Play a favorite song, then pause it. As soon as the music stops, everyone has to freeze like a statue. When the music starts again, everyone dances again.

♦ **Thinking games.** A simplified version of Twenty Questions is a big hit with the preschool set and helps build memory and critical thinking skills. Letter games such as "find me something in this room that starts with the sound the letter S makes, sssssss . . ." are great ways to get those pre-reading juices going. And opposites games can be hilarious. What *is* the opposite of orange?

Can We, Daddy? Can We Please Get a Puppy?

Take a second and think of things from your child's perspective: He drags his stuffed animals around, walks on them, squeezes them, throws them down the stairs, tries to stuff food down their throats, and they never complain. Why shouldn't it be the same with a real pet? Of course, we adults know that there's a big difference, but preschoolers still have a tough time differentiating between fantasy and reality. Plus, their sense of empathy isn't completely developed yet, so it's hard for them to imagine what it might feel like to an animal to have a piece of Lego stuffed into his mouth.

Unfortunately, there's no guaranteed way of protecting your child and any nearby animals from each other. You do, however, have a slightly better chance of training the human than the pets, so let's start there.

To begin with, show your child what good behavior around animals—even his luvvies—looks like. Show him how to pet, hold, and brush them. You might want to check out the DVDs from *All By Myself* (allbymyself.com), which show very young children caring for and interacting with pets. A few specifics:

If you have a cat, teach your child:

- **How to hold the animal.** The best position is with the child sitting with the cat in his lap. He should not hold the cat by the scruff of the neck or by the legs, and certainly not by the tail.
- **To read the cat's body language.** When the ears flatten and the tail swishes wildly, it's time to let the cat alone. The same goes for hissing or wailing.
- **Never to corner the cat or try to drag a cat out of a hiding place.**
- **To let sleeping cats lie, and give the cat some litter-box privacy.**
- **Not to scratch the cat on the tummy.** That can trigger a biting and clawing reflex.

If you're at all concerned that your cat might take a swipe at your child, consider getting some Soft Paws (softpaws.com), which are little vinyl covers that you can superglue to the cat's claws that will keep her from doing any serious damage to your child (and any nearby furniture).

If you have a dog, teach your child:

- **To pet him firmly.** Dogs like that better than light stroking.
- **Not to wake the dog up or tease him.**
- **Not to hug him.** According to Colleen Pelar, author of *Living with Kids and Dogs*, the feeling of being trapped is a common cause of bites. Pelar also recommends against riding the dog or playing wheelbarrow (picking the dog up by the hind legs and walking him around), or dress-up.
- **Avoid petting the dog on top of the head.** The same goes for contact with unfamiliar dogs. Since they can't see what you're doing up there, some dogs may nip.

Whether you have a dog or a cat or are visiting someone who does, teach your child never to get between a pet and his food. Your child also needs to know to approach new animals with caution. If the animal's owner is nearby, always ask permission to approach. If the answer is yes, extend a fisted hand so the animal can sniff it. And always let the animal come to the child and not vice-versa.

You and Your Partner

Although the primary focus of this book is the hows and whys of building strong relationships with your children, let's not forget about one of the most important aspects of being a good father: being a good husband and partner. I've looked at dozens of studies that touch on the critical ways fatherhood and your relationship with your partner are related and influence each other. Here's what the research shows:

- Fathers who are actively involved when their children are young have better, more stable, and more satisfying marriages than dads who aren't as involved with their kids, says researcher John Snarey. Snarey also found that children whose fathers set an example of a positive marriage relationship are better able to establish intimacy later on in their own lives.
- The more you and your partner share the domestic and child-care work-loads, the happier and stronger your relationship with her will be, says University of California, Riverside professor Masako Ishii-Kuntz.
- The happier and stronger your relationship with your partner, the stronger your relationships with your children will be, the more you'll be involved with them, and the more time you'll spend with them. Your children will also be psychologically and emotionally healthier, according to the Child

LIVING TOGETHER BUT NOT MARRIED?

My main objective in all of the writing I've done on fatherhood is to give men the tools and support and encouragement they need to become the fathers they want to be and their children need them to be. Given that so many children are born to unmarried-but-living-together couples, it seems more important to support fathers—whether they're married or not—than to make judgments about people's lifestyle choices.

I still believe that's true. However, if you're not married, there are some compelling reasons to think about making a change:

- **Unmarried fathers aren't as involved.** "Cohabiting partners, even if they are the biological father to the child, do not invest the same amount of time with children as married biological fathers," says family studies researcher Sandra Hofferth, "and they are less warm than the married biological fathers."
- **It's harder to stay involved if the relationship heads south.** In cases of divorce, mothers have primary or sole custody of the children about 80 percent of the time. While divorced fathers frequently feel cut off from their children's lives, unmarried fathers have fewer legal rights and find it even harder to maintain a strong relationship with their children after the breakup.
- **It's good for your health.** Researchers Sotirios Sarantakos and Arne Mastekaasa have found that unmarried couples who are living together are more likely to suffer from depression, and have more health problems than married couples. This may be because "cohabitants put up with behaviour in their partners which husbands and wives would discourage, particularly regarding smoking, alcohol and substance abuse," according to the Institute for the Study of Civil Society.
- **It may keep you alive longer**. Married men have been shown to have longer life expectancies than unmarried men.
- **It's good for your finances.** A number of studies show that married men earn 10 to 40 percent more than single or cohabiting men.

Despite all of this research, no one has a solid idea of why being married makes such a difference. But the connection seems to be there. One last thing: if you're considering getting married, do it sooner rather than later. The longer a couple lives together before the wedding, the more likely they are to get divorced later on.

We do all our own parenting.

Welfare Information Gateway (CWIG). A bad or negative relationship, on the other hand, is a major roadblock to father-child involvement.

♦ Mothers and fathers who are truly partners in parenting have fewer disciplinary problems with their children and generally cope better with their children's development and changing needs as they age, according to researcher Henry Biller, author of *Fathers and Families*.

♦ When their relationship is good, both Mom and Dad are more responsive, affectionate, and confident with their infants; more self-controlled in dealing with defiant toddlers; and better confidants for teenagers seeking advice and emotional support, according to CWIG.

♦ If you have a son, your relationship with your partner and how you handle conflicts becomes a model for how he should treat the women in his life as he gets older, say sociologists Jeffrey Rosenberg and W. Bradford Wilcox.

♦ Rosenberg and Wilcox also found that girls with involved, respectful fathers see how they should expect men to treat them and are less likely to become involved in violent or unhealthy relationships. In contrast, they say, husbands who "display anger, show contempt for, or who stonewall their wives" (giving them the silent treatment) are more likely to have children who are anxious, withdrawn, or antisocial."

♦ Frequent fighting and conflict with the partner can cause fathers to withdraw from their children, says psychologist Joshua Coleman, author of

Imperfect Harmony. And angry mothers are far more likely to try to interfere with their partner's involvement.

♦ Fathers of preschoolers feel more confident in their role as dad when they're happier in their marriages and they believe that their partner sees them as competent, say Canadian researchers Geneviève Bouchard and Catherine M. Lee.

♦ When a woman has a good relationship with her children's father and feels appreciated, she'll be a better mother.

♦ Men think about marriage and family differently than women do. For men, "family" tends to mean a mother, a father, and some kids. As a result, once a man becomes a father he also becomes very committed to keeping his family together. That way of thinking explains, to some extent, why after divorce men remarry sooner and more often than women. Women, however, can imagine themselves parenting without a man around and still consider themselves part of a family. That goes a long way toward explaining why about 75 percent of divorces are initiated by women.

Disciplining Your Preschooler

At one time or another, all parents struggle with discipline—establishing and enforcing limits, and getting their kids to speak to them respectfully and do what they're supposed to do. But remember: discipline isn't only about correction. It's also about teaching kids to control themselves and care about others so they can grow up to be productive members of society. Here are some approaches you and your partner can use to help your kids to do just that:

Do:

♦ **Be clear about your expectations.** "We're leaving in five minutes. Please put away all your trains before we go."

♦ **Keep your child's temperament in mind.** If your child doesn't have any trouble switching gears, you may be able to get him packed up and ready to go in 30 seconds. If he's not, you may need to give ten-minute, five-minute, two-minute, and one-minute countdowns. If you do this, be sure that you stick to the clock (using a timer is a good way to achieve this).

♦ **Be assertive and specific.** "Put down that knife right now" is much better than "drop it!"

♦ **Redirect.** If your child is throwing balls in the house, take him outside and play catch with him. If he's scribbling on the walls, give him some paper.

♦ **Learn to ignore.** You don't have to respond to every rolled eye or smirk or wise-guy comment.

♦ **Try to use natural consequences.** If your child refuses to wear a raincoat, the natural consequence is that he'll get a little wet. Be sure to clearly and simply explain what you're doing and why: "I'm taking away your hammer because you hit me," or "I asked you not to take that egg out of the fridge and you didn't listen to me. Now you'll have to help me clean it up." Natural consequences will grow with your child. Later on, if he breaks a window, he pays to replace it out of his allowance or he works it off.

♦ **Cave once in a while.** Kids can't always tell the difference between big and little issues. So give in on a few small things every now and then (an extra piece of birthday cake at the end of a long day might avoid a tantrum). That will give the child a feeling of control and will make it easier for him to go along with the program on the bigger issues (holding hands while crossing the street, for example).

♦ **Look for patterns.** Does your child have melt downs every day at the same time? Is he insufferably rude when he hasn't had a nap? Recognizing the triggers can help you avoid them. So can padding your schedule. The more rushed you are, the slower your child will move.

♦ **Reward good behavior.** This can be verbal ("I'm so proud of you when I see you cleaning up your toys") or material (making a sticker chart where good-behavior stickers can be traded in for special treats).

♦ **Get your child involved.** "I can see that both of you really want to use the red marker, but there's only one of them. What do you guys think we should do?

♦ **Encourage empathy.** If your child has some kind of altercation with another person, ask questions like, "What would it feel like if someone bit you—would you like it?" A warning: Don't ever demonstrate the things you're trying to get your child to stop doing. Biting him or pulling his hair to show him biting or hair pulling is wrong or doesn't feel good will backfire. Guaranteed.

♦ **Avoid absolute No.** Instead, try something like, "You can't have that candy bar right now, but when we get home, we'll make some popcorn together."

♦ **Give choices.** Kathryn Kvols, author of *Redirecting Children's Behavior*, suggests, for example, that if your child is yanking all the books off a shelf in the living room, you say, "Would you like to stop knocking the books off the shelf or would you like to go to your room?" If he ignores you, gently but firmly lead the child to his room and tell him he can come back into the living room when he's ready to listen to you.

+ **Get down to your child's level.** When you're talking to your child—especially to criticize—kneel or sit. You'll still be big enough that he'll know who the boss is.

+ **Make sure your child eats well and gets enough sleep.** Deficits in either category are major contributor to behavior problems.

Don't:

+ **Warn.** Children have incredibly selective hearing. When you tell your child "If you don't stop that right now" or "If you do that one more time," your child doesn't hear the words "If you." Instead, he hears a challenge: "Don't stop" or "Do that one more time." Such warnings are worse than useless. They ensure that an obnoxious act will be repeated," says family therapist Mark Brenner.

+ **Criticize too much.** Even such seemingly innocuous comments as "I've told you a thousand times . . ." or "Every single time you . . ." gives the child the message that he's doomed to disappoint you no matter what he does. And that completely removes any incentive he might have had to do what you ask.

+ **Make your child feel guilty.** Avoid comments like, "If we don't leave right now I'll be late for work and I'll get fired and we won't be able to pay the mortgage and we'll be living in a refrigerator box under an overpass eating nothing but cat food. Is that what you want?"

+ **Bribe.** It's tempting to pay a child off to get him to do or not do something. But the risk—and it's a big one—is that he will demand some kind of payment before complying with just about anything.

+ **Spank.** It's bad for the kids and bad for you. Children who get spanked are more likely to suffer from poor self-esteem and depression. They're also more likely to believe that it's okay to hit other people when they're mad. Hey, if daddy does it, why can't I?

+ **Make threats you don't really want to follow up on.** If you were planning on going out for a beer with a friend while your child is at a birthday party, not letting him go to the party may mean you'll have to stay home too.

Enough About You, Let's Talk About MEEEE!

What's Going On with Your Child

Physically

♦ No, you aren't imagining it: your four-year-old is even more active than she was at three. She throws, catches, and bounces large balls. She hops on one foot, skips, climbs ladders and small trees, does somersaults, and even bounds over objects five or six inches high. Best of all, she wants to do all of this with you. Just about the only thing she can't do is sit still for any length of time. All in all, it's no wonder that she still needs ten to twelve hours of sleep every night.

♦ Roller-skating is a distinct possibility, as is pedaling and steering a tricycle (or even a two-wheeler with training wheels) at breakneck speed. Fortunately, she's a little more cautious on her way down the stairs, putting both feet on each step.

♦ On the small motor front, she's back to building tall block towers, and can easily thread beads on a string. She loves to paint with big, broad strokes, does a nice job copying circles and squares, and can draw a person with three or four appendages. She may even be able to make something human-looking from clay. She's also comfortable using eating utensils and does a pretty good job handling scissors (child-safe ones, of course). She can get dressed by herself most of the time, although she may still need help with buttons and tying shoes. She can brush her teeth, use the toilet unassisted, and comb her hair, even though she may not want to.

Intellectually

♦ She's up to about 1,500 words now and will boost that to 2,500 by the end of the year. She still uses most of those words to tell you what's going on, but she's starting to participate in—and may even initiate—small conversations with other kids. If you ask her about her day, she may tell you, but chances are she'll make it up and exaggerate all sorts of details. She still can't differentiate between fantasy and reality at times.

♦ She tailors her speech to her audience. She'll tell you, "I fell down outside and cut my toe." But she'll tell a younger sibling, "Me hurt foot."

♦ She's so proud of her language abilities that she starts playing word games, making up silly names for objects she doesn't know. She'll be driven to hysterical laughing by the name-game song ("Bill Bill bo-bill, banana-fana-fo-fil, mee my-mo-mill, Bill").

♦ She identifies a few numbers and most letters—especially the ones that make up her name, which she may even be able to print. She also recognizes a few simple words that she sees regularly, such as *STOP*.

♦ Her grammar is improving. She picks up some irregular plurals ("One mouse, two mice," not "mouses"), but may apply those exceptions to other words ("One blouse, two blice"). She may also have trouble with irregular past tense, saying things like "I goed to the zoo and seed a rhino," instead of "I went" and "I saw." When she makes this kind of mistake, don't correct her; simply repeat the sentence correctly. "Oh, so you went to the zoo and saw a rhino!"

♦ She knows the names of at least six colors, and, as she approaches five, will be able to match colors to similar ones, such as maroon and burgundy as shades of red. She can identify at least three shapes and can count as high as six or seven.

♦ Her attention span is still fleeting, but she'll often focus on one activity for ten or fifteen minutes.

Emotionally/Socially

♦ Your four-year-old is a pretty joyful little creature. But her ability to feel and express emotions is increasing faster than her ability to manage them. As a result, she's often oversensitive, breaking into tears or becoming enraged about something insignificant or laughing for twenty minutes about something that wasn't funny.

♦ She now plays *with* other kids and is trying to figure out what, exactly, friendship is all about. Some nice relationships are developing, almost all of which are with same-sex kids. She'll have a new best friend every day.

And locking another child in a closet so she won't be able to leave is a typical four-year-old way of keeping a play date going.

♦ She's getting better at sharing but doesn't completely understand that other people have feelings that may be as important as hers. As a result, she may exclude (or be excluded by) others from play.

♦ She understands simple rules for games and usually follows them. But she'll often change them to suit herself—but no one else.

♦ Her imagination is on overdrive. Until now, most pretend play had to do with house and taking on the role of Mommy or Daddy. Now she's likely to be a doctor, an astronaut, a spider, a chair, or even a glass of water.

♦ She's still pretty self-centered, bragging about her accomplishments and getting jealous if you pay attention to anyone else. In an attempt to remain the center of attention, she tries to shock people by swearing, using her own made-up profanity like "poopie head." The bigger your reaction, the more she'll do it.

♦ Your preschooler now prefers the same-sex parent and tries to be like him or her in every way. But no matter what gender you are, she loves to hear stories about your childhood—especially the times when you got into big trouble.

♦ She's more curious about sex now and may ask you about the mechanics. Long explanations aren't necessary at this stage. Be warned: boys and girls both may extend their curiosity about sex into the pants of their friends. That's normal. Even so, it may be time for a talk on privacy.

What's Going On with You

Designing Dad

When little girls are growing up, they're surrounded by motherhood role models and images of women caring for children. Of course, not all those role models and images are positive. But most are, and there are articles on various aspects of parenting in almost every women's magazine out there. Most men's magazines, on the other hand, sidestep fatherhood entirely in favor of six-pack abs. (A few years ago I asked an editor at one of the biggest men's magazines why they didn't have more articles on fatherhood—even though most of their readers were dads—and he told me that fatherhood "wasn't cool.") As a result, we're left to look for our role models elsewhere.

Unfortunately, the choices are pretty slim. We can look at the media, where fathers are generally portrayed negatively, as either uninvolved, uninterested,

DEVELOPMENTAL RED FLAGS FOR PRESCHOOLERS

When your child was younger, she was probably seeing her pediatrician at least a couple of times a year. That made it easier for the doctor to identify most potential developmental problem areas. But at this point, your child is probably on a once-a-year-unless-there's-a-problem schedule, which means that it's up to you and your partner to identify issues.

The What's Going On with Your Child sections in every chapter of this book will give you a very good feel for how your child is developing. But as in the other books in the New Father series, they are guidelines only, and the range of "normal" or "average" is quite broad. In other words, the milestones you're reading about in this chapter could apply to a child six to twelve months younger or older. That said, if one or more of the following statements are true about your preschooler, call your pediatrician as soon as possible (we'll have another section on red flags for school-age children later on):

My child . . .

◆ Can't throw a ball overhand or jump in place.

◆ Can't ride a tricycle.

◆ Has a very difficult time separating from me or my partner.

◆ Resists any kind of fantasy play.

◆ Has a tough time holding on to a crayon or pencil between thumb and fingers, or can't make a tower using more than four blocks.

◆ Ignores other children or has no interest in playing with others.

◆ Doesn't use more than three words in a sentence; has trouble using "me," "you," or "I"; or speaks in a way that's completely unintelligible.

◆ Can't describe a recent event, such as a play date with a friend or an outing to the zoo.

◆ Has no self-control, bites or hits or kicks with no provocation, or shows no remorse after hurting someone.

◆ Flinches when hugged, doesn't make eye contact when speaking, or avoids any kind of social interaction (this is way beyond being shy).

◆ Can't follow simple one- or two-step directions.

◆ Can't do basic self-care tasks like hand-washing, putting on clothes, or using the toilet during the day.

dangerous, or dopey. We can look at our male friends who are also fathers, but they're in pretty much the same boat we are. Or we can look at our own fathers, most of whom grew up in an era when putting food on the table and shoes on everyone's feet satisfied the definition of "good father" and constituted all society expected—and allowed—dads to do.

So let's start from scratch. If you were to design the perfect dad—the father you wish you had when you were growing up and the father you want to be for your children—what would he look like? (Even though you're starting from scratch, you're going to be modeling your perfect dad to some extent on your own dad. Whether your relationship with him was wonderful, terrible, or nonexistent, and whether you see him every week, not at all, or something in between, or even if he passed away years ago, the old man's influence on your fathering is alive and kicking. It's completely up to you, though, to decide whether that influence is positive or negative.)

Start by asking yourself three questions about your father:

♦ What did he do that you want to do with your own children?
♦ What did he do that you will absolutely, positively, never ever do with your children?
♦ What did he not do that you wish he would have?

Don't try to do this in a hurry. Spend some time thinking about it. Ask your siblings, your mother, or anyone else who was around for their perspectives. You'll be surprised at all the things you've forgotten. If you're feeling brave, do some "stakeholder interviews"—talk to the people who have a stake in the kind of father you are and want to be, such as your children and your partner—and ask them to answer the three questions above about you.

Once you've gathered all your research, you'll have a good picture of the perfect dad. Then you can decide what you will or won't or can't do to move yourself a little closer to that goal.

Letting Go

As your children get older, it'll become clearer by the day that you can't control everything about their world. You can guide, offer opinions (for a few more years anyway), and make a lot of options available, but little by little, you'll have to handle the decision making—and the consequences of those decisions—over to your child. I know we're in a chapter on raising a four-year-old, and I'm not talking about letting her do her own meal planning, set her own bedtime, and decide whether to or not to go to school or brush her teeth. You're still making the rules in a lot of ways. But starting now, it's important to give your child the opportunity to make certain choices.

When my oldest was four, I wrote an essay about her insistence on getting a haircut (which I didn't want her to do), the importance of stepping back and giving kids limited control over their own lives, and the effects that doing so have on kids and their parents. Here's an excerpt:

Cutting Loose

It started out as a pretty typical day. At breakfast, my four-year-old daughter asked for cinnamon toast, with the crust left on. But by the time I brought it to her, she had changed her mind. "I *hate* crust," she said tearfully. "Cut it off." I took it back to the kitchen. By the time I returned with the crustless toast, she'd changed her mind again. "I wanted the crust *on*," she wailed. Giving up, I put a new slice of bread in the toaster for her and took a bite out of the rejected one. "I didn't say you could eat my toast!" she shouted. All in all, there was nothing particularly out of the ordinary about that day—until my daughter announced that she wanted a haircut, her first ever.

Given that some variation on the morning toast episode happens three or four times a week, you can imagine my trepidation at letting my daughter make a decision that might take years to undo. But she kept insisting, and after all, hair does grow back eventually. . . . So that Sunday, off we went to the hair salon.

The tables in the waiting area were piled high with books, each filled with photos of different hairstyles. Somehow imagining we could get off with just a trim, I leafed through one of the books and showed her some cute shots of girls with neatly styled long hair and bangs just a little shorter than hers. She wasn't impressed. She took the book from me, sneered, and quickly found a photo of a girl with a very short pageboy haircut. "Are you sure?" I said. "Let's look at a few others before you make up your mind." I desperately searched for a compromise, drawing her attention to several shoulder-length styles. She shook her head and demanded we turn back to the pageboy. "This one," she said. "I don't need to keep looking."

Clearly, there was no sense in arguing. So I took a deep breath, helped her into the barber chair, and hoped for the best.

As I sat there, wincing with every snip of the stylist's scissors, it occurred to me that there's a connection between hair and power: it seems that whoever controls the hair controls the body it's attached to. I'd always tried to encourage my daughter to be independent, but I realized that one of the many ways I still maintained control over her was to regulate—at least passively—the length of her locks. Not that this control-the-hair, control-the-person idea is anything terribly original; we all know about Samson and Delilah. And Rapunzel. Locked in a tower by an overprotective witch, the girl capitalizes on her long hair and seizes the first opportunity to take control of her life by letting the prince climb up it. The witch's only chance to reassert her supremacy was to cut Rapunzel's hair off.

I could see then that for my daughter, insisting on getting a haircut was really her first serious attempt to wrest control of her life—and her body— away from me and my wife. "This is *my* body," she seemed to be saying. "I'll do what I want with it." And from there, it's only a hop, skip, and a jump to adolescence, when I can almost see her staring, hands on her hips, head cocked to one side, demanding: "Why *can't* Rob and I lock the door to my room? Don't you trust me?"

The problem is that while my daughter may be ready to start putting her childhood behind her, it's going to take *me* a while longer to get used to the idea. Like many of my friends who have kids, I've greeted each developmental stage with a mixture of joy and sadness. I wildly cheered my kids' first steps, but quietly mourned the end of their crawling (and less-independent) days. Until she was about three, my daughter couldn't pronounce the letter *L*— something my wife and I found incredibly endearing (we must have shot hours of videotape of her saying, "Hey, yook at my yegs!" and "I yuv you"). Every morning, she'd crawl into my bed, nudge me awake, and say "Heyyo, Daddy." One day, though, I opened my eyes to a perfectly pronounced "Hello." I almost cried.

When the stylist triumphantly held up eighteen inches of my daughter's platinum blond locks, the shock literally took my breath away. I hadn't realized until then how much I had loved my daughter's hair. Oh, sure, I remember what a pain it was to wash and how tangled it got afterward, how she cried when her baby sister pulled it, and how it used to snag on her buttons. But in a very real way, her hair was her history—a kind of archaeological dig of her past. Some of the tips had actually been there since the day she was born. I still remember the bath-fresh smell of her hair and the special intimacy we shared as I brushed, combed, or braided it before starting her bedtime story. But now, all that's left of those precious tips—and the ponytail that followed them—is lying lifeless in a plastic bag on top of the refrigerator.

Not surprisingly, the haircut had a dramatic effect on me *and* my daughter. She not only looked older, but began acting more maturely, too. Suddenly, her baby sister was not just some interloper who had displaced her from the center of the Universe. Instead, the baby became *real*, someone to be taken care of and loved. Even her preschool teachers remarked that since her haircut, my daughter seemed different, more self-confident—in a word, more in control.

Now, a few months later, as I look at her and run my fingers through her soft, short hair, I'm filled with a sense of pride at how grown-up she's become. By allowing her to get the haircut she wanted, my wife and I let her make her very first decision involving long-term consequences. And in the end, everything turned out all right. We trusted her, and she didn't let us down. Oh, sure, she still can't make up her mind whether or not she wants the crust on her toast, but when it comes to the big things, she's growing up with confidence in her ability to make decisions. She knows we're there to help and support her, and that we won't second-guess her. She's taking charge of her four-year-old life— strand by strand.

You and Your Child

Why Be Involved with Your Four-Year-Old?

- It'll make her smarter. The more nurturing and caring the father, the higher his children (especially boys) score on tests of intellectual functioning.
- Children whose fathers are involved, helpful, warm, and kind have bigger vocabularies than kids whose fathers are cool and aloof, according to researcher Norma Radin. Part of the reason for this is that although mothers and fathers both adjust their speech and vocabularies to their child's, fathers do it a little less and tend to use bigger words and more complicated sentence structure.
- The more you're involved in your child's education, even at this age, the better she'll do academically and the greater the chance that she'll graduate from high school.
- Having a good, involved relationship with your four-year-old has a wonderful influence on her emotional and social development.
- Expecting your child (especially girls) to be capable and persistent increases her level of intellectual and professional accomplishment as an adult.
- Having clear expectations and boundaries helps girls behave more assertively and helps boys have more perseverance.
- Children with learning disabilities but with actively involved fathers develop a greater sense of self-esteem than those with less involved dads. And regardless of the type of disability (emotional, social, or physical), kids with attentive, encouraging fathers have a much better chance of adjusting successfully than those whose fathers aren't as involved, according to pioneering fatherhood researcher Henry Biller.

Education

Going Back to School:
The Importance of Being an Involved Dad

There's a mountain of research that shows a direct connection between parents' involvement in their children's education and the kids' performance in school; the more the parents are involved, the better the kids do. But in many families, the word *parents* really means Mom. That's a big mistake. There are a number of benefits that are specifically related to *father* involvement. We'll talk about exactly what the word *involvement* means below, but for now, let's take a look at the dad factor in education. When dads are involved, their kids . . .

- Do better in school and enjoy it while they're there. About half of kids with involved dads earn mostly A's, compared to only about a third when dads are not involved. Those children who aren't doing as well in school tend to be less anxious about it than those with uninvolved dads. Interestingly, the chances that children will get top grades have more to do with Dad's level of involvement than Mom's.
- Are half as likely to have ever repeated a grade (7 percent versus 15 percent for children of less involved dads), according to a national survey sponsored by the National Center for Education Statistics (NCES).
- Are much less likely to have ever been suspended (10 percent versus 18 percent for kids of less involved dads).
- Are more likely to participate in extracurricular activities. And children who are involved in extracurricular activities have fewer behavior problems and are less prone to getting involved with drugs or alcohol or to become teen parents.
- Grow up to be higher-performing, more responsible adults who are more likely to have solid marriages.
- Are more interested in exploring the world around them, are more confident, and have better problem-solving skills.
- Tend to do better on standardized tests, have better math and verbal scores, and have higher IQs.
- Get a clear message that you care about them and value education.

Interestingly, these wonderful benefits from father involvement happen whether the dad is married, single, a stepfather, or an adoptive father, and whether he lives with his children or not, according to University of Illinois researcher Brent A. McBride. Overall, that's pretty convincing, don't you think? But wait, there's more. When dads are involved in their children's schools, the dads themselves . . .

♦ Tend to be more involved at home, and vice versa.

♦ Learn a lot of great stuff. The NCES study found that when parents are actively involved in their kids' schools, they "are more likely to visit museums and libraries, participate in cultural activities with their children, and have high educational expectations for them."

♦ Feel more important in their children's lives. "Fathers' participation in early childhood programs will significantly benefit their own sense of contribution to the development of the *whole child*: a child who recognizes that men as well as women can nurture both in the home and in the school environment," write David Giveans and Michael Robinson.

And finally, schools benefit from father involvement too. Teacher morale is higher when they get more support from families, parents have a higher opinion of the teachers, and the schools have better reputations in communities, according to the U.S. Department of Education.

Defining Involvement and Putting It into Action

Okay, now that you know *why* you should take a hands-on approach to your child's education, let's talk about what "involvement in your child's education" looks like, and how to do it. As you might suspect, it's more than just driving the carpool and helping with homework, although that's a great place to start. Actually, defining *father involvement* or *involved father* isn't easy. It's one of those I-know-it-when-I-see-it kind of things. It's safe to say, though, that if you're doing at least three or four things from the list below, you qualify. If you're doing less than that—or if you're looking for ways to be even more involved than you are—here are some suggestions:

♦ **Ask a lot of questions.** What is your child learning in class? What are her favorite and least favorite subjects? Who are her friends?

♦ **Volunteer in the classroom as much as you can.** Be your child's show-and-tell project. Your job may not seem particularly interesting or exciting to you, but to a room full of kids, it could be absolutely riveting. You can read books to preschoolers, tutor grade-schoolers, or spend an hour a week washing paintbrushes. If you have a lot of free time during the day, consider becoming a room parent. (Unfortunately, most schools use the term *room mother*. If you take the job, ask them to change that.) It's very important that your child see you in action. On the most basic level, you're demonstrating your commitment to her, to education, and to helping others.

*Andy plays perfectly well with others—it's others
who don't play well with Andy."*

On a deeper level, the sense of pride that she'll get from having you there is
priceless.

♦ **Volunteer outside the classroom.** Every year for ten years I cooked
three or four spaghetti lunches for my kids' whole school. Be a driver or
chaperone for a field trip, paint the classrooms, help build raised beds for a
school vegetable garden, install new playground equipment. The list is
endless.

♦ **Be in contact with your child's teachers by e-mail or phone.** Check
in to find out what your child's assignments are, when big projects are due,
and how things are going. If all you know is what's printed in the twice-
yearly report cards, you could find that an easy-to-solve problem has been
going on for months and has morphed into something big and ugly.

♦ **Let your child know you're in contact with the teacher.** Have your
child show you her daily planner and ask her to show you her homework
assignments. Don't be too intrusive, though. You want her to know that
you're looking out for her and that you're available to help as needed. At the
same time you want to give her enough room to develop good study habits
and organizational skills on her own.

♦ **Join the PTA** (PTO in some places).

♦ **Go to back-to-school nights, parent-teacher conferences,
concerts, performances, recitals, sports events.** If you want to take

things up a notch, volunteer to serve on a committee or start going to school board meetings.

♦ **Make sure your child always knows what you expect from her academically, and be sure those expectations are reasonable.**

♦ **Give your child's teachers and school administrators a copy of this section.** Many of them have no idea that encouraging dads to get involved is so critical to our children's success.

Bumps in the Road

Knowing how and why to do something isn't always enough. Unfortunately, when it comes to almost anything fatherhood-related, there are still a lot of obstacles that can make it tough to get or stay involved in your child's schooling. Here are some of the barriers you might encounter:

♦ **The workplace.** Even well into the twenty-first century, it's hard for working fathers to get the time off they'd like to have and still be treated seriously on the job. In fact, workplace conflicts are the number-one reason dads give for not being more involved.

♦ **Your education or knowledge.** Generally speaking, the less education you have, the less involved you'll be in educating your child. In some cases there's a shame factor, a feeling of embarrassment at not having earned a college degree or having done poorly in school. Or you might feel intimidated by new math, new teaching methods, and completely unfamiliar topics. For us, biology class involved dissecting frogs. For our kids, it's all about gene-sequencing. If you're finding yourself backing off for any of those reasons, don't. According to Virginia Gadsen, who runs the National Center on Fathers and Families at the University of Pennsylvania, "even when fathers have limited schooling, their involvement in children's schools and school lives has a powerful impact on children's educational attainment."

♦ **Lack of support at home.** If your partner is involved in your child's education, there's a better chance that you will be too. Works the other way 'round as well.

♦ **Divorce/separation.** Children of divorce spend the majority of time with their mother. Having limited time with your children can have an effect on your level of involvement. But a more accurate involvement barometer is the quality of your relationship with your ex. The better you get along, the more she'll support you and the more involved you'll be.

♦ **Being a single father.** Overall, kids in single-parent homes don't do as well academically as those in two-parent homes. But your being a single dad doesn't doom your children. Single dads with custody of their children

ADOPTION AND THE ART OF FATHERHOOD

It used to be that there were two ways to become a father—the old-fashioned, clothing-optional way, or through adoption. But in recent years more and more people are becoming parents by other means. Worldwide, there are two million people out there who were conceived by *in vitro* fertilization (IVF—more commonly called "test tube babies"). And every year about 50,000 babies (more than half of whom are multiples) are born through assistive reproductive technology (ART), which includes IVF, donor eggs, artificial insemination, donor sperm, and surrogate mothers. What that means is that an increasing number of people are raising a child who is biologically unrelated to one or both parents.

Adoptive fathers, and other ARTful dads, develop and change in basically the same ways as biological fathers do. Most—but certainly not all—adoptive parents experience feelings of inadequacy at not having been able to produce their own children. But by now, you're probably over all that. Instead, you and your partner are seeing yourselves as you really are: "eminently entitled and very 'real' psychological parents," as adoption expert Gordon Finley puts it.

Like their parents, adoptive and ART kids are a lot like other kids their age. But there are some interesting and important differences. Research quite consistently shows that children adopted as infants or conceived through ART are just as healthy, well-adjusted, and well-behaved as children being raised by their biological parents. Children adopted after age one, or who were bounced from home to home before finally settling down with one family, are at greater risk for emotional and psychological problems, and may be generally more fearful or anxious, or have behavior problems.

Some of these problems are exaggerated by the normal developmental stage the child is in. Preschoolers, for example, can't really understand what adoption means. They understand the word as it might apply to adopting a kitten from the pound, but they can't truly grasp the idea of having

are actually twice as likely to be involved in their children's schools as dads in intact families. Some of that may be the result of the married dads turning the job over to their partner. But clearly, dads can be involved if they make the effort.

♦ **Schools.** School administrators, teachers, and PTAs often say they'd like to see more fathers involved. But a lot of the time those same administrators, teachers, and other parents are the ones who end up keeping dads away.

had any other family than the one they're living with now. And they can't even come close to grasping the idea of genetic material from people who may not have ever met, swirling around in a Petri dish.

For that reason, you should wait a while longer before you tell your child that she was adopted or conceived through ART. (We'll talk about how to raise that issue and many other adoption/ART-related topics on pages 186–88.)

If you do decide to raise the adoption issue with a preschooler, keep it simple and expect to have an ongoing series of discussions. The most important thing to remember is that you should always emphasize how much you wanted your child and how loved she is. "Preschoolers' reactions to adoption are almost entirely affected by the way their parents feel about the adoption and the way they handle it with their children," according to the National Adoption Information Clearinghouse. "Children of preschool age will be as excited about the story of their adoptions as other children are by the story of their births."

The exception to the wait-a-while rule is if you adopted your child when she was two or older, or if she's of a different race than you and/or your partner. In those cases, it's important that you treat the issues honestly and respectfully. If your child was older when she joined your family, she will have memories of her previous homes. Pretending she has no history will only give your child the impression that there's something wrong. So encourage her to talk about her experiences when she feels comfortable.

For transracial adopted children, raise potentially unpleasant issues before your child hears about them from someone else. Three- or four-year-olds have no problems spotting differences, and she'll notice if she looks different from everyone else in the family. This is a good opportunity to talk about how people in different cultures sometimes look different and have different customs, and that you and your partner love her no matter what she looks like or where she came from.

After a speech I gave on father involvement, a woman came up to me to tell me an anecdote about her husband. He used to volunteer at his children's school but had recently been asked to stop coming. The reason? He was the only man volunteering, and some of the school staff felt "uncomfortable." Over the years I've heard variations on that story from dozens of people. Let me give you a few more examples of school-related barriers you might find yourself facing.

◊ **They don't recruit volunteers in a dad-friendly way.** Typically, schools send out open-ended invitations to volunteer or generic sign-up sheets. But that approach doesn't work for dads. Three for Me (three4me.com), a group that helps parents get more involved in their children's schools, surveyed dads and found that they want invitations specifically inviting dads—not general flyers. They also said that they would make time to be involved if the school were to give them a specific job, utilize their skills, and be clear on how much time is needed and what the expectations are.

◊ **There aren't enough dad-friendly events.** Dads want to do things with their hands, build birdhouses with the kids, paint classrooms, patch drywall, participate in golf tournaments, and so on. Baking cookies and stuffing envelopes aren't nearly as appealing. Dads also don't want to come to a volunteer meeting to schmooze. They want to get right to the point and skip the socializing. But school meetings—most of which are organized by women—tend not to work that way.

◊ **If you do volunteer, you may be the only man.** The guys in the Three for Me study said they wouldn't volunteer if they were going to be the only man present, and they'd be more likely to get involved if asked by another man. As you can see, this creates something of a vicious circle: if no men are involved, none will join in. And if none join in, there won't be any men around to invite the other guys. So do everyone a favor and join—even if you're the only guy. Hopefully you won't have to make too many calls before you're able to corral a couple of other dads.

◊ **They make it tough for divorced fathers.** Many divorced fathers— even those with joint legal and/or physical custody—complain that they don't get to see their children's report cards and aren't notified of school events, conferences, and so on; the notices get sent to Mom's address.

Facilitating Friendships

A few years ago I had this conversation with my daughter, Talya, who was then age four, about her friend Danielle:

DAD: How come you and Danielle are such good friends?

TALYA: Because I like her.

DAD: And what makes you like her?

TALYA: I like her because she's my friend.

DAD: But what makes her your friend?

TALYA (in a rather annoyed tone of voice): Because I like her, okay?

*I like you, Henry—you're one of the few people
around here who actually get it.*

As unproductive as that little chat was, it illustrated an important point: to preschoolers, friendship is fairly black-and-white. Friends are people you like; people you don't like aren't friends. But watch out: These likes and dislikes change awfully quickly, which often means that whomever a child is playing with at a particular time is a friend. And a best friend is probably someone the child played with (without fighting) most recently.

This isn't to say, of course, that kids this age can't or don't have enduring friendships. They do; it's just that with their limited attention spans, it's nearly impossible for them to maintain any kind of intensity with more than one playmate at a time, according to educational psychologist Steven Asher.

Now that your child is in preschool (or involved in a regular playgroup), you'll probably notice a subtle change in where her friends come from. To start with, she's no longer relying on you to introduce her to people. As a preschooler, she's making her own contacts. You'll also see a difference in the gender of her playmates. A couple of years ago your child didn't care whether she was ignoring or snatching toys from a boy or a girl. But at this particular stage, she's especially susceptible to the rigid social standards that preschoolers impose on one another: if you spend time with someone of the opposite sex, you'll get cooties. So don't be surprised if your child seems to be socializing with only kids of her own gender (although she may have a secret favorite from the opposite sex). This is all part of the process of finding things in common. And since she and her friends are too young to register to vote, gender is the next best thing to a shared interest.

As your child matures and develops, so does the definition of "friend." For a typical four-year-old, a friend might be "someone who gives you things." For a seven-year-old, a friend is "someone you like, someone you have fun with." And at nine or ten, a friend is someone who's "nice to talk to and who keeps her promises."

Despite the impossibility of defining the actual word, just about all the experts agree that friends and friendships are extremely important to children's long-term psychological and social development. Here are some of the benefits:

- Children who have friends are more socially competent and have far fewer behavioral problems than those who don't, according to Dr. Willard Hartup, a professor at the Institute for Child Development at the University of Minnesota. "They're more sociable, more cooperative, more altruistic, more self-confident, and less lonely."
- Kids with friends also tend to be far better adjusted in school, and those who are considered "unpopular" are about three times more likely to drop out of school later in life than their more popular peers.
- The feedback your child gets from her peers is becoming more and more important every day. For example, if your child is just learning to ride a bike with training wheels, getting praise from you is terrific. But if she gets a high five from someone her own age, someone who's also interested in riding bikes, that's acceptance. And feeling accepted fuels healthy self-esteem, says psychologist Lynn Borenstein.
- Having friends teaches kids—in a very different way than you or your partner could—a number of valuable lessons about cooperation, tact, initiating and maintaining peer relations, and managing conflicts and aggression. You can explain to your child all day long that it's important to share or be cooperative. But being rejected by a friend will teach her far more quickly exactly what happens when she doesn't share, hits or teases, or hurts another child's feelings.

There's no magic number of friends a child should have, and your child's temperament will play a major role in determining whether she has one or a dozen (more on this below). Your job should be to stress quality, not quantity. Here's how you can help:

♦ **Actively encourage your child to get involved in playgroups, either by setting them up yourself or by joining a group of other parents of preschoolers.** While it comes naturally to some, for others, making friends takes a lot of practice. Kids who don't have ample opportunities to interact with other children may never learn how.

♦ **Keep your child's temperament in mind.** "Active kids who adapt well to new situations have the most friends," says James Cameron, Ph.D., director of the Preventive Ounce in Oakland, California. "But kids who are shy and slower to adapt usually have far fewer—but much deeper— friendships. They often have trouble handling any more than one friend at a time and tend to have 'serial friendships' instead." On a play date, your active child will take off with a new or old friend the minute you get in the door, and she might not even notice when you leave. But if you have a shy child, expect some clinginess and plan on sticking around for a while. Telling both children a story or getting the two of them set up with an art project can really help break the ice.

♦ **If your child is having some trouble making friends, ask her teacher to pair her with another child who's having the same problems.** And when inviting other children over, make sure that you keep the number of guests to one or two. The trick here is to get your child involved in doing something with another child that she would enjoy doing on her own.

Computer Games and Other Tech Toys for Your Three- to Five-Year-Old

From the time she was a baby, your child has seen you spending time staring at a computer screen or doing something incomprehensible on a Palm or Black-Berry. In the same way that she imitates everything else you do, she's inevitably going to express an interest in the computer and other electronic entertainment.

There's a little bit of controversy about whether kids and technology are a good or bad combination. On one side, there's the Alliance for Young Children (AYC), which maintains that allowing young children to use computers is developmentally harmful, causes physical injuries like repetitive stress syndrome, and promotes a sedentary lifestyle and contributes to the rise of childhood obesity. You can download a copy of their rather scary report, *Tech Tonic,* from their Web site, www.allianceforchildhood.net/projects/computers/.

But as far as I'm concerned, the arguments against technology are a bit of tempest in a teapot. For example: yes, it's possible to get repetitive stress

For Father's Day, I'm giving my dad an hour of free tech support.

injuries from heavy computer or video game use. But they are also caused
by musical instruments and by the repetitive motion of sports, according to
Warren Buckleitner, editor of *Children's Software Review*. "Shall we take away
the violins and the tennis rackets, too?" he asks.

Now let me be very clear. I'm not questioning the idea that young children
learn best from hands-on experience. And I acknowledge that computers don't
provide kids with the same kind of socialization and physical activity as active
play with peers or family members. (Although, as we'll see on pages 174–77,
some of the concerns you might have about the drawbacks of technology are
overblown.)

However—and this is a big however—the inescapable fact is that our world
is becoming more and more wired every day, and children who don't have
superior computer skills will be at a disadvantage as they grow up. Children
learn a tremendous amount from using technology appropriately, and depriving
them of those learning opportunities is irresponsible. Of course, the two big
questions are, "What can kids learn from computers?" and "What does 'appropriately' mean?"

Good-quality tech games can help preschoolers master letters and number concepts. They can encourage children to work on projects together and can make learning about other cultures and rituals more interesting and engaging. Well-designed games encourage creative thinking and problem solving. And perhaps most importantly, because games can do a great job of mixing education with fun, preschoolers who have the chance to use them often have a more positive attitude toward learning.

Unfortunately, good-quality games are a rarity. And the problem comes down to a typical business dilemma: a product can be high quality, low cost, or produced quickly—pick two. In an attempt to meet financial goals, many companies opt for quick and low cost and sacrifice quality.

Smart toys, computer games, Web sites, interactive DVDs, and other digital devices are loads of fun, but at this age, your child should spend no more than one hour per day total—always with you right nearby or providing the lap to sit on—connected. And at every age, using any kind of interactive media should be just one of many different ways your child plays, never the only one. If you have a choice between plugging in and reading a book together or taking a hike, you should show your child where the off switch is.

Tech play these days is by no means limited to the desktop computer. And it's a lot more than just software you install from a CD or download from a Web site. As of this writing, there are over a dozen different kinds of game consoles available, and that list will likely grow. Some of the best-known portable devices are Sony's PlayStation (2, 3, or Portable), Nintendo's GameCube or Wii, and Microsoft's Xbox 360. But those are a little advanced for even the most precocious preschooler. So you'll probably be looking more at smart toys such as the various Leap Pad Learning Systems from Leapfrog.

The term *smart toy* can actually have two meanings. First, that the toy itself is smart—it talks, does math, and so on. Second, the toy makes your child smart—by teaching math, reading, geography, mythology, or whatever. When you're evaluating smart toys or any other tech item for your child, keep the following criteria in mind:

- **Ease of use.** Does it work pretty much out of the box, or do you have to plow through a two-hundred-page manual?
- **Speech.** Can you understand what the machine is saying? If not, what's the point?
- **Add-ons.** Do you need to buy other gadgets to make it work?
- **Interactivity.** Does the game or toy encourage your child to get involved and learn and have fun, or does it put on a show that your child sits back and watches? Is your child able to control the pacing and the action?

- **Compatibility.** If whatever you're buying plugs into something like a PC or a television, is it compatible with whatever you have now?
- **Adaptability.** Does the game or toy adapt to different learning styles? Can it be upgraded as your child gets older, or will you have to get a new one every year?
- **Fun.** Is it really fun?
- **Price.** It should be reasonable, whatever that means to you.
- **The whole package.** Looking at it objectively, is whatever you're considering worthwhile? Does it help you and your child to spend quality time together or is it little more than an attempt to separate you from some of your cash?

Here's a short, not-anywhere-near-comprehensive list of interactive media, software, and smart toys for three- to five-year olds. For more reviews and suggestions, check out childrenssoftware.com (fee-based), gamespot.com (free), superkids.com (free), or commonsensemedia.org (free).

ANY OF THE *PUTT-PUTT* OR *PAJAMA SAM* GAMES
Platform: Windows and Mac
In the words of my friend Kenny Dinkin, from Playfirst.com, these games are "accidentally educational." Good, engaging, clean fun that just happens to help children work their way through stories.

MISS SPIDER'S SUNNY PATCH FRIENDS: SCAVENGER HUNT
Platform: Windows and Mac
This game, featuring David Kirk's Miss Spider and her friends, contains nine games on three levels. The player helps Miss Spider's children find a list of items hidden in the woods, using sounds, colors, matching letters, and so on.

ZOOOOS PLAY AND LEARN DVD SYSTEM
Platform: TV-based game
This interactive DVD system comes with a remote game control that works with your DVD player, two DVDs, an interactive book, and an activity pack. The *Sandy Lane School* DVD is a collection of school readiness activities such as counting games, color games, alphabet, and so on. *Sandy Lane Bookshelf*, the second DVD, contains four e-books to read on the screen. Other DVDs are available for this system, such *as Bob the Builder, Thomas and Friends Ride the Rails*, and *San Diego Zoo Animal Explorer*.

PLAYHOUSE DISNEY PRESCHOOL TIME ONLINE
Platform: Web site
www.preschooltime.com
Disney's Web site for preschoolers is all about kindergarten readiness. It teaches language, storytelling, number recognition and counting, spatial reasoning, and more. As of this writing, the subscription fee was $49.95 per year.

TAD'S SILLY WRITING FAIR
Platform: My First Leap Pad
Here's an enjoyable way to learn to write the alphabet, with traceable letters, letter games, and a different theme song for each letter. If your child moves the stylus away from the letter she's tracing, the book will say "Whoops!"

Some other stand-alone smart toys:
- Pretend and Learn Shopping Cart (Leapfrog)
- Power Touch Learning System (Fisher-Price)
- V.Smile TV Learning System (V-Tech)
- Spark Art Easel (Fisher-Price)

Hardwired for Sound?

Remember the Mozart effect—the wildly popular idea that listening to music by Mozart would boost children's IQ? Don Campbell, who took the theory out of the lab and into the shopping mall, sells all sorts of products that supposedly will make your child smarter. Turns out, though, that the Mozart effect does nothing of the kind (although that hasn't stopped Campbell and others from making a ton of money).

Here's what happened. Physicist Gordon Shaw and psychologist/musician Frances Rauscher played ten minutes of a Mozart piano sonata to a number of students and noticed a slight increase in the students' spatial reasoning ability. But—and there are three big buts here—(1) whatever benefit there was disappeared after a few minutes, (2) the students were in college, and there's no indication that preschoolers and grade-schoolers would benefit from listening to Mozart, and (3) no other researchers have been able to get the same results.

So let's dispense with the idea that listening to music is magic. But there's no denying that it affects us. Music has been around about as long as humans have; archaeologists have found musical instruments more than 35,000 years old. And there is no culture in the world that doesn't have music.

Everywhere you go, you can see just how natural music is a part of our lives: that melody you can't get out of your head all day, the woman in the car next to you rocking out while putting on her makeup, your child spontaneously dancing around your living room the second you turn on your stereo, movie sound tracks that get your heart racing or bring tears to your eyes, business owners driving away rowdy teens by playing classical music and Barry Manilow.

At this point in your child's life she's already been listening to music for years, and she definitely prefers some styles over others (probably the same ones you do). If you haven't already done so, I strongly recommend that you expose her to as many different kinds of music as you can—some that you like, some you don't. You can put on anything and everything from Mahler to Mötley Crüe. The only restrictions should be volume (not too loud) and lyrics (if you aren't absolutely sure, listen carefully. When my kids were little, they loved Alanis Morissette, and it was only after they were running around the house one day singing one of her songs that I realized it had a line about oral sex in a movie theater. Needless to say, I did a much better job of screening after that).

Under no circumstances should you limit yourself (or your child) to "children's music." Far too much of it is condescending and dumbed down. There are a lot of wonderful musicians out there making music that's ostensibly for kids but that you'll listen to even when the kids aren't around. Here are some of my favorites:

- Beethoven's Wig, www.beethovenswig.com (a fantastic introduction to classical music)
- Charity Kahn, www.jamjamjam.com
- Debi Derryberry, www.debiderryberry.com
- Ira Marlow, www.brainytunes.com
- Jim Gill, www.jimgill.com
- Johnette Downing, www.johnettedowning.com
- Milkshake, www.milkshakemusic.com
- *Philadelphia Chickens*, a hilarious CD by children's book author Sandra Boynton
- Putumayo Kids label, many artists, www.putumayo.com/playground.html
- Smithsonian Folkways label, many artists, www.folkways.si.edu
- Tom Chapin, www.tomchapin.com
- Trout Fishing in America, www.troutmusic.com

My list of top picks is changing every day, and this one is by no means comprehensive. There are also several great places to get reviews and recommendations and to hear samples. Check out:

- Kids Music That Rocks, kidsmusicthatrocks.blogspot.com
- Zooglobble, www.zooglobble.com
- Common Sense Media, commonsensemedia.org

What Are Daddies Made Of? PART 1

Being an involved dad isn't something you do once; it's an ongoing operation that requires constant change and adaptation as your children get older and as your life evolves. Your definition of *good father* or *involved father* may be very different from mine or a coworker's or even your partner's. So let's not even talk about "good" or "involved" fathers. Instead, let's talk about what makes a *strong* or *effective* father.

I've been researching and writing about fathers for more than a decade. Besides having written this book and the others in the New Father series, I host a parenting radio show (*Positive Parenting*), write a nationally syndicated column ("Ask Mr. Dad"), run a Web site (MrDad.com), and teach classes for expectant and new dads. All in all, I've interviewed dozens of researchers and thousands of fathers and have identified a number of traits I think make a strong father. It doesn't matter whether you're married or not, whether you work full-time or are a stay-at-home dad, or whether you spend as much time with your children as you'd like to.

Below, and in two more sections later on in this book, I'll tell you what it is that strong fathers do. Of course, to paraphrase Abraham Lincoln, you won't be able to do all of these things all of the time—but you may be able to do some of them all of the time or all of them some of the time. Either way, incorporating some of these traits into your life will help you build and maintain a close, lasting relationship with your children.

- **Know your child.** This may sound pretty easy, but you'll probably be surprised at how many gaps there are in your knowledge. Here are a few questions you should be able to answer:
  - ◊ What are the names of your child's best friends? What are their parents' names and phone numbers? According to University of Michigan researcher Jean Yeung, more than half of fathers said they know the first and last names of their children's close friends, and three in four say that when the kids aren't home, they always know whom they are with.
  - ◊ What are your child's favorite and least favorite books, movies, music?
  - ◊ What is your child reading and listening to for pleasure now?
  - ◊ What is your child most proud of about herself?
  - ◊ What does your child like most about herself?

◊ Whom (besides you, of course) does your child admire most?

◊ What would your child want more of from you? Less?

◊ What motivates your child?

Don't worry that you're being intrusive or prying into your child's private business. You're not. And although most kids will never admit it, they'll take your interest in their life as exactly what it is: a sign of your love.

The more you know about your child—and the more areas of her life you're familiar with—the better tuned in you'll be to her needs, the more quickly you'll recognize potential problems before they get too bad, and the sooner you'll be able to jump in to help if need be.

♦ **Be involved in your child's day-to-day life.** This is similar to knowing your child, but it's drilling down a little further. Do you know your child's favorite and least favorite things to take for lunch? Which days she has violin lessons and which she has basketball? When recitals and concerts are? What she's working on in each of her various school subjects? Approximate clothing sizes? The names of her doctor and dentist and when their next appointments are? You should. In sociologist Jean Yeung's study, 80 percent of dads said they help select their children's activities, and 67 percent help choose their children's day care and schools, but only 29 percent say they help their wives select a pediatrician and make appointments for their children. So get out your calendar, get into the car, and start driving.

Not getting involved in the day-to-day decisions that affect your kids' lives can give the impression that you don't think they're important or that you're not interested in being an active parent. And by doing that, you make it more likely your partner will feel comfortable and confident in sharing the nurturing role with you. But make sure to log some private, quality time with the kids. too. Sure, somebody has to schlep them all over town to their ballet lessons or soccer practice, but that shouldn't be the only times you get to see each other.

♦ **Read up on child development.** This may be one of the most important things that you can ever do as a parent, which is why I'm always amazed at how few people do it. At the very least it'll help you understand why your child is doing what she's doing. And chances are it'll reassure you that a lot of those completely insane things she does are absolutely normal.

♦ **Parent the child you have, not the one you wish you had.** Don't compare her to your other children, friends' children, the kids down the street, or

DEALING WITH "I HATE YOU!"

No matter how terrific and involved a father you are, one of these days you're going to walk into the house after a long day of work, and, instead of jumping into your arms and giving you a great big hug, your child will run the other way, screaming "Mommy, Mommy!" And that's only the beginning. No matter what you try to do, whether it's making breakfast, taking her out of the car seat, offering to help with homework, or reading a bedtime story, you'll get "Go away, Daddy, I want *Mommy* to do it!" or a more painful variation like, "I hate you, Daddy!" or "You're not my friend. I only love Mommy!"

As I mentioned in the previous chapter, three-year olds often go through a phase when they prefer the opposite-sex parents. For four-year olds, it's all about the same-sex parent. So whether you have a boy or a girl, at some point or other you're going to get hit with the "I hate you's." The good news is that this phase—and that's exactly what it is—will eventually pass. In the meantime, though, hearing those words and seeing that look in your child's eyes is really going to hurt.

In situations like these, it's tempting to back off as a way of avoiding the pain, to punish your child for speaking to you so disrespectfully, or to try to convince her that she doesn't really hate you. Don't do either; it's important to let your child have the freedom to express her feelings. As coolly and calmly as possible, tell her that you understand that she's angry and that you'll love her no matter how she feels about you. Try as hard as you can to avoid repeating the phrase "you hate me." It's also important that you not let your child see how much she's hurting you. As difficult as it is to believe in the moment, she has no idea of the impact her words are having. Seeing you cry (and believe me, you'll feel like it) or withdraw could actually scare her.

The way to approach this kind of situation is to work through your partner. Ask her to be your advocate, to talk about you when you're not there, to tell your children how much she's looking forward to your coming home, to remind them of all the wonderful things only you can do. The goal is to build you up and to get the kids to look forward to seeing you.

Keep in mind that the role of "preferred parent" usually switches back and forth as children get older, which means your partner will have to deal with a lot of "I hate Mommy" in the not-so-distant future. So mark this page so you can show it to her when it's her turn to be the evil one and yours to be the one who can do no wrong.

some kid you read about in the newspaper. As trite as it sounds, your child is unique. What works for all those other kids may not work for yours.

♦ **Have a support network.** Try to put together a group of people you can rely on, whether it's your parents or in-laws, an organized babysitting cooperative, friends, or just some trusted people you can call up and ask for advice from time to time.

Why Is a Daddy Like a Bottle of Wine?

Most first-time fathers are between twenty and thirty-five when their children are born, but that number is on the rise and has been for a while. Since 1980, the number of babies born to men age thirty-five to forty-nine has increased 40 percent; for men fifty to fifty-four, about 10 percent; and for guys under thirty, the number has *decreased* 20 percent, according to the National Center for Health Statistics.

While some of this trend has to do with men marrying younger women, that's certainly not the only reason—women are having children later in life too. Between 1980 and today, the percentage of first-time mothers between thirty and thirty-four was up about 60 percent; for women thirty-five to forty-four, the birthrate more than doubled. The rate for women aged twenty to twenty-four stayed about the same.

As fathers (and men) we're constantly changing and developing as we get older. That mean that two fathers—one in his twenties or thirties, the other in his forties or fifties—with kids the same age are going to be very different kinds of parents. If I had to sum up those differences in a sentence, I'd dust off a quote from Plato: "The spiritual eyesight improves as the physical eyesight declines." But there's much more to it than that. In the sections below, I'll to explain some of the advantages and disadvantages of being an older dad.

ADVANTAGES

Compared to younger dads, older fathers . . .

♦ Are more relaxed, caring, flexible, supportive, affectionate, expressive, and involved with their children, according to my colleague psychologist Ross Parke.

♦ Are more nurturing with infants and young children. "The impact of these parenting qualities may have lasting effects as the child moves into adulthood," say sociologists Cynthia Drenovsky and Melissa Meshyock. Their research found that as young adults, children of older fathers are more likely to say they had a close relationship with Dad.

♦ Are more likely to have children who were deliberately planned for (as opposed to being a surprise).

♦ Are more established in their careers, have more money, really want to be a dad, and have more free time to focus on their children. Part of the reason for this may be that older dads are painfully aware of how much time they have left, and they're making parenting a priority. Here's how older dad Len Filppu summed it up: "I'm more patient, empathetic, compassionate and wise. I've already been there and done most of that. I've got a bit more money, my affairs are in better order, and my career longevity allows me to juggle work to spend more time with the kids."

♦ Are in more stable relationships.

♦ Are more likely to have older children from a previous relationship. We'll talk more about those "renewed" dads on pages 218–20.

♦ Spend more time reading, talking, and playing fantasy games.

♦ Have children with fewer behavior problems and who feel more appreciated by their fathers.

♦ Use less physical discipline with their children.

♦ Have children who are smarter, happier, and more socially attuned, according to Sherman Sliber, head of the Infertility Center of St. Louis.

♦ Take better care of themselves. Overall, men's lifespan is about five years shorter than women's, and we die younger of every disease. But being a dad gives many men an incentive to eat better, exercise more, and give up risky habits. If you haven't already made these changes in your life, you should. The Men's Health Network (menshealthnetwork.org) has some great resources, including *Blueprint for Men's Health*, a book I wrote for them, which is available as a free download.

DISADVANTAGES

Compared to younger dads, older fathers . . .

♦ Spend less time rolling around on the floor with their kids or playing other physical games.

♦ Have children who may be embarrassed by a dad who's often confused for Grandpa, and who worry that he might die at any moment.

♦ Worry about all sorts of things: their ability to amuse their children, people calling them "Grandpa," whether they'll be able to get down on the ground and play and then get back up again, dying young, living long enough to see their children graduate from high school.

♦ May show a little less affection and warmth toward their partner, according to Jacky Boivin, a psychologist at the School of Psychology at Cardiff

---

LET'S NOT FORGET THE YOUNGER DADS

While younger dads are usually more spry than the older guys and spend more time wrestling and having fun with their children, the picture isn't 100 percent rosy. If you're still in your twenties or early thirties, you may be not very far out of college, not yet solidly established in your career, and you may still be trying to carve out your place in the world. Unfortunately, that often means more time at work and less with the family. But that's getting less and less true.

Several recent studies have shown that more and more of today's young fathers are putting family first. They're turning down promotions and assignments that take them away from their families, and they're more likely to ask for flexible work arrangements to help them better balance their work and family lives.

University in Wales, Great Britain. Boivin also found that some older dads are less tolerant of their children's physical activities and perceive their children to be impulsive and overactive.

♦ Sometimes don't feel they have much in common with the parents of their children's friends, and are less likely to try to bond with them.

♦ May feel good, young, and strong—but are surprised by how old the guy in the mirror looks.

♦ May have completely revised their life plans. Retirement at fifty is looking less and less likely.

♦ May have children with a variety of health issues. As men age, the sperm we produce is more likely to have problems. For example:

◊ Babies of older dads—in their forties and fifties—may be a little less active at birth, according to Yuelian Sun, a researcher at the University of Aarhus in Denmark.

◊ Children born to men over forty have six times more risk of being autistic than children whose dads were under thirty.

◊ Children born to dads age forty-five to forty-nine are twice as likely to have schizophrenia as those whose dads were under age twenty-five.

◊ Older dads are linked with a number of extremely rare genetic mutations, including dwarfism, disorders of connective tissue, a specific type of skin cancer, and a congenital heart defect, according to James Crow, a geneticist at the University of Wisconsin. Children born to older dads also have a very slight increased risk of certain kinds of tumors, cataracts, and being homosexual. Again, all of these risks are minuscule.

Ready, Set, Learn

What's Going On with Your Child

Physically

♦ Even though your five-year-old is about twice as tall as he was at two, this is going to be another slow-growth year—he'll gain only four to seven pounds and creep up just two or three inches. Of course, that's just enough growth to require all new clothes.

♦ He's down to ten or eleven hours of sleep a night, but not because he's any less active than before. In addition to everything he was doing last year, he can catch balls on a bounce, throw overhand, jump rope, climb trees, stand on his head, and balance on one foot for ten to fifteen seconds at a time. He can even walk down a flight of stairs without holding on to the railing, alternating his feet (as opposed to last season's two-feet-per-step approach).

♦ He's now able to take on more complex physical activities such as swimming, skiing, or jumping rope.

♦ He may still like riding his tricycle, but if he hasn't already ridden a two-wheeler with training wheels, he's going to want to soon. That phase will be short-lived—by the end of the year, he'll be ready to get rid of the training wheels.

♦ His new, improved small motor skills include zipping, buttoning, and shoe tying.

♦ Everything is easier than last year. He can cut patterns with scissors and even draw fairly intricate pictures. So what if his people have eyes on the tops of their heads? At least they have necks . . .

♦ As his baby teeth fall out, you'll find yourself paying out good money in the name of someone called the Tooth Fairy. And since the permanent teeth won't be along for a bit, you'll have plenty of time to take pictures of the gaping holes in his smile.

Intellectually

♦ Your five-year-old is a budding lawyer. He loves to argue, reason, and prove his points. *Because* is the big word now, although he may not get the usage down quite right. For example, he might say something like "I'm cold because I'm putting on my jacket," instead of the other way 'round.

♦ He still loves to be read to, but he's getting more interested in trying to read for himself. He understands that books (in English anyway) go from left to right and top to bottom, and that stories have a beginning, middle, and end. He especially likes jokes, nonsense rhymes, and silly stories.

♦ He draws letters and shapes and loves to write, especially his own name and short sentences like "I [heart] daddy." He may even draw portraits of his favorite animals or toys.

♦ He's beginning to understand that actions have consequences. This won't keep him from misbehaving, of course, but at least it's on some back burner for later.

♦ He can memorize his address and phone number—and should do so, for safety reasons.

♦ He can count up to ten and may even have memorized a few more numbers after that. He loves to count and sort and organize everything he can: the number of squares on the sidewalk between your house and the park, the number of dogs you pass on your way there, how many green cars you drove by, how many kids have long hair in his preschool class, how many days until his birthday, and on and on.

♦ He understands the idea of opposites, and can play the "what's the opposite of" game. And "today," "tomorrow," and "yesterday" now mean something to him.

♦ He understands more than 10,000 words and speaks like a little grown-up now, using the correct plurals and tenses that only a year ago had him stumped. While he may no longer sound like a child, don't forget that he still is, possessing a child's logic, and still finding the line between real and pretend a little tough to grasp.

Emotionally/Socially

♦ Friends (still mostly same-sex) are getting to be very important, and your

*You're five. How could you possibly understand the problems of a
five-and-a-half-year-old?*

child will probably have one or two true best friends whom he prefers over
all others. Preschoolers love to get together and construct elaborate fantasy
play. But they spend more time talking about the plotline and who's going
to be whom than actually doing anything.

♦ He's pretty good at sharing and taking turns but still occasionally excludes
some kids from the play group.

♦ He's much more interested in others in general. He now has real conversations with people and may even ask a question now and then.

♦ His sense of empathy is growing. He notices when others are upset and may
try to soothe them. He's also beginning to develop a sense of right and wrong.

♦ Your preschooler has developed a fondness for rules—they offer some security in a world that he seems to have less and less control over. He will
insist that others toe the line, but has no problem bending the rules if things
aren't going his way.

♦ He may be developing a fear of the unknown, which could include loud
noises, the dark, strangers, and even some things he didn't used to fear, like
the mailman or the neighbor's dog.

♦ He likes to test his strength, flex his muscles, and show off how strong and
capable he is. But he's not ready for competition, even with other kids; his

ego is still fragile, and he can't stand not winning. This is not the time for competitive team sports.

♦ He's becoming more aware of the world around him and will notice differences between his family and others' families—this one has two daddies, that one doesn't have any.

♦ He's also becoming more self-aware. He instinctively knows that he needs a little down time every once in a while, and will go to his room or another quiet place where he can be alone.

What's Going On with You

Meet the New You

Close your eyes for a second and imagine that you'd never had kids. How would your life be different? Seems like a simple enough assignment, but a surprising number of fathers I've spoken with have trouble with it. Life before kids seems like part of a different, faraway lifetime or as if it were someone else's life altogether. Even if you can't quite get your mind around how things could have been, there's no question that fatherhood has changed you in all sorts of ways. Here are some of the most common:

♦ **Where you live.** A number of factors go into selecting a child- and family-friendly living situation: neighborhood safety, home prices, proximity to good schools, size of the backyard, size of the house, distance to parks, whether there are criminals or registered child molesters living nearby, whether your neighbors have children, and so on. Those are not necessarily the same factors you would have been looking for if you didn't have kids. And making the decision to put your children first may mean moving across town or across the country or increasing your commute time.

♦ **Your schedule.** You're driving carpools, shopping for clothes, going to teacher conferences and piano recitals, making meals, doing laundry, helping with homework, and a lot more. What on earth were you doing with all those hours before? On a more macro level, having a family means less time to yourself, less time spent on personal development. "As parenting becomes paramount, fathers will tend to be less involved in organizations that focus only on personal recreation, leisure pursuits or self-improvement," says David J. Eggebeen, associate professor of human development at Penn State. "They will also be less inclined to visit friends or coworkers, go to a bar, or play on sports teams."

♦ **Your job.** A lot of guys take a job that they might be less than 100 percent excited about because it pays well or has good benefits. Some guys stay in less-than-ideal employment situations out of fear of losing whatever security they already have. Others work longer hours or take a second job so they can embody the true provider/protector. (The irony here is that men in this situation are so caught up with providing for the family that they end up having less time to spend at home.) But job-related issues aren't always negative. Far from it. In my case, becoming a father gave me a whole new career—took me out of my MBA job and into the dangerous world of self-employment. It was a little scary at first, but I've never been happier. And some guys quit their job entirely to become stay-at-home dads.

♦ **Your relationship with your partner.** As psychologist Jerrold Shapiro once told me, having children tends to make what's good about a couple's relationship better and what's bad about it worse. It could bring you and your partner closer or drive you apart. Or you might find yourself in the middle, staying together for the sake of the children.

♦ **Your friendships.** You probably noticed even before your baby was born that your friendships had begun to change; you spent less time with single friends, less with childless couples. But you also started meeting other expectant couples, or people with kids the same age as yours. And as your child gets older, you'll find that a great deal of your social life revolves around the parents of your child's friends.

♦ **Your family.** You may be spending less time with friends, but many dads compensate by spending more time with family, their own siblings (and the assorted nieces and nephews), parents, and in-laws.

♦ **The larger community.** In the day-to-day process of meeting your child's needs, you're spending a lot of time interacting with people and organizations you might never have come in contact with otherwise: pediatricians, music teachers, coaches, school teachers, PTA, and so on. As a dad, you're also more likely to get involved in community volunteer projects (more on this on pages 136–37).

♦ **Your character.** Most dads say that fatherhood has made them more mature—somehow, having a child makes it pretty clear that you're a grown-up. They also say that it makes them more responsible. They're very aware of the way their actions could affect their family. Many dads I've spoken with say that having children was the catalyst that got them to eat better, exercise more, and generally take better care of themselves. Dads are less likely to take all kinds of risks (I stopped running yellow lights; other dads have given up everything from parachuting and cheating on their taxes to motorcycle riding and recreational drugs), which helps explain researcher

Joseph Pleck's findings that involved dads are less likely to land in the hospital or to be killed in an accident, get arrested or abuse drugs. Some men have said that fatherhood made them more tolerant and compassionate, and less of a perfectionist.

♦ **Having a purpose in life.** Many men say that having a child gave them a purpose in life and a reason to live, helping them clarify what's really important in their lives.

♦ **Your religious life.** As you struggle with the question of how to teach your children good values, you may find yourself spending a little—or a lot—more time involved in religious activities. According to Penn State's David Eggebeen, "Men who are not fathers attend church significantly less than men who live in the same household with their children." More on this below.

Pondering Ye Olde Values, Ethics, Morality, Religion, and Spirituality

Since teaching right from wrong is such a stereotypical dad thing, it's not surprising that a huge majority of dads spend time thinking about it. A lot of time. About 80 percent of the men in researchers Rob Palkovitz's study on new fathers, and a similar majority of the dads I've interviewed, said that they'd made some kind of shift in their basic values or life priorities. Some dads took on a more active role in their children's religious education (most of us tend to leave those things up to our partners), which often meant increasing their own church or synagogue attendance and/or sending their kids to religious school. About half of Palkovitz's sample didn't make any changes at all. Religion was already central in their lives, or they'd had such bad experiences as kids or young adults that they were turned off for good. Younger fathers in particular were less likely to take any big steps either way. Their religious and spiritual views tend not to be as fully developed, and they're not as sure as more mature dads what they're embracing or rebelling against.

A team of researchers in Switzerland did a study a few years ago, hoping to find out whether a person's religion carried through to the next generation, if so, why, and if not, why not. Turns out that by far the most important factor was the father. In families where both Mom and Dad attend religious services regularly, 33 percent of their children will do the same, and another 41 percent will go irregularly. But if Mom goes regularly and Dad is non-practicing or goes irregularly, only two percent of their children become regular worshippers, and about a third will go irregularly.

There are a lot of ways to define the word *values,* but one of my favorites comes from Jeffrey Levine, a career and business coach and my partner in a work-life consulting business called Fathers at Work (fathersatwork.com): "Values are those qualities that must be present for you to have a fulfilling life." But even that way of defining values can be a little slippery, because your values are always changing. Some may disappear completely, while others may appear unexpectedly. To show you what I mean, let me give you an example from my own life.

When I was in high school, I played the violin in an orchestra that performed in several international music festivals. Meeting fellow musicians from all over the world and not being able to communicate with all of them put international travel and learning languages at the top of my list of values, followed by having a fulfilling career. So I learned several languages, lived overseas for a while, and eventually got an MBA in international business, which I thought would position me nicely to live my values. It took me a good nine or ten years to figure out that I wasn't well suited to working for other people. At that point, my wife was pregnant with our first, and I realized that some of my new values were autonomy, being an involved dad, and having time to be with my family. So I gave up the business career and focused on writing. That brought up another couple of values: creativity and wanting to make a difference in people's lives.

How do you know what your values are? Jeffrey Levine suggests that one way is to imagine that you're a hundred years old and one by one, people are coming up onstage to talk about how you inspired them and changed their lives. Another way is to give yourself the homework assignment that one of my kids came home with when she was in fourth grade: Write your *ethical will*, outlining the intangibles—attitudes, philosophies, worldview—you'd like to leave to your child (the assignment was actually for *me* to write the will for her). Try it. It's a wonderful way to help you get clear on what's most important to you, and the way you'd like to be remembered.

Issues for Stay-at-Home Dads

There are over two million stay-at-home dads in the United States, and that number is growing every day. But despite the increasing acceptance, it's not an easy job. To start with, being the primary parent can be an isolating experience. That's partly due to a general lack of resources and support for dads. But the men themselves don't always do much to improve their situation. True to the stereotype, stay-at-home dads—like many other men—don't ask for help. That means that even if they take their children to parks, museums, and other places where there are lots of other kids, the dads aren't likely to connect with many (or any) of the other parents.

The second source of trouble has to do with what I call a crisis of masculinity. As men, we're raised to think of ourselves in terms of how much money we make and to see ourselves in the role of provider/protector. It's very hard for some men to get past this kind of socialization—even when logic and finances say that staying home with the children is the best thing for the family. I sometimes hear from guys who loved being stay-at-home dads in the beginning, but as time went on and their job skills got more and more out of date, they slowly slipped into a funk. Some lost interest in spending time with their children. Some stopped taking care of themselves, quit exercising, began using food for comfort and put on weight, and even took fewer showers. All of those behaviors are classic symptoms of clinical depression.

If you're a stay-at-home dad and you're not as delighted about it as you once were, there's still hope. Your first step should be to get out of the house and connect with some other stay-at-homers or locate some local daddy-child playgroups. Finding out that you're not alone in what you're feeling can make a huge difference and really boost your mood. Slowlane.com and Rebeldad.com are great resources. If you're brave and want to start or join a group, don't be shy about insisting on making it guy-only. I've led dozens of groups and taught hundreds of classes, and I can assure you that when women are in the room, men tend to clam up.

Next, if you can afford it, consider going back to your old employer as a part-time consultant, or start a home-based business. Getting back on (or at least closer to) the career track may make you feel better about yourself and, for lack of a better word, more manly. And that will probably make you a more hands-on (and better-groomed) dad.

You and Your Child, PART 1

Why Be Involved with Your Five-Year-Old?

- ◆ The strongest predictor of your child's ability to feel sympathy and compassion for others is the level of your involvement when he's five.
- ◆ The closer your bond to your child when he's five, the better off he'll be at nine. Belgian researcher Karine Verschueren and her colleagues found that five-year-olds who had a strong attachment to their father were less likely at nine to be anxious, socially withdrawn, or lacking in self-confidence. They also had better friendships and their teachers rated them as being well-adjusted at school. Interestingly, the father effect was greater in this area than the mother effect.

♦ Having a warm, loving relationship with your five-year-old makes him more likely to have a long-term marriage, be a good parent, and form close friendships as an adult, according to researchers Carol Franz, David McClelland, and Joel Weinberger.

♦ Playing with your child in a mature, supportive, challenging way teaches him self-control and how to effectively manage his emotions. It also helps him form closer relationships with others in his preteen and teen years.

♦ Women who rate themselves as having well-adjusted personalities, and men who report "positive personal qualities and behaviors in themselves," tend to have had fathers who were nurturing and interested in them when they were very young.

♦ Being involved with your child at this age will make him more tolerant and understanding later in life.

Education

Is Your Child Ready for Kindergarten?

Despite the title of Robert Fulghum's best seller *All I Really Need to Know I Learned in Kindergarten*, the reality is that you don't really need to know that much to get into kindergarten. Your child will certainly have a leg up if he walks into kindergarten knowing how to write his own name on his cubby or even read a little, able to identify seven different shades of blue, and capable of building a computer by himself. But brains aren't everything, and most teachers are going to be more concerned with whether your child has the emotional and social chops to make it in the kid-eat-kid world of kindergarten. Actually, it's even simpler than that.

A couple of years ago kindergarten teachers in North Carolina came up with a list of what they felt five-year-olds would need to know and do to be successful in school. Ninety-two percent of the teachers put being "healthy, rested, and well-nourished" at the top of their list. I'm assuming that that's pretty much a slam dunk for you. So, aside from that, how do you know whether your child is ready for school? If you can honestly answer yes to most of the following questions, you're good to go. Does my child . . .

♦ Track fairly well with the age-appropriate What's Going On with Your Child sections in this book?

♦ Get dressed (including some snaps, zippers, and buttons), use a fork and spoon to eat, blow his nose, try to brush his teeth, go to the bathroom and wash hands *without help?*

I'll trade you my soy milk for your wheatgrass juice.

- ◆ Play nicely with other children, including sharing, waiting his turn, working together on group projects, and keeping his hands (and teeth) to himself?
- ◆ Generally follow simple directions and rules, help clean up his toys when he's done playing (at least some of the time), and sit quietly for ten to fifteen minutes while you're reading stories?
- ◆ Know his own name and age and the names of his friends and everyone in his immediate family?
- ◆ Communicate his wants and needs using words?
- ◆ Handle it quite well when you pay attention to others while he's still in the room?
- ◆ Keep himself busy for short periods of time without having to be entertained?
- ◆ Know which end of a book is up and which way the text goes?
- ◆ Sing along to familiar songs or tell simple stories?
- ◆ Hear and see well? (Many experts feel that a huge percentage of "learning disabilities" are actually caused by undiagnosed vision and hearing problems.)

YOUR CHILD'S LEARNING STYLE

Most education-related tests are designed to measure proficiency in reading and math. But Howard Gardner, a professor of education at Harvard, believed that traditional tests of intelligence were too limiting. Instead, he came up with the theory that there are actually a number of distinct kinds of intelligence:

♦ **Bodily-kinesthetic** kids are constantly moving, touching, picking things up, bumping into people. Think Michael Jordan or the guys who run sub-four-minute miles.

♦ **Interpersonal** kids are natural leaders who always seem to be involved with other kids, are empathetic, have magnetic personalities, and know how to work a crowd. Think diplomats, mediators, salespeople, schmoozers, and probably cult leaders.

♦ **Intrapersonal** kids are strong-willed, like to be alone, can entertain themselves for hours, and don't need much direction to finish a project. They're self-aware, knowing what they're capable of and what their limitations are. Think entrepreneurs, novelists, memoirists, philosophers, and members of the clergy.

♦ **Linguistic** kids chatter constantly; they love to read, hear, tell, and act out stories; they dazzle you with their incredible vocabulary. Think Shakespeare, Abraham Lincoln, and other great writers and eloquent speakers who have a natural feel for words and how they go together.

♦ **Logical-mathematical** kids love rules and regulations and order. They love numbers and are probably better than you at those addictive Sudoku puzzles. They want to know why and how and why again. Think Mr. Spock, accountants, computer programmers, mathematicians, scientists.

♦ **Musical-rhythmic** kids always seem to be humming or singing or demanding that you change the channel on your car radio from the news to a music station. Think Mozart, J. S. Bach, the Beatles, and people who are proficient at playing an instrument other than their iPod or the radio.

♦ **Naturalist** kids love the outdoors, rain or shine. They're always up for a hike or a backyard wildlife safari. They're fascinated by animals, plants, rock formations, and so on. Think Charles Darwin or TV's Crocodile Hunter, the late Steve Irwin.

♦ **Visual-spatial kids** love drawing and color and puzzles, can mentally rotate objects, and build elaborate structures out of blocks or Lego. Think artists, architects, chess masters, and engineers.

(continued on page 90)

YOUR CHILD'S LEARNING STYLE *(continued from page 89)*

Hand in hand with the now widely accepted theory of "multiple intelligences" is the somewhat less-widely accepted idea that there are also multiple ways of learning and that what is best for one child may not work at all for another. Here are a few examples:

- **Auditory learners** learn better by hearing things, such as lectures, being read to, listening to books on tape, and so on.
- **Visual learners** learn by watching and looking. For these kids a picture—or a video or a graph or chart or a 3-D model—really is worth a thousand words.
- **Musical learners** may need to have music playing while they're reading or studying. They'll learn best if lessons can be taught through songs or rhythm.
- **Linguistic learners** are pretty good at acquiring information verbally or orally, but putting it in writing really cements it.
- **Bodily learners** learn best when they're moving around and are often good at multitasking. Teaching about fractions by cutting an apple into pieces is clearer than looking at a chart.

If you had a lot of nos or I'm-not-sures, you may want to consider waiting to enroll your child in kindergarten. But while you're making up your mind, talk to your pediatrician and ask specific questions about the areas that concern you. He or she will be able to give you a more definitive answer about your child's readiness for school.

Making the Transition

Whether it's this coming fall or the next one, start getting your child prepared as far in advance as possible for the big jump from preschool (or day care or staying at home with your partner or you). You can do this by:

- Talking with your child about how his life is going to change, the new routines, rules, and expectations, schedules, bedtimes, friends, and so on. You'll have this discussion a few dozen times. Then start easing your child into the new routine a few months before the first day of school.
- Visiting the school, preferably while it's in session, so your child can see the teachers in action and get to know the classroom.
- Encouraging your child to talk about anything that might be worrying or frightening him.

- Telling your child all about your experiences as a kindergartner.
- Reading books about the preschool-to-kindergarten transition.
- Reinforcing the skills your child will need to use, such as sharing, taking turns, cleaning up toys, speaking respectfully to adults, following instructions and rules, and so on.
- Having a special first-day-of-school ritual. In my family we always had cookies baked into the shape of letters, a tangible demonstration that learning is sweet.
- Leaving your schedule open for the first day of class. You may need to spend a little extra time saying good-bye to your child. Actually, this could continue for a few weeks.

The Weaker Sex? It May Not Be the One You Think

Back in the 1970s, it started to come out that girls were lagging behind boys in math and science, but were a little ahead in reading and writing. As a result, a huge effort was made to restructure our education system to improve girls' performance. It was amazingly successful. Maybe a little *too* successful. The edge boys had in math and science has almost completely disappeared,

I don't have to be smart, because someday I'll just hire lots of smart people to work for me."

and the reading-and-writing gap has widened. In short, boys are being left in the dust.

To give you an idea of how deep that dust is, here are some statistics I gathered from the U.S. government and other sources that may surprise (and probably shock) you. Compared to girls, boys:

♦ Get the majority of D's and F's in schools.

♦ Are twice as likely to be in special ed or remedial programs.

♦ Are less likely to do homework and come to school with the supplies they need.

♦ Are 50 percent more likely to repeat a grade in elementary school.

♦ Are 30 percent more likely to drop out of high school.

♦ Are twice as likely to be identified with a learning disability and twice as likely to be prescribed Ritalin or some other attention deficit/hyperactivity disorder (ADHD) drugs.

♦ Are three times more likely to be diagnosed with an emotional disturbance and account for about 80 percent of discipline problems.

♦ Are more than twice as likely to be suspended from school and three times more likely to be expelled.

♦ Are more likely to have been victimized criminally in school.

♦ Are far less likely to be involved in extracurricular activities like student government and performing arts. The only area where boys are more involved than girls is sports, and that gap is closing fast.

A little later in life, males . . .

♦ Are about 50 percent less likely to earn an associate's degree.

♦ Are about 30 percent less likely to earn a bachelor's degree.

♦ Are four times more likely to commit suicide.

♦ Are fourteen times more likely to end up in jail (even higher for African-Americans).

♦ Are 50 percent more likely to be homeless.

A Solution? How About Single-Sex Education?

When people think of single-sex schools, they usually have girls in mind. Girls in girls-only schools tend to do better than those in coed schools. What about boys? Well, not many people know about it, but the results are similar: boys in boys-only schools do much better than boys in coed schools. In fact, the bump kids get from single-sex schools is even greater for boys than it is for girls, according to an exhaustive study by English researcher Graham Able.

There are a number of advantages to a single-sex education. According to

He's at that annoying age where they're always testing you.

the National Association for Single Sex Public Education (NASSPE—www.singlesexschools.org), the three biggest ones are:

♦ **Boys and girls learn differently, and teachers can custom-tailor their teaching style to the boys.** Here's how the NASSPE described what a boy-friendly classroom might look like: "Most boys will perk up and show some interest if you talk about things that are dangerous, or immense, or 'yucky.' The boy who was bored by biology at the coed school will be interested if you bring in some black garden snakes. The boy who fell asleep in chemistry class will be energized if you give him an assignment to do a PowerPoint presentation on dynamite, with lots of pictures of things blowing up. Most boys enjoy blowing things up (or at least imagining blowing things up)." (See pages 89–90 for more on learning styles.)

A **girl-friendly classroom "is a safe, comfortable, welcoming place.** Forget hard plastic chairs: put in a sofa and some comfortable bean bags. Let the girls address their teacher by her (or his) first name. The teacher should never yell or shout at a girl. . . . Girls will naturally break up in groups of three and four to work on problems. . . . If you're assigning class presentations, let two girls give a joint presentation. The format of one student giving a presentation to an entire class doesn't work as well (for girls) as two students giving a joint presentation to a smaller group."

♦ **The single-sex classroom promotes a more diverse and well-rounded educational experience.** Boys and girls in coed schools spend a lot of time worrying about what the other gender will think of them. Girls may worry that if they're smart, boys won't find them attractive. They may dumb down their own performance in some subjects and avoid others (like math and science) altogether. Boys try to impress girls by being tough, and they stay away from "girly" activities like chorus, drama, debating, and foreign languages. They may also underperform, worrying that being a straight-A student will make them seem nerdy to the other boys. The bottom line is that in single-sex schools, girls can be girls and boys can be boys.

One other important advantage of single-sex education for boys is that there are likely to be more male teachers than in a coed school, where 80 percent of teachers are women. "Learning from a teacher of the opposite gender has a detrimental effect on students' academic progress," according to Thomas Dee, an economist at Swarthmore College. Dee, who's been ruffling a lot of feathers with his research, also found that when a class is headed by a woman teacher, boys are more likely to be seen as disruptive. And disruptive children often end up in remedial classes or getting Ritalin or some other drug to "control" their behavior.

Henry Biller points out that in Japan, where about half of elementary school teachers are men, boys' and girls' reading scores are equal. In Germany, where the majority of schoolteachers are men, boys not only score higher than girls, but they are also less likely to suffer from severe reading problems.

And Speaking of Teaching . . . How About Manners?

When our children were very young, we didn't much care about their manners. As infants, their loud burps (and other bodily sounds) would usually elicit laughter, and as they learned to speak, we considered their inadvertent insults or seemingly rude behavior rather adorable. But as children get into preschool and start having play dates and doing the birthday party circuit, manners become increasingly important.

Children who don't learn respect, good manners, and how to behave with others run the risk of being shunned by their peers as children and having trouble in social situations as adults.

Unfortunately, teaching kids manners isn't easy. If preschoolers could draw a picture of the universe, they'd put themselves at the very center. They want to be first, best, strongest, and they want everyone around them to notice. They aren't particularly interested in anyone else's needs.

The good news is that you've probably already started teaching your child manners. When he wants more green beans (okay, white rice), you prompt him to say, "Please." And when he receives a present, you encourage him by asking, "What do you say to Grandma?"

While saying "Please" and "Thank you" is a great start, there's more than that to good manners. Overall, teaching manners is about instilling good behavior in a variety of situations. Here's how to do it:

- **Start off easy.** For three-year-olds, "Please" and "Thank you" are first, then add in "Excuse me." Learning to share, "Nice to meet you," telephone etiquette, and thank-you notes are still a ways off.

- **Give them some strategies.** The second you answer the phone or start talking with someone, your preschooler will develop a sudden, irrepressible need to talk to you or show you something. Trying to stop that need is as futile as trying to keep earthquakes from happening in California. What you *can* do, though, is teach your child to politely say, "Excuse me," or squeeze your arm instead of screaming. As he gets older, you can explain the difference between good reasons to interrupt and bad ones. A fire in the kitchen is a good one. Needing a snack is not. If your child uses one of the polite strategies, respond immediately. Ignoring a gentle arm squeeze sends the message to your child that screaming is a better option—at least it gets your attention.

- **Talk the talk.** Use *please, thank you,* and *excuse me* with your kids and everyone else you come in contact with. If you don't say "Please" when asking your child to pick up his toys, or you skip the "Thank you" when your spouse gives you a Valentine's Day present, you're undermining all the great lessons you've struggled so hard to teach.

- **Walk the walk.** Similarly, holding the door for the people behind you and helping an old person cross the street models polite behavior. Screaming at the bozo who cut you off in traffic does exactly the opposite.

- **Be consistent.** Manners and good behavior aren't only for company or for going out to eat. They need to be part of your everyday routine.

- **Give a little warning.** If you're brave enough to take your child to a fancy restaurant or to meet your rich uncle or someplace else where good manners are expected, tell him so before you arrive and let him know exactly what you expect. You may not get it, but you'll at least up the odds.

- **Skip the lectures.** Too many parents launch into long-winded sermons like, "Stop that yelling! How many times do I have to tell you to be quieter in the house?" Short, to-the-point phrases like, "Inside voice, please," are much more effective. Same with behavior. If your child picks up his food with his hands, instead of lecturing him on the history of flatware in the United States, just hand him a fork.

+ **Lay it on thick.** Preschoolers really want to do the right thing—even if they don't know what the right thing is—and they're suckers for compliments. So when yours behaves nicely, be lavish with praise. And be specific: "I'm so proud of the way you said 'Excuse me' when you were trying to get my attention," or "You did exactly the right thing when you told your baby brother you were sorry you dropped a block on his toe."

+ **Respect your child.** If he behaves rudely, take him aside and discuss the issue privately. Criticizing your child in front of others will embarrass him and could cause him to be even ruder later on as a way of trying to get back at you.

+ **Establish—and enforce—consequences.** The manners bar should get higher as your child gets older. So if he demands that you go to the living room and bring the stuffed animal he left there, tell him he'll have to get it himself. And if he doesn't thank you for pouring him the big glass of milk he asked for, take it away until he does.

Finally, keep your expectations reasonable. Although there are books and DVDs out there that claim they'll produce a well-mannered, delightful child in a matter of days, save your money. The reality is that teaching good manners is a process that will take years. In the meantime, you'll need to be prepared to remind your child dozens of times every day before the message really sinks in.

You and Your Child, PART 2

Keeping Those Pearly Whites Pearly White

Okay, here's something you probably didn't know: dental caries (better known as tooth decay or cavities) is a *disease*, not just a hole in a tooth. Actually, it's the single most common chronic childhood disease—far more prevalent than asthma and obesity, according to the California Dental Association. And to make matters worse, tooth decay is contagious, just like the measles, the flu, and smallpox. The bacteria that cause decay can be passed from one person to another by kissing or sharing drinking cups or silverware.

Pain and suffering due to untreated tooth decay can lead to problems in eating, speaking, and paying attention in school. In other words, cavities hurt.

And having them filled hurts too. (New laser treatments are promising to make cavities and fillings pain-free. But don't mention that to your child.)

One way to avoid cavities is to make sure your child brushes twice a day, every day, with a soft brush. This comes directly from the top, the American Dental Association (ADA). Unfortunately, until your child is about six years old, he won't have the coordination to brush his teeth on his own. He can get the process started, but you'll need to give his mouth a good once-over to make sure the job gets done right.

As your child gets older, show him how to brush with a fluoride toothpaste and floss on his own. There are all kinds of flavored flosses out there that you can buy to make the task less onerous. You also might want to pick up some *disclosing tablets* or drops at your local pharmacy. You may remember these tablets from grade school. When you chew them or swish the drops around in your mouth, unbrushed spots on the teeth will show up red. Use the tablets or drops every day for the first week that your child is brushing solo. Then cut back to once or twice a week.

If your child refuses to brush, you've got a few options.

1. **Sticks.** Take away some privileges or treats until the teeth start gleaming.
2. **Carrots.** Give incentives and rewards for doing the job right. That's generally more successful than punishment.
3. **Scare tactics.** Caring for your teeth and gums does more than improve your smile and your breath. The bacteria that cause tooth decay can get into the bloodstream, where they increase the risk of ulcers, pneumonia, digestive problems, heart disease, stroke, and diabetes. This is absolutely true.
4. **Gum and candy.** Yep. But not just any kind. It has to be sugar-free and sweetened with *xylitol*, a natural sweetener that keeps bacteria from sticking to teeth. Chewing gum with xylitol for five minutes after each meal has been shown to reduce cavities.
5. **Sealants.** About 80 percent of cavities in kids are on the tops of their molars, and studies have shown that sealing these teeth with a special kind of resin is extremely successful in preventing cavities.

Playing with Your Five- to Six-Year-Old

Four important things to keep in mind about playing with your five- to six-year-old:

♦ **Don't do too much teaching.** According to psychologist Lawrence Cohen, play is "children's main way of communicating, of experimenting, and of learning." That means that your child will be soaking up knowledge from almost everything you do. So there's no need to be heavy-handed about it.

♦ **Let your child run the show.** You can make suggestions, but don't insist on doing things your way (unless what your child wants to do involves juggling knives or some other health and safety issue).

♦ **Have a *beginner's mind*.** "In the beginner's mind there are many possibilities," writes Zen master Shunryu Suzuki. "In the expert's mind there are few." One of the great things about playing with a child is that it gives you a chance to see his world from his point of view, to marvel at the things he marvels at. You can't do that if you're trying to corral your child into doing something *you* want to do or if you're trying to show off how much you know.

♦ **If what you're doing isn't fun anymore, stop.**

Here are some activities that will provide hours of entertainment (and plenty of education) for you and your child.

♦ **Go fly a kite.** Build a kite with your tyke and take it to the park on some windy weekend afternoon. Spend a little time running and trying to catch the wind, but don't be surprised if your child would just as soon do some of his running without the kite.

♦ **Don't get rid of the dress-up box yet.** Imaginative play is still enormously popular at this age, and is much more elaborate than it was at three or four. You'll see some gender stereotyping, with girls wanting to be princesses or ballerinas or slipping into Mom's clothes and putting on makeup. Boys may want to dress in your clothes, but they'd probably rather be a cop, a robber, or a superhero. Interestingly, that gender stereotyping won't apply to the rest of the cast of characters, meaning you can expect to spend a lot of time having your nails painted, hair braided, and feet squeezed into your partner's shoes.

♦ **Get out the cards and boards.** Enjoy those lazy Sundays at home by teaching your child how to play checkers and some simple board games (Candyland, Chutes and Ladders) and card games (Uno, Go Fish, War). If you're a chess or backgammon player, give it a try, but you might need to hold off another year or two. Your child is beginning to understand rule-based games, so now's the perfect time to institute a regular family game night, a tradition that will hopefully go well into your child's teenage years and beyond.

♦ **Progressive storytelling.** This is a great one for long car trips or those endless hours waiting in airports. One person, usually an adult, starts the story ("Once upon a time there was a young wolf named Max . . .") and continues for a minute or two or until a climactic point in the tale. The next person, usually a child, picks up the action and continues the story.

+ **Twister.** Once your child has a good handle on his primary and secondary colors, and can consistently tell left from right, he's ready for this classic game. It's best played with a group of people. You can be the referee and flick the spinner. Or someone else can do it while you risk pulling a few muscles by playing. Either way, you'll spend a lot of time laughing yourself silly.

+ **Don't forget about all those ball games.** Catch, basketball, football, T-ball, soccer, dodgeball, tetherball, badminton, four square, or golf. If you're feeling adventurous, you might even try some tennis. But have your child use a child-size racquet or a racquetball racquet—it'll be a lot easier for him to handle.

+ **Start making some noise.** You can produce literally hundreds of sounds without ever leaving your house. Have your child close his eyes, then you do something and have him guess what you're doing. Drop a coin on the floor and have him tell you whether it's a penny, nickel, dime, or quarter. Pour some rice into a metal container. Smack a pickle with a carrot. Then you close your eyes and have your child handle the sound effects. There's no end to the possibilities.

+ **Build something.** Children this age often show an interest in real tools—especially if they've seen Dad using them. Get a book of simple-to-make wood projects and pick out a basic birdhouse. Then make a list of what you need, go together to the lumberyard or hardware store, and pick it up. Show him how to read the plans, how to use tools safely, and let him do as much of the real work as possible. (If he's going to try his hand at hammering, you should get the nail started and then have him use a very small hammer. And be sure you and your child wear goggles or safety glasses.) The two of you will feel an incredible sense of pride when the first robin lands on your birdhouse. If you don't know one end of a nail from the other, not to fear. Places like Home Depot and Lowe's often have dad-child classes where they take you through a simple project from beginning to end.

+ **Skate on by.** Your five- or six-year-old is coordinated enough to take to the streets or the ice, and you can help him soar. So dust off those ice skates, roller skates, or in-line blades, or find out when a local rink is open. Be sure everyone's got a helmet, gloves, and knee and elbow pads.

+ **Call for reinforcements.** Did you know your house came with a fort? Your child does, and at any given moment, a pirate garrison may appear in your living room, dining room, bedroom, or any other place where there's a blanket, a table, some chairs, and some pillows. If you learn nothing else from this book, remember this: Grown-ups are not permitted in these forts unless they're specifically invited. This means you.

♦ **Put on a show.** You do a little magic, your child does some card tricks, little sister does a dance. Get your timing down, then invite Mom, Grandma, Grandpa, and some neighborhood kids over to enjoy.

♦ **Develop his sense of humor.** At this age your child likes riddles, knock-knock jokes, and bathroom humor. Pick up a couple of good books of jokes. This is the perfect time to introduce the Three Stooges.

♦ **Spend some time in the kitchen.** This can teach your child many valuable lessons about textures, measuring, and how things change shape when they're mixed, heated, or cooled. Jell-O is particularly well suited because it doesn't even require cooking. Be patient: making food with a child can be a tremendous mess—but an even more tremendous amount of fun.

♦ **Do some art.** Take a pad of paper and something to draw with and go to a museum. Find a picture your child really likes and copy it. Then walk through the galleries and see how many dogs, or cats, or horses your child can find. Before you go, you might want to take a look at a wonderful series of interactive books called *How Artists See* (*Animals, People, Families, The Elements, Cities,* and others). You can, of course, do this activity anywhere.

♦ **Take up a collection.** Could be coins, stamps, dried leaves, bottle caps, stones, or anything else. If you have a collection of your own around, show it to your child. But if it has any value, don't turn your back for very long, unless you want your uncirculated proofs to wind up in a piggy bank or your rare stamps stuck to your child's forehead.

♦ **Leave him alone—kind of.** Although it's tempting to want to spend every waking hour playing with your child, remember that he needs plenty of down time. So once in a while, take your child to a park, flop yourself down on a bench, and read the paper while he runs around like a maniac, skips, climbs trees, goes down the slide, makes sand angels, and plays hide-and-seek with some new friends.

Reading to Your Five- and Six-Year-Old

OH, WHERE, OH, WHERE HAVE THE DADDIES GONE?
The very first article I ever had published appeared in *Newsweek* and was called "Not All Men Are Sly Foxes." It was all about what I perceived to be the negative stereotyping of fathers in children's literature. I spent an entire day in the children's section of my local library talking to the librarians and reading

children's books, and found that for the most part dads were completely absent. Of the books where a parent appeared, Mom was almost always the only one. Dad, if he was there at all, was much less loving and caring than Mom.

The library had a special catalog of children's books with positive female characters—heroines *and* mothers. As the father of a daughter, I thought that was great. But as a father who was sharing the child-care responsibilities equally, I found it incredibly frustrating that they didn't have a catalog (or even many books) with positive *male* role models. Even my three-year-old wanted to know why there weren't more daddies in the books we read.

Unfortunately, in the more than thirteen years since that article came out, not much has changed. Oh, sure, we now routinely refer to "firefighters" and "mail carriers" (instead of firemen and mailmen), and we show women working in every conceivable job. There are dozens of books that feature positive portrayals of the disabled, minorities, and people from other religions and cultures. Only the portrayals of fathers have stayed the same.

The one thing that *has* changed is that I'm not the only one complaining about these negative stereotypes anymore. In 2005, researchers David A. Anderson and Mykol Hamilton did an exhaustive study of the portrayals of parents in two hundred children's books and found pretty much what I had: fathers appeared in half as many scenes as mothers. When present, they were portrayed as "unaffectionate" and "indolent" and were "relatively less likely than mothers to touch, hug, kiss, make other contact with, talk to, or feed children." In fact, there wasn't a single action that fathers did more than mothers, and dads were *never* seen kissing or feeding a baby.

So the big question here is, Does any of this make a difference? In my mind there's no question that it does. A number of researchers have found that when kids are exposed to books that contain gender role stereotypes, they end up with negative attitudes toward women. But when they see women in nontraditional roles, they have a positive view of women. Seems perfectly reasonable to assume that the same thing is going on with regard to portrayals of fathers: when kids are bombarded with negative images of fathers (we'll talk about movies and television in a later chapter), how could our children's attitudes be anything but negative?

The only way to correct this situation is to expose our kids to positive images of fathers in a variety of situations. In the Resources section, on pages 245–47, I've included a list of books that feature all sorts of good fathers.

Now that your child recognizes letters and even some words (some children this age may even be reading quite fluently), it's important that you adapt your reading style to his changing abilities and needs.

♦ **Add some subtle education.** Read some alphabet books with your child. When reading other books, run your finger under the words to show your child where you are on the page. If your child asks you what a particular word means or points to a word and asks you to tell him what it says, do it. Be sure to point out letters, especially those in your child's name. You can turn this into a game by asking your child to find certain letters or words on the page. But be sure not to turn your reading time into a drill session.

♦ **Shake things up a little.** Who says you have to read books from front to back? Your child will find it incredibly funny if you read one of his favorites from end to beginning ("Hat the in Cat The"). And be sure to vary the pace. Faster can increase the tension, slower can heighten the drama.

♦ **Add a little variety.** Try reading a picture book one night, and a couple of chapters from a longer storybook the next. When reading longer books, have your child do a recap of where you are before starting the next chapter.

♦ **Get your child involved.** Rather than just read to him, stop now and then and ask questions: "What do you think is going to happen next?" "What would you do in that situation?" "How come Bruno got sent to his room?"

♦ **Let him see you read for pleasure.** There's no better way to set an example. If you have boys, it's especially important to show them that real men read.

♦ **Make a list.** Keep a running tab of the books you and your child read together. Take yourselves out for a treat to celebrate certain milestones.

♦ **Create themes.** Spend a week reading all the books by a particular author. Or check out a week's worth of books on princes or princesses or trains or sports or magic or travel or any other topic your child seems interested in. If you want to go a little deeper, spend some time focusing exclusively on illustrations— watercolors one week, woodcuts the next, photographs after that.

Below are a few dozen more books (none with negative portrayals of Dad) that are sure to be hits with your five- or six-year-old.

GENERAL
The Adventures of Super Diaper Baby, Dav Pilkey
Amazing Grace, Mary Hoffman
Archaeologists Dig for Clues, Kate Duke

Baseball Saved Us, Ken Mochizuki
Bears, Ruth Krauss and Maurice Sendak
Can You Say Peace? Karen Katz
The *Captain Underpants* series, Dav Pilkey
Cloudy with a Chance of Meatballs, Judi Barrett
Dear Tooth Fairy, Pamela Duncan Edwards
Dinosaur Bob, William Joyce
Eloise, Kay Thompson
Flat Stanley, Jeff Brown
The Frog Wore Red Suspenders, Jack Prelutsky
Grandfather's Journey, Allen Say
Moon Plane, Peter McCarty
Mrs. Katz and Tush, Patricia Pollaco
My Father's Dragon, Ruth Stiles Gannett
Nate the Great, Marjorie Weinman Sharmat
Night Driving, John Coy
In the Night Kitchen, Maurice Sendak
Owen, Kevin Henkes
A Pocketful of Kisses, Angela McAllister
Sheila Rae, the Brave, Kevin Henkes
The Story of Ferdinand, Munro Leaf
The Story of Ruby Bridges, Robert Coles
The Three Little Wolves and the Big Bad Pig, Eugene Trivias
Throw Your Tooth on the Roof: Tooth Traditions from Around the World,
    Selby Beeler
Thunder Cake, Patricia Pollaco
Time Train, Paul Fleischman
Tough Boris, Mem Fox
What's the Big Idea, Ben Franklin? Jean Fritz
Wingman, Daniel Pinkwater
Wings, Christopher Myers

STARTING KINDERGARTEN

I Am Absolutely Too Small for School, Lauren Child
The Kissing Hand, Audrey Penn
Miss Nelson Is Missing! Harry Allard
Vera's New School, Vera Rosenberry
Will I Have A Friend? Miriam Cohen

You and Your Partner

Sex: The Marital Barometer

If you watch much television, it's easy to get the impression that everyone out there is having sex three times a day with five different partners. Real life is a little different. Sixteen percent of couples haven't had sex in the past month, and a lot more people are rolling in the hay once or twice a month.

Some people put the blame on the various pressures put on working couples, and even came up with a clever acronym: DINS (Dual Income No Sex). Turns out, though, that isn't true. A huge problem is simple fatigue, which stay-at-home moms and dads have at least as much of as those who spend sixty hours per week at the office. And, contrary to the stereotype, women aren't the only ones keeping their knees together. Denise Donnely, a researcher at Georgia State University, found that men stop sex at least as often as women.

But regardless of how it starts, low levels of sex in your relationship could be an indication that all is not right. If your sex life is suffering from some neglect, getting it back on track is going to take communication, planning, and lots of patience.

- **Make sure there are opportunities for verbal as well as sexual intimacy.** And while you're at it, get rid of the idea that there's always a connection between the two.
- **Stop thinking about it (for a while).** Spend some time getting used to being affectionate with each other in a nonsexual way.
  - ◊ Hold hands.
  - ◊ Stroke her hair.
  - ◊ Kiss her when walking through the kitchen.
  - ◊ Give each other massages, back rubs, and so forth.
  - ◊ Make out. . . .
- **Schedule sex.** It doesn't have to be spontaneous to be fun.
- **Go on dates** (see page 217 for more).
- **Go for quality over quantity.** You may only be able to make love a few times a month, but make them count.
- **Try to keep it regular.** Your sex organs are muscles, and they need some regular working out to operate at peak capacity.
- **Flirt.** Remember when you and your partner were just falling in love? Recapturing some of those feelings isn't as hard as you think. When you see her getting out of the shower, tell her how good she looks; let her catch you looking down her shirt or staring at her butt; put some love notes in her

Hey look, before this goes any further,
I should probably tell you we're married

wallet so she'll find them when she's at work. By the time the two of you get
home, you'll be all over each other.

♦ **Argue a little.** In Donnely's studies, couples who didn't have much of a sex
life also didn't argue about it much. They may have just given up.

♦ **Get some help.** In researching his book, *VoiceMale: What Husbands*
Really Think about Their Marriages, Their Wives, Sex, Housework, and
Commitment, author Neil Chethik found that twenty-five percent of men
had gone to marriage counseling together. Three-quarters of them said it
was helpful.

♦ **Get out of the house—or at least the bedroom.** Your house and your
bedroom are filled with too many distractions. So have sex in the back
seat of your car, or in the shower, or on top of the washing machine. You get
the point.

♦ **Take turns pleasuring each other.** She may not want to "go all the way," but she might be interested in trading a back rub for a somewhat more intimate kind of rub. And of course the same holds true if she's in the mood at a time you aren't.

♦ **Just do it.** Despite the exhaustion and everything else, sometimes just starting to go through the motions—touching, stroking, kissing—can be enough to get you aroused.

The Famous Mr. ED

Generally speaking, your sex life is a reflection of your overall health—the healthier you are, the better it will be. But good overall health isn't a guarantee of a good sex life.

Sometimes called *impotence,* erectile dysfunction (ED) means that you can't regularly get or keep an erection long enough to satisfy your sexual needs or those of your partner. All men—whether they admit it or not—have an occasional erection problem. But for about 30 million American men—10 percent of all men, 30 percent of men over sixty—ED is an ongoing problem. It can start at any age and can develop slowly over time or suddenly.

There are a lot of myths out there about ED. Some people insist that it's all in your head. Others say that it's just what happens when you get older. The truth is that about 90 percent of the time, ED is the result of a physical problem that can almost always be treated. Heart disease, high blood pressure, smoking, alcoholism, back injuries, testosterone deficiency, prostate problems including surgery, and over 200 prescription drugs can all contribute to or cause ED.

Even though physical problems are the primary culprits, psychological factors, including depression, still play a role. Men who suffer from ED often feel inadequate and less sure of themselves. That can make them anxious, tense, angry, or worried that they can't satisfy their partners. Those feelings only make the ED worse.

If you're experiencing ED, do yourself and your partner a favor and schedule a visit to your doctor right now. Chances are, he'll be able to get to the bottom of your ED problem in just one or two visits. He'll ask you a lot of questions about your health habits, your diet, drugs you take, how often and under what circumstances the ED happens, and so on. He may also order tests of your blood, urine, heart function, and hormone levels.

Treating ED

In many cases, taking steps to improve your overall health will help reduce or even eliminate ED. This means:

♦ **Eat a low-fat, low-sodium, low-cholesterol diet.**

♦ **Quit smoking.** Chemicals in cigarette smoke can narrow blood vessels, making it harder to maintain an erection.

♦ **Drink less alcohol.** Alcohol slows your body's reaction times.

♦ **Get more exercise.** Exercise builds muscle, improves blood flow, and helps get the cholesterol out of your blood. It also improves your mood, which will make you feel better about yourself.

♦ **Cut back on coffee.**

If these lifestyle changes aren't successful, your doctor may prescribe one or more drugs that have been used successfully to treat ED. These include Viagra, Cialis, and Levitra. Each has advantages, disadvantages, and potential side effects that your doctor will explain. Alternatively, he could prescribe injections, vacuum devices, or one of a number of surgical options.

How Your Sex Life Changes as You Age

There's no question that your sex life will change as you get older. You probably won't respond to sexual stimulation quite as quickly as you did when you were younger. You may lose your erection after sex sooner, and it may take longer for you to get another one. But none of this means that you can't have an active sex life. The key is to keep it going. As mentioned above, without regular workouts, your sexual muscles will get weaker.

As men, having a positive self-image is a very important part of our sex life. But the two are connected in a kind of loop: the more attractive and desirable we feel, the better we'll perform. At the same time, the better we perform sexually, the more attractive and desirable we feel. For this reason, it's especially important to make contact with your doctor if you experience any sexual problems. Remember, most are treatable.

Your Amazing, Stretching Child

What's Going On with Your Child

Physically

- Your six-year-old is stretching out. Her legs are growing longer, and she's packing on more muscle and getting stronger. That, combined with lots of physical activity, has eliminated most of her baby fat and makes her look gangly.
- You should have a good idea by now of whether she's a righty or a lefty, and her hand-eye coordination is getting better all the time. She can catch small balls and connects fairly regularly with a baseball bat.
- Her small motor control keeps improving. She can print her name and lots of other words, and handle a pair of scissors without drawing blood. Most of her artwork may actually look like what she claims it is. Still, she prefers doing things that use the more developed large muscles (legs and arms).
- She loves to play outdoors. Her balance is pretty terrific now, and if she hasn't yet, she's ready to learn to ride a bicycle without training wheels.
- Her mouth is still mostly filled with baby teeth, but they're slowly but surely falling out.

Intellectually

- Language is becoming increasingly important. When she was younger, she learned by doing and seeing. Now a lot of her new knowledge comes via words. Speaking of words, she understands about 15,000 and uses over

Benjamin, we've discovered, is quite gifted at third base.

2,000. She loves magic, card tricks, and competitive games but still can't stand losing.

♦ She craves knowledge and loves learning, adventure, and new ideas. She is pleased to show off what she has learned at school. Questions are constant. With her increased attention span, she spends a lot of time reading and writing, though she may still reverse lowercase b and d. She may also write other letters backwards (E, N, R, Z).

♦ She can separate fantasy and reality but may not want to—especially when fantasy yields money and prizes, as in the case of the Tooth Fairy or Santa Claus.

♦ She knows and understands the days of the week, can count to 100, and can tell time on an analog clock, yet persists in asking time-related questions (How long till we get home?).

♦ She's something of a rigid thinker, dividing everything in her world into black and white, good and bad, with very little room for compromise. She finds security in rules, makes up complicated games with extensive, ever-changing regulations, and may get upset if you break them.

♦ She can tell her own right and left apart, but may have trouble applying the concept to other people.

♦ The notion of "men's work" and "women's work" is beginning to dawn on her, and she may have some trouble dealing with the idea of a male nurse or a female firefighter.

Emotionally/Socially

♦ For the first part of this year, your six-year-old is a highly emotional being, given to angry outbursts, mood swings, and difficult behavior. Fortunately, as she heads toward six and a half, she'll stabilize somewhat.

♦ She wants to be the biggest, be the strongest, and have the most, and she is easily hurt by criticism. She adores being flattered and becomes infuriated if you don't notice—and praise—her often. She wants to tell you all about her day and everything (and I mean *everything*) that happened to her, and expects you to stop everything you're doing to listen. She's discovered that tattling is a great way to get your attention.

♦ Her emotional range is fairly limited, and she tends to express herself physically more than verbally. She's likely to hit or push rather than discuss problems. And when playing, she's not a particularly gracious loser. Even so, she's becoming better at identifying her emotions: happiness, sadness, anger, frustration.

♦ Though still fairly self-centered, she can now, at least sometimes, see things from others' points of view and has a greater (but not too great) respect for their needs.

♦ Those first, tentative steps away from her insulated little world and into the bigger world of school and peers may scare her and even undermine her confidence.

♦ Her playmates are still mostly of the same sex. She plays better with one friend at a time and demands loyalty ("If you play with her, you can't be friends with me").

♦ Her sense of right and wrong has taken a giant leap since five, and she knows that she has—and makes—choices.

What's Going On with You

Who Am I Going to Be This Week?
The Evolution of a Confused Father

For the first five or so years of your child's life, you had two dominant ways of interacting with her: caregiving (feeding, changing diapers, driving to the doctor, walking around trying to get her to stop crying, and so on) and playing (wrestling, rolling balls back and forth, playing hide-and-seek, reading stories, and so forth).

But now that her needs are different, you'll have to recalibrate your parenting—again. One of the big shifts, according to researcher Robert Bradley, is that your role in her life will evolve "from caregiver and organizer of experiences to that of mediator and guide." As she gets older, your role in disciplining her will increase (not in a harsh way, but in the way the word was originally used: to train or instruct.) "During these middle years the father can be a teacher, coach, confidant, and pal as well as an authority figure," write psychologists Bryan Robinson and Robert Barret, authors of *The Developing Father*.

Most dads instinctively understand all this and respond to their school-age kids' changing needs by making fundamental changes to their own personalities, and by altering the way they see themselves and the ways others see them.

Here's how this plays out for a lot of dads:

♦ **Honing your skills as a role model.** You've always known that what you do influences your child. Just think about the way she imitates your mannerisms and of all those times you've heard her swear and then realized that she's repeating *your* words. But seeing your child pretend to smoke a cigarette or drink a beer or copy any of your bad habits, or hearing from her teacher that she launched into a profanity-laced tirade at someone who cut in front of her in line at the cafeteria, is going to make you think a lot more seriously about the way you behave. Of course you never fudged on your taxes, but some dads who did think twice about that now.

Fatherhood researcher Rob Palkovitz found that a lot of dads give up destructive or risky behavior, criminal activity, drug abuse, or bungee jumping. A lot of young dads also change their attitude about their health. Most men don't go to the doctor (for themselves anyway) unless a woman in their life forces them. But our kids often motivate us more than we or anyone else can. Many dads of school-age kids start having regular physicals, or at least they're more receptive to the idea when their partner brings it up. All of a sudden being around for their kids seems a lot more important. They may start exercising more regularly, eating better, and even cutting down on the amount of artery-clogging trans fats that make their way home from the grocery store—partly for themselves and partly to encourage their kids to get into the same good habits.

Knowing your child is watching your every move could get you thinking more deeply about a lot of things you take completely for granted. I've always stressed to my children the importance of keeping their promises and following through on commitments. On a family trip to Indonesia a few years ago, I got into a huge argument with a *tuk-tuk* (kind of a cross between a bicycle and a taxi) driver. He'd quoted us one price before we got on but was demanding more money at the end. I kept the argument going so long because I was trying to show the kids that everyone—even *tuk-tuk* drivers—needs to hold up his or her end of a bargain. But after about five minutes, I suddenly realized that we were squabbling over about 50 cents. In any other circumstance, 50 cents wouldn't have been worth haggling over. But to that man, it might have made the difference between feeding his family that day or not. I gave him his money and had some interesting discussions with the kids about knowing when to make exceptions to rules.

♦ **Slowing down and smelling the roses—for a millisecond.** A lot of men find the start of their children's school career to be very stressful; they suddenly realize that they haven't spent as much time with the kids as they wanted to, and now the kids are practically leaving home.... In a way our kids give us a time limit. You may not feel that you've aged since becoming a dad, but seeing how quickly your child has grown makes you realize that she— and you—aren't going to be young forever. A lot of men I interviewed said they tried to take it a little easier, sometimes cutting back at work or working a more flexible schedule, and even turning down promotions or transfers that would take them away from their families. I remember becoming a lot less obsessed with being on time and insisting that everyone else was too.

♦ **Expanding your (previously narrow) horizons.** The personality overhaul that your school-age child has triggered in you is going to rub off in other areas of your life too. If your years of parenting have taught you only one thing, it's the value of contingency planning, just in case Plan A goes terribly wrong. This is a skill you may have already brought to your workplace. You might find yourself interested in mentoring younger coworkers, taking them under your wing. You're likely to be a more outspoken and confident advocate for your children, whether it's at a parent-teacher conference, or asking a waitress to take back an undercooked steak. Because you love your child more than anything in the world, you're going to learn to think more flexibly and creatively. You'll teach yourself to accept her rejection while swallowing your pride and supporting her at the same time. That newfound ability to adapt your thinking and responses to other people's irrational behavior might make you a little more tolerant when those around you act like complete idiots. And as your child picks up new abilities and skills and brings home new interests and passions, you may find yourself learning about things you never heard of or never cared about before. Who knows, you could find yourself studying the rules and strategies of soccer, learning to tie fourteen kinds of slipknots, becoming an expert rock climber, solving quadratic equations, or conjugating irregular Latin verbs.

My Child Dumped Me; or, Coping with Your Separation Anxiety

Even though your child has been trying to establish her independence since she was born, she still spent most of her time at home, with you and your partner. You were her primary source of information about the world, and you still had a lot of control over her life—where she went, who her friends were, what she learned. But at the ripe old age of six, things are changing. Fast. Even if she's had some experience with preschool or day care and has spent some good chunks of time away from the house, there's still something about starting first grade—that's "real" school, after all—that is very different.

A lot of dads I've spoken with have said that while the start of their children's school years was a happy occasion, it was also a little devastating. On the one hand, we're proud that our kids are getting bigger and smarter and stronger and better looking. On the other hand, we have this helpless feeling that they're slipping away. The issue isn't the number of hours away from home. It's that slowly but surely, we're becoming aware that our kids don't need us as much as they used to, and we're losing our ability to influence them.

From here on out, school will be the focus of her life, and what her friends and teachers say will carry more and more weight in her mind. She'll also be influenced by her own reading—over the next few years she'll go from being barely able to read her name to plowing through 200-page novels. Between the friends, the teachers, and the books, your child will be exposed to all sorts of new ideas and thoughts and philosophies that you have very little control over.

As your child careens unsteadily into her new world, you've got a lot of adjusting to do. To start with, it's going to take a little doing to get used to relinquishing control over your child's education, but you can handle it. What's going to be a lot tougher is to come to terms with her budding independence. It wasn't all that long ago that she wanted to hold your hand all the time and have you watch every somersault and hang up all those "You're the best daddy in the world" notes that she made for you all by herself.

But now, as she develops deeper relationships outside the home, her relationship with you and your partner will change. There'll be no more—or at least a lot less—snuggling in bed as a family to read stories or watch videos together, she may become self-conscious about being hugged or kissed by you, especially in public, she may not want to talk to you about her day, she's very clear on how much everything about you embarrasses her, she always has someplace else she'd rather be, and she may hardly want to spend any time with you at all.

She's developing her own social life—one that often won't include you—and she's perfectly capable (or at least she thinks she is) of scheduling her own engagements and other activities. The fact that you might have other things to do than chauffeur her all over town won't even occur to her. Getting recognition and acceptance from you won't be nearly as important as it used to be. Instead, life will be more about fitting in with the new crowd and being accepted by them. She needs to prove to herself and others that she can make it in that big world out there. In her mind, the only way to show her independence and be accepted by her friends is to reject you. Doesn't make a lot of sense from the adult perspective, but those are the cold, hard facts. And let me tell you, it's going to hurt.

Novelist Charles Chadwick did a great job of capturing this dynamic in his book *It's All Right Now*. "My son has stopped asking me about my work. A long time ago he stopped asking me how strong I am." But as normal as it is for your child to push you away, it's just as normal for you to feel confused. You'll be proud that your child is growing up, and you'll want to encourage her independence. At the same time, you'll want to keep her close to home where you can protect her from the world. But watch out: you may have other, more selfish reasons for not wanting to let your child go. You'll mourn the loss of your close relationship, and you'll feel hurt by her rejection. Having a child dependent on you made you feel important and needed, and you don't ever want to forget how her hugs and kisses melted you.

It can be very tempting to take your child's rejection personally and "get even" by pulling back emotionally or even physically. Big mistake. Try to remember that you're the grown-up here, and you've got to behave like one. Your child may act as though she doesn't need you, but deep inside she does—and she knows it. So don't stop being affectionate (just respect her wishes and don't kiss her in public), don't stop trying to communicate, and show up at her games or performances even if she's asked you not to. Your new and improved role now is to set boundaries, while keeping the door open, to steel yourself against the sting of rejection but remind your child that you love her and that you'll always be there for her. You need to show that support unobtrusively, without feeling hurt, disappointed, or angry, according to the Group for the Advancement of Psychiatry (GAP). You also have to discipline yourself not to expect much back from your child. It won't be easy, but you'd better try: "Parents who need reassurance of the child's faithfulness are the unhappiest people in the world," writes the GAP.

DADS ON SCREEN

In the previous chapter, I talked about the (mostly negative) ways dads are portrayed in books for children. The good news is that books aren't the only place kids get messages about fathers. The bad news is that portrayals in other media—most notably television shows, commercials, and movies— are at least as bad.

American children spend an average of about four hours watching television every day, and for the most part, the fathers they see are incompetent, absent, uncaring, and unnecessary. Their children routinely outwit them and rarely look to them for advice. Their wives don't respect them, and treat them like another child in the family.

Commercials, which take up about 20 percent of a broadcast hour, are even worse, in part because kids see them over and over and over. Overall, women are far more likely than men to be shown as parents, far more likely to be shown nurturing or comforting children, and six times more likely to be shown teaching kids. As with television shows, when dads are in a parenting role, they're usually the buffoon.

Movies are more of the same. Researchers at the Annenberg School for Communication did an exhaustive study of G-rated films and found all sorts of bad news. Overall, male characters outnumber females three to one. Seventy-two percent of characters with speaking parts are male, as are 83 percent of narrators and characters in crowd scenes. Sounds like discrimination against girls, right? Not really. About four times more males than females are portrayed as violent or physically aggressive. But males are half as likely to be identifiable as parents, married, or in a committed relationship.

Still, if you look for them, there are some positive father characters out there. To help make your search a little easier, I've put together a list of films that show good, warm, engaged fathers. Not all the dads are perfect—and they shouldn't be. But they're all trying to find ways of caring for their children. The list is on pages 247–48 in the Resources section.

You and Your Child

Why Be Involved with Your Six-Year-Old?

♦ Schoolchildren whose fathers are involved in their lives have a greater tolerance for stress and frustration in school. They're confident in their ability to work on their own, are more willing to try new things, and are better able to wait their turn for the teacher's attention, according to fatherhood researcher Henry Biller.

♦ Children whose fathers were involved during the first three years of their kids' lives have higher cognitive and verbal function at this age, according to Lisa Crockett and her colleagues.

♦ When it comes to raising empathetic children, father involvement is the most important ingredient. Richard Koestner and his colleagues studied 379 people over twenty-six years and found that dads who spent time alone with their kids doing routine child care at least twice a week had children who grew up to be the most compassionate adults.

♦ Children with involved fathers are less aggressive, more generous, and more popular and well liked than children with less involved dads.

♦ When fathers are supportive and involved, their children are less likely to have excessive absences from school, and they tend to do better on exams.

♦ For children with attention deficit/hyperactivity disorder (ADHD), supportive fathers can have a stronger positive influence on their adjustment to school than mothers, according to Israeli researcher Malka Margalit.

♦ Even when dads aren't available as much as they'd like to be, their children still benefit, says Biller. They have an easier time adjusting to new experiences, have more stable emotions, and generally get along better with others.

Military Dads

As a former U.S. Marine, my heart goes out to all the dads (and everyone else, for that matter) who are deployed overseas and separated from their families. Being a father who works outside of the home is hard enough as it is, but having to be away from home for months at a time can be nearly unbearable for some guys. There are over 700,000 children under five in military families who are separated from their mother or father. Here are some ways to keep in touch, keep relationships going while you're away, and prepare yourself and your family for your absence.

♦ **Go high-tech.** Before you deploy, pick up an inexpensive webcam and a good CD and/or DVD burner or tape recorder (remember those?). That way, your family can keep you in the loop by sending audio or video recordings of life at home. Or they can create a Web site and post movies, favorite songs, report cards, and lots more. Depending on where you're stationed, you may be able to set up some video conferences with your family. But even without conferencing, you can have some of your buddies film you, or you can take advantage of programs like the U.S. Army's Knowledge Online, which allows active-duty, National Guard, and Army Reserve soldiers to create video messages. The files are stored on a server, and you can e-mail the link to your family. The upshot of all this is that if you look around, you may be able to stay actively involved in your kids' lives and participate in any big (or small) decisions that affect them.

♦ **Go low-tech.** Before you leave, write a whole bunch of messages for your kids and hide them around the house so they'll find them in unexpected places. If your child can't read yet, another option is to put all the messages in a special basket. Your partner can read a new one to your child every day, or your child can take one out herself anytime she wants a little virtual hug.

♦ **Sit down and talk with your kids before you leave.** Explain to them exactly what's happening and why. If you need some help finding the right words, check out some of the books in the Resources section on page 236.

♦ **Use the mail.** Technology is great, as far as it goes, but it's no substitute for a good, old-fashioned package from Dad. Little things—a dried leaf from a tree near your barracks, a film canister full of sand—are great ways to let your child know that you're thinking of her no matter where you are. They also give her a tangible sense that you're somewhere, in a real place. This is particularly important for younger children.

♦ **Take a good book on child development with you and read it.** This one, for example. That way, you'll be able to keep up with how they're changing and you'll have a better chance of hitting the ground running when you get back.

♦ **Ease your partner's burden before you go.** Your not being there is going to cause increased stress on your whole family. Your wife will have a lot more to do, and everyone will be anxious and worried about your safety. If there are any household tasks that are your responsibility, make sure your partner is up to speed on how to handle them (where bank statements are, when bills are due, and so on). Make sure your paychecks are automatically deposited to your joint account. And if you can set up your rent and other bills to be paid automatically, so much the better. Lastly, write a will.

♦ **Get some support.** It's important to have a strong network of family, friends, and/or community. On one level, these people can help your family cope with your absence. On another, knowing they're there and keeping an eye on your family will put your mind at ease. If there's a support group for non-deployed military spouses on your base, get the details and let your partner know about it. Your synagogue or church may have a support network available. In the Resources section on pages 235–37 you'll find a number of very helpful resources for yourself and your family.

COLOR ME MALE . . . OR FEMALE

Until fairly recently, it was politically incorrect to even suggest that there could be significant biological differences (besides actual gender) between boys and girls. Differences in behavior, career choice, and so on were supposedly largely the result of the varying ways our society treats both genders. But in the past five to ten years, researchers using high-tech brain imaging and other techniques have identified a number of physical differences between boys' and girls' brains, differences that may be responsible for some of that stereotypical "boy" and "girl" behavior.

For example, boys' and girls' brains seem to be wired differently for sound. Several studies have shown that when preemies are exposed to music therapy (soft music playing in the nursery or someone holding them and humming), they're able to leave the hospital an average of about six days sooner than those who don't hear music. But psychologist Leonard Sax points out that the six-day figure doesn't tell the whole story. "Premature girl babies . . . left the hospital *twelve days earlier* on average than girl babies who weren't. But premature boy babies . . . didn't leave the hospital any earlier than boys who weren't."

Boys' and girls' eyes are also very different. Boys' retinas are thicker than girls' and more responsive to motion. Girls' eyes are more sensitive to color and texture. "We're not talking about small difference between the sexes with lots of overlap," says Sax. "We're talking about large differences . . . with no overlap at all."

How these eye differences play out is absolutely fascinating. When you look at drawings by kindergartners and first-graders, you'll see that girls generally use many more colors than boys. They also tend to draw curvier forms, while boys prefer more angles and straight lines. Girls often draw

Can Being a Committed Father Save Your Life?

It just might. In fact, it did just that for a lot of dads who served in World War II. In her book *Parenthood: Its Psychology and Psychopathology*, Therese Benedek talks about how these soldiers' thoughts and fantasies of their children helped them overcome the hardships and deprivation, and made them more resourceful when they were in actual danger. Each of these fathers knew he might not be able to see his wife or child again for years, if ever. But his sense of responsibility for his family kept him going. I get e-mail and letters from soldiers in Iraq, Afghanistan, and other places. What I find fascinating is that more than sixty years and dozens of wars after World War II, the contem-

groups of people or objects, standing still, and facing straight forward. Boys usually draw their subjects farther apart and from the side, indicating motion. They also include many more monsters, weapons, rocket ships, and anything else that moves. In one study, researcher Ireneusz Kawecki asked eight- to eleven-year-old children to draw a picture of water. "Girls drew calm rivers and oceans, boys drew storms at sea."

The differences in boys' and girls' brains also influence their behavior on the playground. Overall, girls play face-to-face and talk a lot with their friends. Boys play shoulder-to-shoulder and talk a lot less. Psychologist Janet Lever found that boys fight *twenty times more often* than girls. Even more interesting, boys who fight with each other one day are actually *more likely* to play with each other in the days after the fight. With girls, fights have a better chance of ending the relationship. For boys, physical play is a way of being intimate. So when boys knock into girls or pull their pigtails, they usually aren't trying to do any damage. Instead, they're trying to say, "I like you." And "when girls are under stress, they want to be with friends," says Sax; "when boys are under stress they want to be left alone."

Even the stories boys and girls tell (and the scenes they act out with their toys when they're alone) are very different—and they tell us something very important about the kids. Researchers Kai Klitzing and Kimberly Kelsay found that five- to seven-year-old girls tell stories that are "more coherent" and much less aggressive than boys' stories. That's not much of a surprise. But here's the kicker: Girls who told less coherent, more violent stories were more likely to have significant behavior problems than girls who told the more stereotypically female stories. The level of violence in boys' stories didn't predict behavior problems at all.

porary military dad has the very same concerns. If he were to die, who would support his wife and children? Would his children remember him, would he have made a difference in their lives?

Education

Hey, Whose Homework Is It Anyway?

Once you've bought into the idea that homework—at least in reasonable doses—is important, you've got two important issues to deal with: Should you

B. Smaller

My parents didn't write it—they just tweaked it.

help your child? And if so, how much? It's very easy to get impatient with a child who doesn't seem to be "getting it" as quickly as you'd like. And it's just as easy to cave in to a child's whining and just give her the answers.

So let's get something straight right up front: your child's homework assignments are for her, not for you. If you've already slipped into the mode of offering help or answers too quickly, stop it now. Helping too much or jumping in and taking over will sabotage her ability to learn good study habits. It could also leave her unable or afraid to complete any assignments without your help, and send her the message that you don't think she's smart enough to do her assignments by herself. If she's started to believe you, rebuilding her homework independence will be tougher. The same holds true for boys and girls.

Your goal should be to get your child to the point where she can complete her own assignments and ask for help only when it's absolutely necessary. What she really needs when she gets stuck isn't answers and impatience, it's support and explanations. Start by trying to figure out exactly what she doesn't understand and why. Help her break her assignments down into more manageable chunks and give her a lot of praise when she gets through each one. Ruth

HOMEWORK: TOO MUCH OF A BAD THING?

These days more grade-schoolers are doing homework than ever before, and they're doing more of it. In the mid-1990s, about 34 percent of six- to eight-year-olds had homework on any given day. In 2002 it was up to 58 percent, and in 2006, 64 percent. In 1981 children six to eight were doing an average of nine minutes of homework per day (forty-five minutes per week). By 1997 it was up to about twenty-five minutes per day (about two hours per week).

As you might expect, there's plenty of controversy about homework. Some say that it teaches students responsibility and time management, and improves their ability to retain information by reinforcing concepts learned in the classroom. Others, including Harris Cooper, a professor at Duke University and one of the country's leading experts on homework, believe that "there is no evidence that any amount of homework improves the academic performance of elementary students."

Research from the National Assessment of Educational Progress (NAEP, an agency of the U.S. Department of Education) goes one step further, finding that too much homework may be counterproductive, especially for grade-schoolers. (Actually, the battle against homework has been raging for close to a hundred years. From about 1900 to 1920, teachers were generally opposed to homework. And in 1930, the American Child Health Association [which no longer exists] equated homework with child labor.)

In 2000, for example, fourth-graders who did fifteen minutes per day of math homework scored an average of 232 on the NAEP scale. Those who did thirty minutes scored 230, and those who did no homework at all scored 228. Not much of a difference. But students who did from forty-five minutes to over an hour per day scored only 217—worse than the zero-homework group. (Harris Cooper has found that doing homework starts paying off in middle school and high school.)

Does this mean your child should bag homework altogether? Not at all. It just means that you should encourage her teachers to keep assignments reasonable. As a guideline, go with ten minutes per night starting in kindergarten and first grade, and add ten minutes per grade (thirty minutes for a third-grader, and so on).

Peters, author of *Overcoming Underachieving*, suggests interspersing easy assignments with harder ones or allowing for a few minutes of fun before moving on to the next task.

If your child has gotten so dependent on you that she balks at doing her homework without your help, you need to get tough. Cut back on play dates or weekend fun until she starts getting back in the groove. Ask her teacher to help out too, perhaps by keeping your daughter inside during recess until her homework gets done.

This process is probably going to be a little unpleasant for everyone and may involve your child screaming at you, either demanding help or accusing you of hating her (otherwise you'd help her, right?). But don't give in. Helping your child rebuild her confidence in herself is one of the best things you can do for her.

Here are a few other not-too-intrusive ways you can help your child with homework:

- **Make sure your child gets plenty of sleep every night.**
- **Monitor extracurricular activities.** Your child should be a student first, athlete (or musician or dancer or whatever else) next.
- **Have a regular time and place for homework.** It should be comfortable, well lit, distraction-free, and stocked with supplies, including pencils, paper, dictionary, thesaurus, calculator, textbooks, Internet connection, and anything else your child might need. You don't need to have a separate room. In fact, if she's out in public, it'll be extremely easy for you to keep tabs on her.
- **Give your child some freedom to study the way that works best for her.** If she's the kind of kid who will sit down and work for two hours at a stretch, great. But if she needs to take a break every ten minutes or works best lying on her back listening to her iPod, let her alone—provided that she gets the assignments done well and on time.
- **Monitor your child's assignments.** This means checking every day to see what's being assigned, talking about the assignments and what your child thinks about them, and following up to make sure the work has been done.
- **Enforce a homework-first, everything-else-after rule.** Otherwise, if you don't, you'll be dealing with a child who suddenly "remembered" two minutes before bedtime that she had a hour's worth of reading to do.
- **Support your child's teacher.** If you think an assignment is stupid or useless, keep your thoughts to yourself in front of your child but phone or e-mail the teacher and ask a few pointed questions. Calling your child's teacher a moron will undermine his authority.

Daddy's way of helping you with your homework is not to help you.

What Are Daddies Made Of? PART 2

Here are some more traits for strong fathers:

♦ **Be mean to your kids.** As dads, our natural inclination is to want to do everything we can to protect our children. But sometimes our provider/ protector mode can get in the way of our children's development. One of the most important things you can do as a dad is to allow your children to fail. They need to know that we all fall on our face sometimes, and that making mistakes doesn't turn you into a bad or unlovable person. So if your child falls down (actually or metaphorically), don't jump in right away. Not giving her a chance to pick herself up sends the message that you don't think she can take care of herself—and that can undermine her self-confidence in every area of her life.

This point is beautifully illustrated by Bud Schulberg in his short story "A Short Digest of a Long Novel." In the story, one of the characters plays a game with his daughter in which she jumps off a table and into his arms.

"He would not even hold out his arms to catch her until the last possible moment. But he would always catch her. They had played the game for more than a year, and the experience never failed to exhilarate them. You see, I am always here to catch you when you are falling, it said to them, and each time she jumped, her confidence increased and their bond deepened."

You can apply this wait-a-few-seconds-before-jumping-in rule to all sorts of situations. For example, you're out with your child, and she announces that she has to pee. Right now. You know your child; if she's doing the I'm-really-really-going-to-explode-any-second dance, you'd better find the nearest bathroom (or bush). But if you're pretty sure she can hold it—even if she says she can't—wait a minute or two. Sometime in the not-too-distant future she'll have to go, and you'll be in a place with no bathrooms. You'll be able to remind her about that time that she thought she couldn't hold it but did.

Similarly, imagine that your child has smacked into something and is crying. If you rush over and start offering bandages and ice packs, you're effectively telling her that you're worried and that she should be too. That'll escalate the tears. But calmly saying something like, "Ouch, that must really hurt," or "Show me where it hurts," gives your child much more control over the situation and will almost always result in drier eyes.

One important caveat here: I'm not talking about torturing or humiliating your child. Never tell her "Big girls don't cry," or that whatever is bothering her is silly, or to just "Get up and walk it off." You should always be compassionate and comforting. The trick is in the timing.

♦ **Teach while you still can.** You've still got a few years before your child decides she knows everything better than you do. (As acclaimed musician Charles Wadsworth put it, "By the time a man realizes that maybe his father was right, he usually has a son who thinks he's wrong.") Until then, take advantage of her relatively open mind to take her to interesting places, show her interesting things, and teach her as much about the world as you can.

♦ **Talk, talk, talk, talk. And then talk some more.** Have some serious conversations about drugs, alcohol, sex, peer pressure, and all the other things you dread talking about. Let your kids know clearly what the rules are in your home and what kind of behavior you expect from them when they're elsewhere. You may have had some of these discussions before, and you'll probably be having some of them again, so get used to it. According to the Office of National Drug Control Policy, "Kids who learn from their parents or caregivers about the risks of drugs are 36 percent less likely to smoke marijuana, 50 percent less likely to use inhalants, 56 percent less likely to use cocaine, and 65 percent less likely to use LSD than the kids who don't learn about these drugs from their parents." Make sure these conversations are actually that. If you start preaching, your child will tune you out before you even get through the "When I was your age . . ."

♦ **Be a good communicator.** School-age kids have a lot they want to talk about—and they have a lot of interesting things to say, too. So set aside some time every day or at least every few days to turn off the cell phone and the television and the computer and focus 100 percent on your child. Resist the urge to give advice—just listen carefully. Dads tend to want to jump in and solve their children's problems. But in your attempt to fix things, you may miss the emotional message your child is trying to give you. Show your child that you understand by repeating important phrases or asking follow-up questions. For example, "So what I hear you saying is . . . ," or "Do you mean . . . ?"

Try, also, to stay away from questions that your child can answer with "Yes," "No," "Fine," "I don't know," or a silent shoulder shrug. Sometimes you can skip the questions and start off with a statement: "Tell me something you learned today," instead of "How was school?"

♦ **Show your love. . . . Every day.** More often, if you can. When the kids are little, hug them and kiss them as much as possible. That'll help you build up a reserve to assist you through those times when your child won't want to be seen standing next to you, let alone get kissed. But even when she's in the leave-me-alone-Dad phase, a wink, a pat on the shoulder, or some other kind of brief physical contact can remind your child that you love her. Skip the fake Hollywood air kisses. And make those hugs last—let your child be the one to squirm away, not you.

♦ **. . . And talk about it too.** Seventy-five percent of the dads in University of Michigan researcher Jean Yeung's study said they hug their children or show physical affection every day. But only about one-third say they actually *tell* their kids every day that they love them. We do all sorts of things for our family. We work, we teach, we play, and so much more. And we often assume that they'll understand that we're doing all those things out of love. They may, but don't underestimate how important it is for people to hear the words.

♦ **Acknowledge your mistakes.** If you lose your temper or say or do something you know you shouldn't have, apologize later. Too many parents feel that apologizing to a child is a sign of weakness, or worry that they'll lose their children's respect. Neither is true. In fact, apologizing when appropriate shows kids that you're human and that you take responsibility for your

GET OUTA HERE!

Childhood today is very different than it was when you were growing up. And one of the biggest differences is the amount of unstructured play time—especially time spent outside. Back in 1971, for example, about 80 percent of seven and eight-year olds walked to school on their own. But in the early 1990s, it was only about 9 percent, according to Mayer Hillman, a researcher and urban planning expert. There are, of course, a lot of reasons for that decline: school days are longer and kids have more homework and more extracurricular activities, they watch a lot more television and play video games, and more of us live in urban areas where parks are harder to find. Fear of lawsuits has forced cities across the country to shut down playgrounds or make them so "safe" that no one wants to play on them. And fears that the world is a much more dangerous place than it used to be makes parents keep their children closer to home (although, as we'll see in Chapter 7, those worries are largely unfounded). Things have gotten so crazy that in Manhattan and other places, specially trained "play workers" have been hired to teach children how to engage in fantasy play. If there's one thing kids *don't* need, it's to be told how to play.

It's looking like singer Joni Mitchell was more right than she ever imagined when she sang, "They took all the trees, put 'em in a tree museum." The phrase "go outside and play" has become as old-fashioned and out-of-date as "dialing the phone" (as opposed to pressing buttons), typewriters, and carbon copies. And that created a big, big problem, one that Richard Louv, author of *Last Child in the Woods*, calls *Nature Deficit Disorder*.

own actions—even the less-than-perfect ones. Hopefully, that will make it more likely that your children will do the same.

♦ **Give your children opportunities to be responsible.** In the preschool years, this could mean simple jobs like washing hands before meals, setting the table for dinner, getting ready for bed, brushing teeth after meals, and getting dressed in the morning. Add age-appropriate opportunities as your child gets older. Early elementary-schoolers could do occasional chores like caring for a pet, helping a younger sibling get dressed or doing a puzzle, helping with meal prep, cleaning up their bedroom, vacuuming the living room, gardening, weeding, taking out the trash, or walking to the store to buy milk and bringing back change from a $20 bill. Older kids might prepare a simple meal on their own, get a job watering the neighbor's garden, plan a family outing, or even do some other chores without having to be

A mountain of research shows that playing outside, particularly in green areas, has tremendous benefits to children. Here are just a few examples.

- Children who spend more time in nature have fewer behavior problems and better cognitive skills, are less anxious, and are less likely to be depressed than children who do their playing indoors or on pavement. They also have better hand-eye coordination and balance, and fewer absences due to illness than kids who spend less time outside.
- After spending time in nature, children with Attention Deficit Hyperactivity Disorder (ADHD) have fewer symptoms, are more self-disciplined, and concentrate better, according to Andrea Faber Taylor and her colleagues at the University of Illinois. The more green they're exposed to, the less severe the symptoms.
- Children who spend more time in nature are more creative then those who don't, and they deal better with stress. Again, the more nature they get, the greater the benefits.
- Exposure to nature stimulates children's powers of observation, fosters creativity, and "instills a sense of peace and being at one with the world," according to developmental psychologist William Crain.

Now I'm not suggesting that you go out and hug trees, but there's no question that climbing a few of them will do your whole family a world of good. So try to log at least a few hours every week just hanging out in nature. No agenda, no expectations. Just take a walk, go fishing, or sit on a rock and read a book.

reminded. The point of all this is to keep putting your child into situations where she can demonstrate responsibility. The more she accomplishes, the better she'll feel about herself.

- **Create family rituals.** Although the word *ritual* is usually associated with religious observance, it doesn't have to be. As far as I'm concerned, a ritual is any kind of meaningful activity you do on a regular basis. Reading stories to the kids every night could be a ritual; so could having your parents over for dinner every Friday, making waffles and hash browns for breakfast on Sunday mornings, or going to the same spot for summer vacation every year. You get the point.

Family rituals help bring everyone in the family together, make them feel closer, and should be something everyone looks forward to. For young kids, they're comforting. If you imagine the family as a business, you might even look at rituals as branding, something that differentiates your family from others. We're big Lego players. We love Hitchcock movies, and so on. (Not all rituals are enjoyable, though. You might visit with your in-laws every Thanksgiving and spend the entire weekend hiding in your room trying to avoid yet another family blowup.)

You should have at least one family ritual that involves everyone in the family. But not all have to. You could go for Sunday hikes with one child and compete in five-kilometer road races with another. Rituals can be simple or elaborate. I meet my wife every Thursday for a dim sum lunch in Chinatown. And every morning when I take my preschooler to school, we read two stories. If one of the stories was *The Three Billy Goats Gruff*, she'll become the Big Billy Goat Gruff and head-butt me, the poor troll, out the door. Otherwise she'll just give me a shove. It helps if I do a theatrical backward stagger and sprawl out on the ground. Then I have to push her back inside.

Of course, with everything else going on in your life, creating a family ritual may seem like one more pie-in-the-sky idea. But if you think about it, you can probably find a way to make it happen. For example, hopefully you're reading stories to your child every day. And at *some* point, your kids will have to go to sleep. So creating a bedtime ritual where the whole family gets together to read a story won't take any more time than you're spending now. You'll just move things around a little.

And think about things you're already doing. Could you tweak them a little to make them rituals? For several years my daughters had piano lessons every Tuesday evening. To save time, we'd stop at Subway on the way home and have sandwiches for dinner. That became our Tuesday Night Subway ritual, which kept its name even when the lessons got changed to Thursdays.

♦ **Don't devalue the things you like doing with the kids.** Understand that you're not a substitute for Mom—and she's not a substitute for you. Men and women have different but equally important ways of interacting with their children. Men tend to stress physical and high-energy activities more, women social and emotional experiences. But don't let anyone tell you that wrestling, bouncing on the bed, or any of the other "guy things" you love to do are somehow not as important as the "girl things" your partner does (or wants *you* to do). Overall, you're just as good at taking care of your children's needs as their mother; you just do it a little differently. though, both kinds of interactions are indispensable, and it's a to try to compare or rate them.

breaks. Airline flight attendants always advise parents to put n oxygen masks before helping their kids put on theirs. The same logic applies here: You can't be an effective parent if you can't manage the stresses in your own life—regardless of where they're coming from. If you're stressed at work, you may take out your frustrations at home, snapping at everyone including the dog and generally being a drag to be around. If you're stressed at home, you may take out your frustrations at work, staring at your screen saver, checking your e-mail or sending out resumes instead of doing you're really supposed to be doing, and generally slacking off. The whole thing quickly becomes a very negative feedback loop. Stressed at home leads to poor performance at work. Poor performance at work leads to increased pressure and stress there, which leads to stress at home. . . .

In the Workshop

One of the best times for dads and children—boys or girls—to bond is when you've got a minor home repair to do. For a lot of us, there's an endless list of things that need to be tightened, installed, replaced, painted, or tweaked, and many kids are thrilled to get a chance to work on grown-up projects like this with Dad. For preschoolers, just pulling out the right tool from your toolbox or even holding the flashlight while you're on your back under the sink might be enough. As they grow older, they'll get a real thrill from driving in a couple of screws, hammering a few nails, taking measurements, or pouring a quart of oil into the engine.

Of course, it's going to take a little more time and a lot more patience to finish a project when you have a junior helper on board, but there are some great benefits. First, you'll need to get a camera with a wide-angle lens to capture the smile on her face after she helps you. Depending on the project, there may be something for her to point at for years to come and tell anyone who will listen how she helped you. Finally, you'll be teaching her valuable skills that will last her a lifetime. And every time she drives a screw or puts up blinds, she'll remember that you taught her how to do it.

Even if you're not the handiest guy in the world, you can still share some knowledge with your child. (Just the fact that you're older and have better hand-eye coordination will give you a leg up.) And if you happen to have a child with an aptitude for tools, your own skills might improve as the two of you spend more time together on various projects.

I can't emphasize enough that everything I'm saying here applies equally to boys and girls. Sure, some girls would rather play with dolls, but there are plenty who would be delighted to help you out with anything—just so they can be with you. Little girls love getting attention from their dad as much as their brothers do. And, as they grow older, knowing their way around a toolbox will be a big help when they eventually become car or home owners.

Finally, if you have more than one child, resist the urge to have them both help at the same time. Having too many kids around can make even the smallest project hard to manage. Plus, the last thing you want is for your kids to start squabbling in an area where there are a lot of sharp objects around. So pick just one child to help you this time, and let the rest of the kids know that their turn will be coming next time.

You and Your Partner

Small Steps

It seems like the traditional American family—Mom, Dad, 2.5 kids, and a dog—is a thing of the past. Today, cats outnumber dogs, and about half of all marriages are remarriages for at least one of the partners, most of whom have children. That helps explain why more than half of American children will spend some time in a stepfamily before age eighteen. Given all that, there's a good chance that you could be starting your fatherhood experience with someone else's child. Or, your new partner might be the incoming stepparent.

Marriages that include children are twice as likely to end in divorce as those without. (As Oscar Wilde put it, "Marriage is the triumph of imagination over intelligence. Second marriage is the triumph of hope over experience.") So, if you're already a stepfather, are about to become one, or are involved with a soon-to-be stepmom, there are a number of important issues that you may find yourself dealing with. Ignored, they can get out of control and interfere with your new partner, her kids, and even your own kids, if you have any. (Interestingly, though, at least one study shows that after the first five years, stepfamilies are actually *more* likely to last than first marriages.) While an in-depth discussion is beyond the scope of this book, simply being aware that these potential problems areas exist will go a long way toward helping you and your new partner stay out of the traps that too many stepfamilies fall into.

You

♦ Don't make the mistake of thinking that you're going to ease into your new situation right away and that your new, blended family will behave just like a regular biological family would. In reality, this hardly ever happens. The truth is that stepfathers have a very difficult time figuring out just where they fit into the new family structure. Being a father and raising your own children is hard enough. Stepping into a prefab family and trying to be a father to someone else's kids—who may already have a father somewhere else—borders on the impossible.

♦ As a stepfather, you won't have any kind of legally established authority (unless you adopt the stepchildren); this authority stays with the biological father. And even if their place were clearly prescribed and protected by law, most men, even if they're fathers themselves, don't have much practice or training in parenting other people's kids, which is very different from parenting your own.

♦ A lot of stepfathers are also surprised when the love they expected to feel for and from their stepchildren doesn't materialize—either as soon as they'd hoped or at all.

♦ You may feel guilty that you're not living with your biological children.

Your New Partner

♦ She may resent the time you spend with your children, feeling that it's time that you won't be available to spent with her, her children, or any children the two of you have together. Or you may resent the time she spends with her kids instead of with you or your children.

♦ If your own children don't live with you, you may feel guilty about spending more time with her kids than your own.

Her Kids

♦ They may be absolute angels before you and their mother get married or move in together, and then become vicious immediately afterward.

♦ When it comes to setting limits and enforcing them for your own children, you're in charge. But what about disciplining your stepchildren? Most stepfathers are unsure about where they stand on this issue. And if you haven't had a lot of time to get to know your stepchildren and earn their respect, disciplining them may be difficult.

♦ You may not know exactly how much affection to show your stepchildren (assuming you want to show them any at all). Too much would be insincere, too little isn't a good idea either.

♦ Her children may be angry, resentful, and jealous that you're taking their mother away from them. One of the most important factors in children's adjustment to a stepparent is trying to maintain the one-on-one relationships they had with her natural parents. Kids often feel that they're losing their biological parent to the new stepparent. And the truth is that in a way they're right. Before, it was just them and their mother, but now they have to share her with some interloper—you. The longer she was a single parent, the more covetous the kids will be of their mother, and the less they'll want to share her with you.

♦ Children may feel that showing you any affection (or even just liking you at all) is betraying their biological father. As a result, they may lash out at you for what seems like no reason at all. Even stranger, these explosions often happen just when you think your relationship with your stepchild is getting better. If (when) they happen, try to take them as a compliment.

♦ At the same time, you may resent her kids for cutting into your time with their mother.

♦ You may also resent the complete lack of gratitude they show when you do things for them. (Of course, if you have children of your own, you're already very used to that kind of treatment.)

Your Kids

♦ Because your children's mother probably has more time with your kids than you do, and because your new partner has more custody of her kids than her ex does, you'll undoubtedly be spending more time with your new partner's children than with your own. Your children, especially if they aren't living with you, may feel that since you have "new" kids, you don't or won't love them anymore. As a result, they may develop a strong rivalry with or even a dislike for their stepsiblings.

♦ Your kids may not be terribly excited to be part of a new family. This is especially true if you've been a single father for a long time or if you're barely out of your relationship with their mother.

♦ In some cases, you may be so scarred by your relationship with your ex that you feel as though you'd be better off starting a completely new life, without anything—kids included—to remind you of the past.

♦ If you're beginning to get close to your new partner's children, you might be feeling as though you're betraying your own kids and that there won't be enough love to go around.

♦ A lot of kids, regardless of their age, fantasize that their parents will get back together. Your getting remarried dashes that hope. Same goes the other way around.

The Exes

♦ We all secretly want the women we get involved with to have been virgins before we met them, but the existence of her kids can make it kind of hard to keep that fantasy alive. And the existence of her ex-husband—especially if he wants to be as involved with his kids as you do with yours—makes it impossible.

♦ If he is involved with his kids, you may have a tough time seeing him all the time and hearing what a great guy he is.

♦ If your ex is involved with someone, he's going to be stepfathering your children. How are you going to react if your ex wants the kids to call him "Daddy"?

♦ Remember that it's hard for you not to be affected in some way, real or imaginary, by your partner's ex or by your ex's new partner. You may wish he'd disappear, but that would only hurt his (or your) kids. And by the way, it's perfectly normal for you to hate him: Whether or not you've met is completely irrelevant.

Finances

♦ The issue of who pays for what or whom is a frequent source of trouble in stepfamilies. How are you and your new partner going to arrange the finances of supporting two families?

♦ If you're paying child support, will your new partner resent that all of your income isn't available to your new family? Will you have to get a new (or second) job to be able to support kids in two households?

♦ If your kids are living with you, how will she feel about the money you spend on their private school tuition or other expenses that neither she nor her children get any benefit from?

♦ And how will you feel if the situation is reversed? How are you going to feel about spending your money on things for her children?

♦ What kind of gift-giving strategy will you have? You don't want your step-children to feel like the poor cousins. But you also don't want your biological children to feel that they're getting the short end of the stick.

Society as a Whole

♦ Whether you're a brand-new stepfather or have been at it for years, you'll have to deal with people's suspicions that you're a child abuser, especially if one or more of your stepchildren is female. The truth is that while stepfathers are more likely to abuse their children than biological fathers, *neither* is as likely to harm their children as the children's own mothers.

♦ Besides this unfortunate and inaccurate suspicion, society seems to have even worse stereotypes about stepmothers than stepfathers. Just think of *Cinderella, Hansel and Gretel, Snow White,* and a host of other fairy tales.

The Thinker

What's Going On with Your Child

Physically

+ Your seven-year-old is getting lankier, with long arms and legs that seem to go everywhere. Still, he's becoming more coordinated in his gross motor play. He's shaping up to be a pretty good swimmer and batter, and an expert tree climber. But most likely, he's zipping around the block on his two-wheeler or skateboard. He likes to test his limits, and enjoys his growing mastery of physical abilities. Translation: he may become something of a daredevil, experimenting with various stunts. Be sure he wears a helmet.
+ This can result in some exhausting days, so make sure he eats well and gets plenty of sleep.
+ He's fine-tuning his small motor skills. His handwriting is getting better, and so is his mastery of scissors and tiny jigsaw puzzle pieces.
+ Here come those permanent teeth! All those adorable spaces in his mouth will soon be occupied by what look like enormous chompers. Don't worry: his mouth will most likely grow to accommodate them.

Intellectually

+ There are pouts galore as your seven-year-old becomes increasingly taken with the notion that people are unfair and favor everyone else—especially younger siblings.
+ His vocabulary keeps growing, and his attention span is longer. His ability to process information and think abstractly is starting to develop. He can

compare two objects and tell you how they're similar and how they're different.

- He's a good reader and writes well, but may still have trouble with spelling.
- He thinks logically and is a good problem solver, and he loves puzzles, riddles, and name and number games.
- Sometimes he's distracted by every bug that flies by. Other times, he'll get so absorbed in a project that nothing—even your repeated requests to come to dinner—can pull him away.
- He's getting mighty curious about reproduction and birth, but fortunately, that's about as far as his interest in sex goes.
- He has a good understanding of actions and consequences of behavior, meaning you have a better chance of reasoning with him.
- He can tell time and knows his seasons, the days of the week, and the names of the months.

Emotionally/Socially

- Last year's boisterous six-year-old has now become quite introverted. As he approaches eight, he'll become more outgoing again, but seven is definitely his first reclusive, thoughtful year. He may prefer solitary activities to playing with his friends.
- In keeping with his inward nature, he wants more privacy and will develop a sense of modesty (no more running naked through the house!). It's important to respect those desires.
- With all this introspection, his sense of empathy has deepened. He feels others' pain and may even cry at a sad movie or story.
- Your seven-year-old will stand for nothing less than perfection in himself. He wants to please you and his teachers, and can be very hard on himself when he doesn't live up to his own expectations. He still doesn't take criticism well, feels shame when he makes mistakes, and will go through more erasers than you ever would have thought possible. If he loses a game, he may sequester himself in his room, or under the dining room table in his homemade fort.
- He has "real" fears, such as not having friends, or that something horrible that happened somewhere else (like 9/11) will happen to him, which are slowly replacing those garden-variety childhood fears of witches and monsters and being flushed down the toilet.
- One might think of seven as the "middle age" of childhood. At seven, he is utterly self-aware, as well as being aware of the world at large in ways he's never been before. He's not sure he likes what he sees.

♦ If he has siblings, there's bound to be some tension in the house. He squabbles and fights with them frequently. Outdoor play, for both siblings and friends, is bound to have a more positive outcome. He's more patient with his friends and has less trouble waiting his turn.

♦ As if his life wasn't complicated enough as it is, your seven-year-old may develop an interest in the opposite sex. Boyfriend-girlfriend relationships are more common, as are crushes on teachers, movie stars, musicians, and even the mother or father of a close friend.

What's Going On with You

Making the World a Better Place after a Long Day . . .

Remember how you used to roll your eyes when you were little and your parents started blathering on about "When I was your age…" or "Back in the day…" ? Well, it's finally happened: *you're* the droning fossil now, looking back and comparing the world you grew up in with the one you're trying to raise your child in. It seems so much bigger than it did then, with so many more opportunities. At the same time, life feels less secure, more dangerous, and more threatening. Think about all those things you never noticed when you were a kid, but have suddenly become important now that your child is taking his first tentative steps into the larger world: war, drugs, alcohol, crime, terrorism, poverty, overpopulation, homelessness, and on and on. And while you're at it, throw in the dangers that didn't exist back then but that do now (AIDS, global warming, and so on). When you put it all together, the world may seem like a pretty scary place for a kid to be in all by himself.

That thought can be a real wake-up call, a kick in the butt to get you to change things, to do whatever it takes to improve your community and the larger world. This is a time when dads "become more aware of, more vocal in, and more vigilant regarding community issues," writes researcher Rob Palkovitz. "Men become more community centered when they have children growing up in a community, not only for the interest of their own children, but for the good of the children in the community."

Other researchers have reached similar conclusions. "Those men who live with their biological or adopted children are significantly more likely to belong to service clubs and school-related organizations," says David J. Eggebeen, a research associate at Penn State. "Children are the mechanism that lead men who are fathers to become a Cub Scout leader, Scout Master, community league basketball coach, Little League coach and school board member."

*Things were done very differently on the farm
when I was your age, Kenny.*

Roughly speaking, there are two types of community involvement. Formal involvement, according to Palkovitz, includes things like building ball fields and playgrounds, putting up speed bumps, joining neighborhood watch groups, coaching, scouting, and getting involved in the PTA. I talked to dads who volunteered at homeless shelters, led Outward Bound expeditions, cleaned up litter from local freeways, became Big Brothers, took petitions door to door, and even ran for city council. It was as if there was a sudden shift from, "Someone ought to do something about that!" to "*I'm* going to do something about that, damn it!"

Not everyone reacts this way, of course. Palkovitz found that even dads who don't participate formally get involved informally. "Informal community involvement was represented by more awareness and outgoingness within neighborhoods, encouraging kids to come in off the streets into gyms, and so forth." Other informal activities might be talking to parents and the police about unsafe or questionable behavior or conditions and trying to keep drug dealers out of the neighborhood.

Embracing the Plan Gone Awry

Your child's growing independence and the ways he and you handle it play a major role in how both of you develop—he from a child into an adult; you as you change and grow as a father. Besides that, though, there's another major issue that you've dealt with before and that you'll be dealing with for the rest of your life: the difference between the way you planned or imagined or hoped that your life would turn out and the way it actually is.

The years between about thirty-three and forty—which is probably about where you are right now—are what author and psychologist Daniel Levinson calls the Settling Down phase. This is typically the time when fathers (and men in general) focus their energy on becoming a man in society: on "making it," on advancing in the workplace, on family and friends, on success, whatever that means to you. The days of figuring out what you're going to do when you grow up are pretty much gone. You no longer have infinite choices. Any door you open, any choice you make, requires closing other doors and missing other opportunities. The worst part about this phase is that each choice makes you grow up a little, and the more you grow up, the more you have to give up. This isn't all bad, of course. For every one door you close, you open a dozen windows—you may lose out on one opportunity, but you'll have all sorts of other ones you never knew existed.

Are you the kind of über-father you imagined you'd be ten years ago? Had you even planned on being a father at all? Are you able to spend as much time with your family as you want? Do you have the kind of relationship with your kids that you thought you would? How does your relationship with your partner compare to the way you pictured it would be? Are you living in your dream home in your dream neighborhood? Are you sending your kids to the kind of schools you'd planned on? Are you giving them the life and the things you wanted them to have? Are you keeping the promise you screamed when you were a teenager to never, ever raise your children the way your parents raised you, or have you forgotten and slipped into doing exactly what they did? Do you have the education you wanted? Have you traveled everywhere you wanted to go? Where are you in your career? Are you as far along as you'd hoped? Are you even doing the kind of job you thought you'd be doing?

And then, of course, there are all the questions about your child. Is he as successful as you wished him to be? Is he excelling in the things you hoped he would? Is he on track to make a ton of money so he can support you and your partner in your old age? Is he making you proud, or do you secretly feel disappointed?

Your life today may be superlative, or it may . . . not. But no matter what it's like, chances are there are at least a few things about it that have turned out differently than you'd planned—not necessarily better or worse, just different.

The difference between fantasy (or even your best-laid plans) and reality can cause a tremendous amount of conflict, and there are three basic ways to deal with it. First, you could get absolutely paralyzed and horribly depressed that your life hasn't turned out the way you'd hoped. Second, different or not, you might choose to be perfectly happy with life just the way it is. Third, you can adopt a kind of serenity-prayer attitude: enjoy the things that are going better than expected, fix the things that aren't, learn to accept the things you can't change, and get clear on the difference between what's changeable and what's not. Life is far from over, and there's still plenty of time to fulfill at least some of those dreams.

You and Your Child, PART 1

Why Be Involved with Your Seven-Year-Old?

♦ The most influential factor in getting girls to be involved in sports and take care of their bodies is having a dad who actively plays with them (whether it's wrestling, playing touch football, ice skating, or shooting baskets doesn't matter). And when girls are involved in sports, they're much less likely to get into trouble (drugs, alcohol, early sex) as teenagers.

♦ It builds proficiency in math. "One possible explanation is that fathers tend to engage in more physical activities with their children and this appears to enhance the children's comprehension of spatial relations which is related to mathematical ability," writes researcher Norma Radin.

♦ Girls with involved fathers are less likely to have mental health problems later in life, and good relationships with their father can prevent boys from getting into trouble with the police, according to research conducted by the Centre for Research into Parenting and Children at the University of Oxford, in England.

♦ Your involvement with your seven-year-old has a direct impact on how far he'll go in his education by age twenty. It also decreases the chance that he'll ever be homeless or on welfare.

♦ Fathers who have warm relationships with their children, who monitor what their kids are doing at school, and who spend time playing and socializing with their kids have children with fewer behavior problems, according to Jean Yeung, a researcher at the University of Michigan. Behavior problems include lying, being overly active, crying too much, feeling no one loves them, being fearful or anxious, or having a tendency to withdraw.

♦ It's good for children's moral development. When fathers emphasized how behavior can affect other people's feelings, their school-age daughters were regarded by their classmates as "very unselfish," according to The Institute for the Study of Civil Society (Civitas). And boys with involved dads were

It's very important that you try very, very hard to remember where you electronically transferred Mommy and Daddy's assets.

able to develop more patience. By getting involved in their day-to-day activities, you're setting a great example of how to honor commitments.

Education

Of Social Promotion and Retention

If your child isn't doing particularly well in school, you're probably going to become very acquainted with the phrases *social promotion* and *academic retention.*

Social promotion means moving poorly performing children on to the next grade even when they haven't mastered the material or met the minimum standards, in order to keep them with their peers. Social promotion fell out of favor in the late 1990s, which led to an increase in academic retention, which is just a nice way of saying "flunking," making a child repeat a grade.

Unfortunately, neither approach is particularly successful in dealing with children who are having trouble in school. According to the U.S. Department of Education, the costs of social promotion are quite high. To start with, a child who can't handle the work in one grade will have an even tougher time keeping up in a higher grade. Socially promoting children frustrates them and sends the message that no one expects much from them. "As a result, students fail to grasp the importance of working to achieve academic goals and learn they can get by without working hard," according to a U.S. Department of Education report. Kids who are socially promoted are more likely to drop out of school. Those who do graduate often don't have the skills they need to get good jobs, go to college, and become productive members of society.

The seemingly logical alternative to social promotion is to hold a child back and have him repeat a grade, which is exactly what happens to over 2 million American school children (about 5 to 10 percent). But that approach might even be worse. A study by the University of Georgia found that children who had to repeat a grade fell even further behind the second time through. Overall, according to Australian researcher Helen McGrath, students who repeated a year were 20 to 50 percent more likely to drop out of school, compared to similar students who didn't get held back.

Most children know when they aren't doing well in school, and a lot of them worry that their poor performance means they must be stupid. So being forced to repeat a grade tends to confirm their worst suspicions. Besides that, kids going through a grade the second time often feel out of place, since they're usually taller and more mature than their classmates. They miss their friends, and they often get made fun of by other students. The stigma of repeating a grade is so big that in one study, grade-school children who had been held back rated retention as the single most stressful event of their lives, even worse than the loss of a parent or going blind, according to Gabrielle Anderson and her colleagues at the University of California at Santa Barbara.

The same team of researchers found that by adolescence, "experiencing grade retention is predictive of health-compromising behaviors such as emotional distress, low self-esteem, poor peer relations, cigarette use, alcohol and drug abuse, early onset of sexual activity, suicidal intentions, and violent behaviors." Oh, and it gets worse from there. Adults who repeated a grade are more likely "to be unemployed, living on public assistance, or in prison" than those who didn't. Pretty scary stuff.

Okay, so what are you supposed to do if your child's teacher suggests that your child be retained? It's a four-step process:

1. **Set up a meeting with the teacher and ask exactly why.** Is it a question of social skills, physical skills? Behavior? Academics? You need to know what the problems are before you can start addressing them. Then ask the teacher whether she thinks that repeating a grade will actually resolve the problem. If the issues are academic, be very

clear about which subjects. It's extremely unlikely that your child is lagging in all subjects by the same amount. He might be a year behind in math but two ahead in reading. Making him repeat an entire grade because of weakness in one subject will do more harm than good.

2. **Get your child tested.** You want to rule out hearing or vision problems and learning disabilities. If your child has any of those, repeating a grade won't help. Check with your school district before you plunk down a pile of money on private testing and evaluation. If your child is in public school, they'll almost definitely pick up the tab. And in some cases even private-school children can be evaluated at state or county expense.

3. **Determine whether there's anything going on at home or at school that could be affecting your child's performance.** For example, if you and your partner are having relationship problems, if there's a new sibling in the house, or if your child is being bullied, holding your child back will only make things worse.

4. **Get your child the help he needs in the specific areas he needs it.** In some cases, tutoring or remedial classes will be paid for by the public schools. In others, you may need to hire a tutor at your own expense or do the tutoring yourself.

Throughout this whole process it's important that you be a powerful advocate for your child. If you strongly object to having him retained and you can make a strong case for why it's a bad idea, most school administrators will back down.

However, if after you've gone through all of these steps—especially the tutoring—and you and your child's teacher agree that repeating a grade would be in his best interests, it's important that you talk to your child in the most positive way; your attitude will make a huge difference in how he reacts to and deals with the decision. Focus on the things your child does well, then talk about how everyone needs a little extra time now and then, and staying back a year will give him the time he needs to catch up. The last thing you want is for him to feel like a failure.

An Ounce of Prevention

If you're worried about your child's school performance, here are some steps you can take that may help you avoid problems before they start.

♦ Make sure your child eats well and gets enough sleep.

♦ Make sure he gets to school on time every day.

♦ Be in regular contact with his teacher. Let her know right away if you see that your child is having trouble with assignments. And ask her to give you regular updates about what's happening in the classroom.

♦ Create a kid-friendly work environment. Your child should have a desk that's large enough to allow him to spread out a little, good lighting, and plenty of paper, pencils, erasers, and other supplies he might need.

♦ Check his homework every day.

♦ Demonstrate your respect for education in general and his teachers specifically. If you don't take it seriously, he never will.

Skipping a Child

As we've seen in other sections in this book, having a child who's a little (or a lot) behind in one or more subjects poses some real challenges. But having one who's ahead of the curve can be just as challenging. And interestingly, many of the issues are the same. Should a bright (or brilliant) child stay with his agemates, or should he be skipped ahead a year or two? What about a child who's way ahead in one or two subjects but right where he's supposed to be in others?

At the end of the day, making sure your child is academically challenged is critical. If your child is ahead in one or two subjects, that could mean getting special advanced tutoring, putting him in a higher grade just for those areas, or even doing some homeschooling. If he's ahead in everything or almost everything, skipping could be your best alternative. But before you make your final decision, be sure to take the following into consideration:

♦ **His social development.** If he's very adaptable and makes friends easily, he probably won't have many problems fitting in to the higher grade. If he's not particularly adaptable, he could have a rough time leaving old friends behind and trying to get plugged into an environment where most of the kids already know each other. Ask your child's teacher about this one, since she sees your child interact with peers and other kids more often than you do.

♦ **His ego.** A lot of bright kids are like the big fish in the small pond: they're used to being the center of attention. If you bump your child up a higher grade, how will he react to suddenly being a small fish in a big pond?

♦ **His physical development.** Will he be much less physically mature than his new classmates? Will they make fun of him for being a runt? This is an especially big concern if you're thinking about skipping more than one grade or if you've got an off-the-charts nine-year-old who's going to high school.

♦ **What does your child think of the whole idea?** If he's bright enough to skip a grade, he's bright enough to participate in a discussion about his life. This doesn't, of course, mean that you have to go along with your child's wishes—you and your partner still have 51 percent of the votes. If you and your child end up on opposite sides, he deserves an explanation.

♦ **The school administrators and teachers.** How will your child's old and new teachers feel about moving him from one grade to another? Having them on board will make a huge difference. What's the school's philosophy about skipping grades? Also, does your child's school have a special accel-erated program? Would your child have to apply or be tested to get in?

♦ **Your child's strengths.** Is he ahead in every subject or just one or two? If it's the latter, he'll probably do well in those subjects in the higher grade but could be extremely frustrated the rest of the day.

Let's get back to the first bullet for a minute. One of the biggest questions that comes up about bright or gifted kids is that skipping grades could harm them socially. No question, that's true for some children. But some interesting new research is showing that *not* skipping these kids might be even worse. When bright kids are bored out of their minds, their academics often slip, and they may start acting out. When that happens, the best-case scenario is that you'll be hearing a lot of comments from teachers like the ones my parents heard: "Armin has such great potential but doesn't do anything with it." (If the word "slacker" was being used back then, it certainly would have been spoken in my direction.) Worst case is that your child will develop behavior problems and could end up getting tossed out of school.

To find out more information, check out the National Association for Gifted Children (www.nagc.org) or the Hoagies Gifted Education Page (www.hoagiesgifted.org).

Overweight Backpacks

About one in six schoolchildren will miss class time due to a backpack-related injury, and nearly half of all schoolkids complain of pain caused by their back-pack, according to Matthew Dobbs, an orthopedic surgeon at St. Louis Children's Hospital. Overweight backpacks have been getting so much atten-tion that the American Occupational Therapy Association has established an annual National School Backpack Awareness Day. Other organizations have followed suit. The Congress of Chiropractic State Associations went even fur-ther, creating National Backpack Safety *Month.* And several major textbook industry groups are evaluating ways to make books lighter.

Children, mostly under age fourteen, are reporting backpack-related pains that result from repetitive strain—schlepping packs from home to bus to school to classrooms to bus to home a couple times a day, five days a week.

Shanahan/Dorin

Besides causing back pain, leaning forward or over to one side to support an overstuffed pack can actually injure the spine, neck, and shoulders or cause changes in posture. Symptoms can be so severe that the kids have to be treated in emergency rooms.

Ideally, your child's backpack shouldn't weigh more than 10 to 15 percent of his body weight (before putting the pack on). But plenty of kids routinely haul around packs that weigh as much as 40 percent of their body weight. Get out your calculator; if you had to lug 40 percent of your body weight in and out of cars and up and down stairs all day long, you'd be in some serious pain too.

Fortunately, there may be some ways to save our kids' backs:

- **Weigh your child's backpack once in a while.** And keep it under the 10–15 percent guideline.
- **Keep nonessentials to a minimum.** Does your child really need to carry all those books at the same time? Will he use every one of them that day? If your child won't tell you, make a few calls to his teachers.
- **Investigate whether your child can share books with one or more of his classmates**. That way each kid can carry a smaller portion of the total load.
- **If possible, arrange to have duplicate books at school.** Or invest in a few paperbacks (particularly of literature) and have your child keep the hardcovers at home.

- **If your child really does have to carry a lot of books, at least be sure to get the right kind of backpack.** Single-strap packs cause the most discomfort because they're carried on one shoulder, which means that the child is always leaning to one side. The best—and most comfortable—packs have two padded straps and an abdominal belt.
- **Load it right.** The heaviest items in the pack should be closest to the body.
- **Lift properly.** When picking up the pack, make sure your child squats and lifts with his legs, not the back.
- **Exercise.** Back- and ab-strengthening exercises may help ease the pain.
- **Get a rolling backpack if your child's school allows it.** Some don't, though, because they're worried that students will get injured, trip, or fall over them in the classroom or the hallways. Why they aren't worried about the kids' backs is beyond me. But be careful that your child doesn't turn the rolling bag into an excuse to stuff even more junk into his pack. Wheels or not, you're going to have to pick it up sooner or later.
- **Treat your child to a nice neck/shoulder/back massage.**

Interestingly, injuries to the back account for only a small percentage of all backpack-related injuries. The Consumer Product Safety Commission (CPSC, cpsc.gov) collected data from one hundred emergency rooms across the country and found that the most common backpack-related injuries were to the head or face (22 percent), followed by the hand (14 percent), wrist/elbow (13 percent), shoulder (12 percent), and foot/ankle (12 percent). Back injuries were in sixth place, with 11 percent. The most common cause of injury was actually tripping over the backpack. Wearing the pack caused just as many injuries as being hit with it.

Now, before you go out and buy your child a heavier backpack, remember that the CPSC was tracking only emergency room visits. Many doctors believe that wearing overloaded packs is responsible for chronic back problems—not the kind of injury that would land someone in the ER.

You and Your Child, PART 2

Playing with Your Seven- to Nine-Year-Old
- **Take game night into overdrive.** Two-person board games like chess and backgammon are great choices. Your child's ego is a lot stronger than it used to be, so it's okay for you to win once in a while. But to keep him from

getting too frustrated while he's learning the ins and outs of strategy, add a twist. Have a rule that at any point, either player can turn the board around 180 degrees and play the other's pieces. That'll certainly make life a little more interesting.

♦ **Board games.** There are dozens of possibilities, many of which you probably haven't played since you were a kid. Others you may never have heard of. So start with the old classics like Monopoly, Parcheesi, Risk, Life, Clue, Chinese checkers, and Scrabble. Move on to newer classics like Trivial Pursuit, Boggle, Pictionary, and Scattergories. Then add in some current classics like Cranium, Apples to Apples, The Settlers of Catan, BattleLore, and Carcassonne. And from time to time, throw in some of the up-and-comers like BaffleGab and Don't Quote Me.

♦ **Card games.** Some use a regular deck (rummy, bridge, hearts, spades, Crazy Eights, euchre, poker, cribbage, canasta, pinochle, Hand and Foot, and even Concentration) while others use a special deck (Uno, Skip Bo, Coup d'Etat, Magic, Phase 10, Pokemon, Set, Yu-Gi-Oh).

♦ **Jigsaw puzzles.** Five-hundred-plus-piece puzzles, even complicated 3-D ones, are perfect for your "middle-aged" child.

♦ **Make a little music.** Even if your child plays an instrument, experimenting with pinging glasses filled with different amounts of liquid, or blowing across bottles, can be great fun.

♦ **Magic.** Pull a rabbit out of a hat? Yank out the tablecloth without breaking, spilling, or moving anything? He loves the spotlight and will enjoy performing magic for family and friends. There are plenty of tricks he can do with everyday household items, or you can splurge on a magic kit (rabbit not included). Mastering magic tricks (and practical jokes, too) is tremendously satisfying for your child—and fun, too.

♦ **Team sports.** Many kids this age go out for soccer, baseball, swimming, football, and even ice hockey. At seven, team sports should be played for fun, but by nine, the stakes are higher, and the old expression, "It's not whether you win or lose, it's how you play the game," will fall on deaf ears. Your involvement in your child's sports experiences makes a huge difference in how he sees himself as an athlete. "[S]pecific behaviors by dads, such as shuttling their kids to games, coaching sports teams, going to games, and buying athletic equipment for their children, were really important in how both boys and girls viewed their own athletic abilities," says University of Michigan psychologist Kathleen M. Jodl. In addition, your attitude has a tremendous influence over whether your child sees sports as fun or a chore. Encouraging him to get involved, working with him to

Just remember, son, it doesn't matter whether you win or lose—
unless you want Daddy's love.

improve his skills is great. But make sure he plays because *he* wants to and
not because he wants to please you.

- **Clubs.** Children who aren't interested in organized sports may get involved
  in clubs based on common interests. Most of the clubs will be single-sex,
  with girls gravitating toward the Barbie Club and boys toward chess or computer clubs.

- **Don't get rid of the lab coat yet.** Your child is getting more curious by
  the day, and experimentation is the name of the game. Kitchen chemistry is
  still a great dad-child activity. Take two identical pieces of cheese. Leave
  one out on the counter, put the other in the fridge, and keep track of each
  one's mold progress. Soak an uncooked egg in vinegar for twenty-four hours
  and see what happens to the shell. Make some muffins and see what happens if you leave the baking power out. While you've got the baking soda
  and vinegar out, find out what happens when you mix the two together. If
  you're really brave, try dropping a Mento into a bottle of Diet Coke. Be
  sure that you and your child are wearing goggles, and that you keep a safe
  distance. On your way out of the kitchen, grab a couple of refrigerator

magnets and experiment with switching the poles—one way they attract, the other they repel. Take your child on a nature walk and keep track of how many bugs you see and whether they have six legs or eight. Find a dead bird and observe how the ants reduce it to a skeleton over the course of a few days.

♦ **If you build it . . .** Your child's excellent hand-eye coordination means it's time for those special Lego kits. They are surprisingly complicated, and some even come with working motors. Since your child has some experience with tools, you and he can construct more intricate projects with wood.

♦ **If you plant it . . .** Your child may have grown a potato or an avocado pit in a cup when he was younger, but now he's ready for the big time: a real vegetable garden. Take a look at some gardening books and select some vegetables or vines that are appropriate for your climate. Lettuce, zucchini, cabbage, green beans, tomatoes, carrots, radishes, corn, sunflowers, and strawberries are pretty easy. And there's nothing more satisfying than sitting down to a plate full of something you grew in your very own backyard.

♦ **Put together an arts and crafts kit.** My mother was the artist in the family, and to this day, she's got dozens of jars filled with feathers, buttons, pieces of broken tile, pine cones, lanyards, fabric samples, sand, paint, sea shells, and more. At the very least, we always had something to do on those cold, rainy winter days.

♦ **Make a puppet theater.** If your child has a flair for the dramatic, he may enjoy having his own stage. A few big cardboard boxes, a couple of two-by-fours, some glue, and whatever else you've got in the arts and crafts kit, and you're good to go.

♦ **Get out of here!** You won't have to persuade him to join you. Go for a bicycle ride together, play ball, take a hike, go fishing, teach him to play golf. There are endless possibilities in the great outdoors. Your child will thrive, and you'll benefit from it too.

♦ **Hang out together.** Go on a picnic in the woods, take a trip to the zoo, go to a lake and feed the ducks, go garage-sale or flea-market hopping, or get a basic book on constellations and see how many you and your child can identify.

♦ **Take a break.** As we discussed in earlier chapters, your child needs some down time. So from time to time, give him the option to do a solo art project or watch a movie by himself. The best thing you can do in this situation is honor his need for solitude.

Lazy Kids

Once upon a time, even the youngest kids had clear-cut duties around the house. It might have been bringing in firewood, feeding the chickens, or whitewashing fences. For better or worse, however, those days are long gone.

Today, it's a lot more likely that getting a child to do a chore as small as loading the dishwasher or taking out the garbage once a week will be like pulling teeth. Even worse, when you do ask a kid to do something, there's a good chance he'll demand to know, "How much am I going to get paid for doing this?" Frustrating, but at least you can take some comfort in knowing that that your child has a firm grasp of how the free enterprise system works.

Sure, special jobs, like painting that shed in the backyard, might involve some type of payment (which could be cash or perhaps a trip to a ball game), but most jobs around the house should fall under the general heading of "family duties." No one gets paid for setting the table, making dinner, or washing the dishes. These are things that family members do to contribute to the running of the house. A child's weekly allowance should be independent of chores. In other words, don't tie taking out the garbage to a direct payment.

The trick to instilling a domestic work ethic in your child is twofold: Lead by example, and start early. From the earliest age, your kids look at you for clues on how to act. If they see that you don't put your things away, drop your clothes in a pile in the bathroom, leave your dinner dishes on the table, and so on, they'll get the signal loud and clear that they can leave stuff around for someone else to pick up—and that someone is going to be you.

On the other hand, if you got started a few years ago by making your toddler put away his toys when he was done playing with them and having him straighten up his room once a day, you've already instilled the habit of chipping in when there's work to be done. As the kids get older, their duties around the house should expand to fit their abilities.

If you have more than one child, you're going to hear complaints from the older ones about how unfair it is that they have to do more than the younger ones. Start with a vocabulary lesson: the word *fair* does not mean "the same." Then remind the older kids of some privileges they have that that the younger siblings don't. More privileges go hand in hand with more responsibility.

Of course, contrary to the accusations your kids will sling at you, you probably don't really want to turn them into little domestic slaves. But having a clearly defined list of chores (posting a written list is often helpful), along with who's responsible for doing each one, is an important facet of family life.

As you're putting your list together, take a second to ask yourself whether you're slipping into any gender stereotypes. Frank Stafford, an economics professor at the University of Michigan's Institute for Social Research, found that parents tend to assign chores like fixing things or mowing the lawn to boys, while assigning dishwashing and cooking to girls. Boys are also more likely to be paid for doing their chores, while girls are expected to do theirs for free. Overall, girls six and older do two more hours of chores per week than boys do. The study measured averages and didn't compare differences between boys and girls in the same family.

Finally, build some flexibility into your system. If one of the kids needs to spend a lot of time on a big project, make some allowances. You might offer to do the child's chores for him in exchange for an equal amount of time spent on other household chores later on.

Pitching in: Instilling That Volunteer Spirit

Volunteering as a family—serving meals at a local soup kitchen, for example—is a great way to show your kids that your commitment to your values is more than just talk. Besides that, it can give children of all ages an opportunity to discover hidden talents, develop skills, learn about cooperation and problem-solving, and gain some appreciation of how lucky they are. Volunteering as a family does as much good for the family as it does for the community. Here are some things to consider as you search for the right volunteer opportunity.

- **Look into causes or issues that are important to you.** What better way to pass your values on to your children than by getting involved in an organization that works with issues you care strongly about. If you need some suggestions, call your local United Way. Chances are they'll have a volunteer center that can hook you up with organizations that need help.
- **Look into causes that are important to your children.** Kids have big hearts too. Letting them pick whom they want to help will make them that much more committed.
- **Consider your children's career interests.** Volunteering is a great way to expose your children to careers they seem interested in. Later, if they're still interested, the volunteer experience will enhance their college applications and first resumes.
- **Think about trying something new.** Learning a new skill can be an exciting family project, and many organizations are looking for people who are willing to learn. Realize, however that you may need to devote a lot of time to get trained before the actual volunteer assignment begins.
- **Don't overcommit.** It's better to start off slowly and add time later than to agree to take on more than you can possibly do.
- **Look at volunteer-from-home opportunities.** If volunteering together

doesn't fit into your family's schedule, or you can't find the time to transport your kids to and from their own volunteering activities, try using your computer as a volunteer tool. Servenet (www.servenet.org) is a great place to find listings of volunteer positions. Plus, it has an entire section devoted to virtual volunteering.

Reading to Your Seven- to Eight-Year-Old

A lot of parents assume that as soon as their children can read on their own, it's time to stop reading aloud to them. Big mistake. Reading aloud to your emerging reader is important for a number of reasons:

+ **It's a great way to stay connected with your child.** You may not have him sitting in your lap anymore, but you can still snuggle up together under a blanket on the couch.
+ **It's a great way to keep your child interested in books.** Although your child is reading now, for the next few years there's going to be a big disconnect between the books he's capable of reading on his own and the ones that really interest him. Your reading to him bridges that gap. This is especially important if your child is having some reading trouble.
+ **It's a great way to build vocabulary.** Your child is more likely to get the meaning of unfamiliar words when hearing you read—either by the context or by asking you—than if he were to encounter the word in a book he was plowing through on his own.
+ **It's a great way to broaden his horizons.** Who says you have to read novels? The morning paper is filled with articles you can read to—and discuss with—your child over breakfast.
+ **It's a great way to build focus and memory.** I read my kids the first four Harry Potter books and the first eight volumes in Lemony Snicket's Series of Unfortunate Events. Even at a two- or three-chapters-per-night pace, it would take us a more than a month to get through one book. Keeping all those characters straight in our heads for that amount of time was a great exercise.

Reading to your child now that he's seven or eight isn't all that different than it was when he was younger. Here are a few ideas for how to keep it fun for everyone.

+ **Keep it lively.** Do voices, accents, and sound effects. Vary the pace; add drama and suspense. This is especially important when you're reading back-and-forth dialogue, where it wouldn't be clear who's speaking to someone who can't see the page.

- **Don't abandon picture books.** As your child gets older, the amount of text on the page will increase. But kids (and adults too) love illustrations. They're also great conversation starters.
- **Take some detours.** It's perfectly fine to stop in the middle of what you're reading to talk about something one of the characters did or a situation she's in.
- **Turn the tables.** Alternate pages with your child. You read one to him; he reads the next one to you.
- **Visit the library.** Not long ago, your child heard the stories you read to him. Now he's old enough to get recommendations from friends, teachers, and librarians.
- **Read everywhere.** Waiting for the dentist, stuck in traffic, and so on.
- **Put away the books sometimes.** Tell a story from your life or have your child provide you with a person, place, and thing and make up your own story.
- **Don't forget about nonfiction.** There's a myth out there that kids only like fiction, but the truth is that they absolutely love facts and the real world (this is a little more true for boys than for girls). A book about trucks, trains, costumes, baseball players, scientists, venomous snakes, or anything else your child is interested in will be as riveting as any novel. Try putting together pairs of books on the same topic—one fiction, one nonfiction. Read them both and talk about the differences between the two. For example, read Dan Guttman's *Babe & Me: A Baseball Card Adventure* and *Home Run: The Story of Babe Ruth*, by Robert Burleigh. And don't forget all those newspapers and magazines.
- **Be flexible.** If you have children of different ages, read to each of them separately. If you don't, you'll be reading to one and boring the other at the same time. As Jim Trelease, author of *The Read Aloud Handbook*, put it so beautifully, "If you can't squeeze your kids into the same size underwear, don't try to squeeze them into the same size book."

Here are some great titles to add to your home library, or to check out from a school or public library:

Abbie in Stitches, Cynthia Cotton
The Adventures of Ali Baba Bernstein, Joanna Hurwitz
Almost Gone: The World's Rarest Animals, Steve Jenkins
Behold the Bold Umbrellaphant, Jack Prelutsky
Bittle, Patricia McLachlan
Book of Bad Manners, Stoo Hample

Cal and the Amazing Anti-Gravity Machine, Richard Hamilton

Charlotte's Web, E. B. White

Chowder, Peter Brown

Cornelia and the Audacious Escapades of the Somerset Sisters, Lesley M. M. Blume

Cricket in Times Square, George Selden

Flotsam, David Wiesner

Flush! The Scoop on Poop through the Ages, Charise Merical Harper

Freckle Juice, Judy Blume

The Frog Wore Red Suspenders, Jack Prelutsky

Golem, David Wisniewski

Harry the Poisonous Centipede Goes to Sea, Lynne Reid Banks

Henrietta, There's No One Better, Martine Murray

Henry and the Kite Dragon, Bruce Edward Hall

Hiawatha, Dennis Brindell Fradin

How a House Is Built, Gail Gibbons

If You Decide to Go to the Moon, Faith McNulty

John Henry, Julius Lester

Kite Flying, Grace Lin

Knights of the Kitchen Table, Jon Scieszka

Koko's Story, Francine Peterson

Little Sap and Monsieur Rodin, Michelle Lord

The Magic Hat, John Burningham

Millions to Measure, David Schwartz

Mr. Popper's Penguins, Florence and Richard Atwater

Mr. Williams, Karen Barbour

Oh, No! Where Are My Pants? And Other Disasters: Poems, Lee Bennett Hopkins

The People Could Fly: American Black Folktales, Virginia Hamilton

A Place Where Sunflowers Grow, Amy Leetai

Ramona the Pest, Beverly Cleary

The Something, Natalie Babbitt

Starry Messenger, Peter Sis

Stuart Little, E. B. White

The Summer My Father Was Ten, Pat Brisson

Theolonius Monster's Sky-High Fly Pie, Judy Sierra

Traction Man Is Here! Mini Grey

The Wall, Eve Bunting

Weatherford, Carole Boston

When the Horses Ride By: Children in the Time of War, Eloise Greenfield
When I Was Nine, James Stevenson

SCHOOL

The New Kid at School (the first volume in the Dragon Slayers' Academy
   Series), Kate McMullan
Get Ready for Second Grade, Amber Brown, Paula Danziger
My First Day of School, Patrick Hallinan

Making Music Part of Your Life

In Chapter 2 we talked about the importance of *listening* to different kinds of
music. Now, if you're looking for something that has a good chance of benefit-
ing your child in the long term, *playing* music (an instrument, not a CD) on a
regular basis is the way to go. Here's what the research shows:

   ♦ Premature babies who are exposed to music put on weight more quickly
   than babies who don't hear music. (See also Chapter 4, pages 71–73.)

   ♦ Children who take music lessons score 27 percent higher on fractions tests
   than those who aren't taking lessons.

   ♦ Kids who play in a band or orchestra are less likely to drink alcohol, smoke,
   or experiment with drugs.

   ♦ Skipping ahead a few years, high school music students score 57 points
   higher on the verbal section of the SAT and 41 percent higher in math. The
   connection between math and music is fascinating. "Both are about
   patterns, recognizing patterns, applying patterns, creating patterns," says
   Charity Kahn, a mathematician *and* a wonderfully talented children's music
   artist. Quarter notes, whole notes, eighth notes, half notes—it's all math.
   When you're unconsciously nodding your head along with a favorite song or
   banging out a drum part on your steering wheel, you're doing math. You can
   feel the difference between a piece of music in 3/4 time (like a waltz) or 4/4
   (any rock song)—math again.

When should you start your child on making music? Depends on the child.
Any preschooler will love going to music-and-movement classes with you. If
your child can sit still and focus for fifteen to twenty minutes straight, this is
the perfect age to start him on the piano or the recorder. Both are simple and
allow him to make reasonable-sounding music almost immediately. The
Suzuki method is a time-tested approach that teaches children to play by
ear—the same way we learn to talk—before learning to actually read music.
If your child hasn't got the concentration or you just don't want to start him on

lessons, have him toot around on a kazoo or imitate you when you tap out various rhythm patterns on the front porch.

Three important things to keep in mind about music lessons:

1. **Find a good teacher.** Look for one whose philosophy and approach are a good fit with your child's learning style (see pages 89–90 for more on that). The Music Teachers National Association has some wonderful resources for evaluating and selecting teachers (www.mtna.org/choosemt.htm).

2. **You do *not* need to be a musician or even be able to carry a tune to support your child.** If you don't play an instrument, now's a good time to start. If your child does Suzuki, parents learn the same lessons as the children so they can practice together.

3. **Do it because it's fun.** Yes, there may be some academic benefits, and who knows—your child might be a rising star. But keep your expectations reasonable, and life will be a lot more enjoyable for everyone.

We're all born with a certain amount of natural musical ability, and our capacity to understand and respond to music develops gradually. Sandra Trehub, a researcher at the University of Toronto, found that that babies as young as four months prefer music that is melodic and in tune, and can actually tell when a song is out of tune.

Preschoolers rarely sing in tune, but they can tell the difference between high and low notes and can respond physically to rhythm. They really enjoy add-on songs, like "The Green Grass Grows All Around." In the first verse there's a tree—the prettiest little tree you ever did see. The tree's in a hole and the hole's in the ground and the green grass grows all around, all around, and the green grass grows all around. In the next verse there's a limb on the tree and the tree's in the hole, and so on, adding something new with each verse. You can get lyrics and music for every age and on every topic at Songs for Teaching (www.songsforteaching.com).

Kindergartners and first-graders can carry a tune, remember some melodies, and still sing for the fun of it. By age seven or so, the inner critic will kick in, and they'll be very concerned with making mistakes. Some kids this age may point out that "Twinkle Twinkle Little Star" has the same melody as "The A-B-C Song" and "Baa Baa Black Sheep." By age seven they may notice musical references that most adults don't. For example, the notes of the first two lines of "Twinkle Twinkle" are the same—just in a different rhythm—as the first two of lines of Louis Armstrong's "Wonderful World." Try it, and you'll see what I mean.

Twinkle, twinkle little star
How I wonder what you are

and

I see trees of green, red roses too
I see them bloom for me and for you

By seven or eight, children have a good grasp of the emotional side of music, and they can tell you how a particular piece makes them feel. At this age, kids are finally able to practice an instrument regularly, although most won't unless you figure out some way to make it enjoyable. The right teacher should be able to help you with that.

Monitor the Media

This does *not* mean turn it off. It *does* mean do it together. Watching television and movies with your child can be a great way to talk about issues of morality, right and wrong, politics, and a great way to transmit your opinions and world-view to your child. Don't believe everything you hear about how video games, superheroes, comic books, and make-believe violence in the media lead to aggression. Some research shows that contrary to what we've all come to accept as the truth, fantasy violence sometimes gives kids important coping skills.

Advertising is a completely different situation. The average American child watches between 20,000 and 40,000 television commercials every year, and sees hundreds of thousands more on billboards and in magazines, newspapers, and movies. In 1990, U.S. advertisers spent about $100 million trying to reach children. Today it's over $10 *billion*. And boy, are they getting their money's worth. Pediatrician and children's media expert Victor Strasburger has found that children who watch a lot of television want more toys seen in advertise-ments and eat more advertised food than children who don't watch as much TV. And psychologist Allen Kanner says that by the time children are three years old, they recognize an average of over one hundred brand logos. To put it in more concrete terms, children under twelve spend about $40 billion of their own money and influence the spending of another $300 billion ("Can I have it, Daddy, please Daddy, I really need it, pleeeeeease?").

The worst part is that children under eight don't really understand that advertising is designed to get them (and you) to buy stuff and that ads are sometimes misleading. The result is that children are becoming more material-istic every day. They feel that they always need to have the latest and greatest, or whatever their friends have, and they feel bad about themselves (or angry at you for not whipping out your wallet) if they don't get it.

Helping your children understand what they're seeing and advertisers' agenda is critical. Here are a few ideas to help you get the process started.

- ◆ **Look at your own buying patterns.** Are you an "early adopter," the guy who has to have the newest gadget the second it comes out? Do you have a closet full of clothes you don't wear? Your behavior is going to tell kids much more than your words.
- ◆ **Have lots of family activities besides shopping.** A lot of dads (including me) pack up the kids and head down to Costco or Home Depot on weekends. While it's important to feed the family and maintain the old homestead, you don't want the kids to get the idea that shopping is all people do when they aren't working.
- ◆ **Don't keep up with the Joneses (or the Smiths or the Ignetowskis or anyone else).** Just because they have something doesn't mean you have to. If need be, dust off one of your mother's old sayings, like "I know little Joey bought a brand-new gizmometer and you want one too. But if little Joey were to jump off the Golden Gate Bridge, would you do that too?"
- ◆ **Talk about the messages you're seeing.** As you're watching a commercial or when you see a print ad, ask your child what's being sold. Point out how his favorite cartoon or movie characters are being used to sell products. And ask whether he thinks those $150 shoes will really make him play basketball better.
- ◆ **Point out product placement.** Draw his attention to subtle ads, such as when people in movies mention brand names, or when the camera lingers on a corporate logo, or when dolls are holding Coke cans and action figures are sporting the Nike swoosh.
- ◆ **Do comparison shopping.** When you're in the store and your child demands some big brand-name product, show him how the price lines up against the store brand.
- ◆ **Do blind taste tests.** Bring home a major brand and the generic version that comes in a nearly identical package. Without letting your child see the containers, have him taste both and tell you which one he likes best.
- ◆ **Watch the PBS/Frontline program *The Persuaders*.** It's a powerful, disturbing program that you and your kids should watch and discuss. You can view it at www.pbs.org/wgbh/pages/frontline/shows/persuaders.

You and Your (Former) Partner

When Things Don't Go According to Plan

Hopefully you won't ever need any of the information in this section. But just in case you and your partner break up, read on. The most important piece of advice I can give you is to do everything possible to keep things civil between you and your ex. Divorce is hard on everyone, but especially children. And the level of conflict between the two of you is the biggest predictor of how well your kids will cope after the divorce.

Fortunately, in order to be a good coparent, you don't have to love each other, or even like each other. Here are some steps you can take that can help you build a successful, long-lasting coparenting relationship with your ex. You'll find more suggestions in "Taking the High Road," below.

- **Treat her like a business partner.** Your children, of course, are the business.
- **Write a parenting agreement.** If you and your ex can't sit down together, have a mediator help you.
- **Come up with some ground rules for resolving conflicts.** You're going to have plenty of disagreements, so you should have a plan—probably including mediation—for how to handle them in place from the very beginning.
- **Know your limitations.** There are certain things you're capable of doing and certain things you're not. Be very clear on the difference.
- **Agree on a fair custody schedule.** If the kids are going to be living with one of you more than the other, there are dozens of scheduling options, and you'll have to pick the one that works best for you. If you're dividing custody fifty/fifty, two are especially good. One week at your place followed by one at your ex's is fine for kids over eight. But for smaller kids, a week away from either of you is too long, so switch every two or three days.
- **Have regular meetings.** These can be formal, informal, in person, or on the phone.
- **Respect each other's privacy.** You don't want your ex asking a bunch of nosy questions about your private life, so don't ask her any either.

Broken Marriages, Not Broken Children

Your relationship with your child's mother may end, but your relationship with your child never will. Not being able to see your kids as often as you'd like can make you angry, sad, and frustrated. But no matter how bad you feel, don't fade

away. Divorce is very hard on kids, and the impact can last for years. Here's
how you can make things easier for them:

- **Encourage them to talk to you about their feelings and make sure
  they know that the breakup is not their fault.** Show them that you
  love them and that they're important to you no matter how much time you're
  able to spend together.
- **Never badmouth your child's mother, and never use your children
  to deliver messages or spy on her.** The better you get along with your
  ex, the better your kids will be able to cope.
- **Come up with a parenting plan that makes you and your ex happy.**
  But don't give in too easily. Your kids need you as much as they need
  their mother. If you don't get to spend much time with them, they'll think
  it's because you don't love them anymore. If you can't agree on a plan, try
  mediation.
- **Pay your child support.** Not paying will hurt your children, not your ex.
  If she's preventing you from seeing your children or if you're having trouble
  making payments, contact your lawyer or the local district attorney right
  away. You'll also want to contact those same people if you're supposed to be
  receiving support from your ex and she's not paying.

Taking the High Road

Communication and cooperation are supposed to be two-way streets, but things
don't always turn out the way they should. No matter how much of a jerk your
ex is and no matter how horribly she treats you, it's critical that you learn to be
a *mensch* (a Yiddish word that means "a decent human being" or "someone
who does the right thing"). Here are some things that can help make you the
mensch you and your kids need you to be: *Remember that everything you do
has to be done with the best interests of your kids in mind.*

- **Respect each other's relationship with the children.** Hopefully she'll
  do the same for you. She may have been a rotten partner, but that doesn't
  mean she's a rotten mother. Unless your ex is doing something dangerous or
  damaging to the kids, let her parent them the way she wants to.
- **Honor your commitments.** This means not being late, keeping your
  promises, following the exact terms of your parenting agreement, and making your child support payments in full and on time. Expect the same from
  your ex.
- **Share information.** Send your ex a copy of any information you get about
  your kids that you think she doesn't have or would be interested in. This
  includes report cards, notices of parent-teacher meetings, school

photographs, and even copies of the kids' art projects. The effort will be greatly appreciated—guaranteed.

- **Remember that you can't control her, but you *can* control yourself.**
- **Keep your comparisons to a minimum.** Yes, she may be living in a mansion while you're sleeping in your old bunk bed in your parents' garage. But that's just the way things are.
- **Be flexible.** Kids get sick, and plans change. Emergency trips, illnesses, out-of-town guests, weddings, and other impossible-to-foresee events can mean asking your ex to keep—or to let you keep—the kids a few extra days. Whether you're asking for help or offering it, be nice, and the favor will probably be returned. But don't be so flexible that you let your ex take advantage of you. Stand up for your rights when it's appropriate to do so.
- **Don't deliberately do things that you know will annoy or hurt her.**
- **Give her the benefit of the doubt—at least for a while.** Don't assume that she's doing things to deliberately hurt you.
- **Listen to what she says to you.** Try to find the truth in it. Who knows, she may actually come up with something that can help you.
- **Get some help.** If your anger toward your ex is so consuming that it gets in the way of your parenting, you really need some help dealing with it.
- **Apologize to her if you've done something wrong.** It might hurt you to do this, especially if she never apologizes to you, but it's the right thing to do.
- **Don't assume you know what she'll say or how she'll react in a given situation.** Yes, you may have been together for years, and yes, she may have reacted that way every other time, but people can and do change. Give her a chance. If she does react the way you thought she would, at least you won't be surprised.
- **Force yourself to make reasonable compromises.** Granted, now that you're a single parent, you've lost one of the biggest natural incentives to cooperate with your ex: the desire to keep your relationship together. But learning when to compromise may be more important now than it was then.
- **Try to keep from getting defensive.** One of the most painful things your ex can do to you is to question whether you have what it takes to care for your children. If she ever makes this kind of accusation, before blowing up, take a second and honestly ask yourself whether there's even a glimmer of truth to what she's saying. If there are areas you really need help in, you might want to sign yourself up for a parenting class at your local community college.

- **Stop relying on her for approval.** You're a big boy now, and it's up to you to do what you think is right.
- **Learn to work around her anger.** Do not get dragged into a shouting match, no matter how tempting. There's absolutely nothing good that can come from it. Instead of responding to her unreasonable demands, ignore them. And remember, you can always take a walk. You do not have to stick around and be abused—verbally or otherwise.

Ultimately, no matter what you do, your ex is still her own person, and there's nothing you can do to force her to behave the way you want her to. But hopefully, if she sees you taking the high road for long enough, she'll eventually decide to join you there.

Energy to Burn

What's Going On with Your Child

Physically

♦ If you look closely, you may see hints of the adult your child is becoming. Most girls this age are at about 75 percent of their full adult height. Boys won't hit that mark for another year.

♦ She's in between growth spurts now, and the lull makes it easier for her to control her body. Coordination and small motor skills are excellent. She can use both hands at the same time, which should help her make great advances in playing musical instruments.

♦ As hard as it is to believe, your eight-year-old is even more active than she was a year ago. And she still acts like a child, with energy to burn, fidgeting and in constant movement. She does everything fast, shifting quickly between activities. Endless projects are started; few get finished.

♦ All this activity takes its toll on both of you. Even though she needs to be reminded that it's bedtime, she'll crash hard at the end of the day. But because she doesn't need quite as much rest this year as last, she may wake up in the morning fresh and ready to go. You're another story altogether.

♦ All that energy translates into her appetite, which is enormous. Keep healthy snacks available at all times—otherwise she'll go for the junk food. Her table manners have improved, especially when she's at someone else's house.

♦ Since most of her permanent teeth have come in, it's a good idea to visit the orthodontist (and to start squirreling away some cash for braces.)

Intellectually

- She still loves praise but is starting to grasp the painful notion that the entire world doesn't revolve around her. She loves competitive games and can now tolerate losing once in a while.
- Her awareness of time is growing. She knows her bed- and wake-up times and may write out detailed hour-by-hour schedules of her day. Sequence and order make sense to her now, which enables her to concoct very elaborate stories about why she was late for school. It also enables her to comprehend death.
- Money intrigues her, and the more she understands what it does, the more motivated she'll become to do what it takes to get some of her own. Resist the urge to bribe her.
- Girls are more aware sexually than boys. Boys love to tell dirty jokes. Both genders are a little shy when it comes to sexual themes.
- Her mind is growing, and she uses it every chance she gets. She loves memorizing and now reads to acquire information, as opposed to reading for entertainment. She prefers active learning (going to see the lions at the zoo) to listening to adults drone on and on. Beware of the know-it-all attitude this new knowledge gives her.
- Her spelling skills are getting better, and she rarely reverses letters anymore.
- She's developing a sense of right and wrong! She tells the truth more often and exaggerates less.

Emotionally/Socially

- She's outgoing and cheerful most of the time but sometimes seesaws back and forth between emotional highs and lows. The good news is that pouting is replacing violence as a way of expressing anger.
- She can be impatient too, with a little trouble delaying her own gratification, and she's jealous of the time her younger siblings spend with you.
- Her confidence is growing, particularly about what she's learning at school. Her teacher can do no wrong, which means that should you ever disagree with either of them, you'll suffer her wrath.
- She enjoys hanging out with her family, but as friends take on a more central role in her life, she'll spend less and less time with you. At this age boys and girls love to gossip and send notes (or text messages or IM). This is prime time for creating secret clubs.
- As her desire to fit into the group increases, her confidence in herself decreases. And there's still an awful lot of drama. She tattles, is quick to

DEVELOPMENTAL RED FLAGS FOR SCHOOL-AGE CHILDREN

As before, it's important to remember that the range of "normal" and "average" is a big one. You, your partner, and your child's teachers will be in the best position to identify possible problems. So, if one or more of the following are true about your school-age child, call your pediatrician. My child . . .

♦ Is failing in school.
♦ Is aggressive or violent with people, animals, or property.
♦ Has no friends, avoids contact with just about everyone, or seems socially isolated.
♦ Engages in excessively risky behavior or does things to deliberately hurt herself.
♦ Has trouble knowing the difference between right and wrong.
♦ Seems unable to pay attention, has problems concentrating, or is easily distracted.
♦ Has lost (or never had) interest in schoolwork, friends, or other daily activities.
♦ Frequently complains of stomachaches, headaches, or extreme fatigue.
♦ Lies, cheats, or is manipulative.
♦ Flat-out refuses to comply with basic, reasonable rules.

judge others, her feelings are easily hurt, and she often exaggerates the wrongs people are doing to her.

♦ Boys and girls both develop an interest in things in the past. For boys, dinosaurs are always a big hit. For girls, it's often the characters in *Little House on the Prairie* or other historical figures.

♦ Even though there's some tentative interest in the opposite sex, most eight-year-olds still play and hang out with same-sex children. Boys' friendships are fairly smooth. Girls have endless spats, breakups, and make-ups. She has a handful of friends and a worst enemy. The lineup changes daily.

What's Going On with You

Breaking the Mirror
(Why Your Kids Are Not a Reflection of You)

There's very little that feels as nice as having someone come up and tell you what a great kid you've got. Makes you feel good all over, doesn't it? Yeah, you're proud of your child for whatever it is that she did so well. But deep down inside, you also take that observation about your child as a comment on what a great dad you are. On some level, you're right: people *do* see our children as reflections of us, and when they say, "You've got a great kid," they *are* complimenting your fathering skills. Unfortunately, this cuts both ways. When your child shoplifts, shoves crayons up her nose, bullies a classmate, or grinds a grape into a friend's white shag carpet, that also reflects on you— pretty negatively. All of a sudden, that sense of pride magically turns into disappointment.

One of the biggest challenges for dads is to get out of the habit of living vicariously through our children, seeing them as extensions of ourselves. We know we shouldn't do it. We know we need to support them as they grow into their own people and not try to turn them into Mini-Me's. But we do it anyway, at least sometimes. We all secretly want to take credit for the good things our kids do, and distance ourselves from the bad.

Is it possible to get to a place where you can still be proud of your child's positive accomplishments but *not* get disappointed at the less-than-positive? Probably not entirely. But it's important that you try. Allowing your child's accomplishments—good or bad—to dictate how you feel about yourself is putting your child in charge of your life and your happiness. And it's a guarantee that you'll be miserable. There's *always* going to be something you wish your child would have done or not done. The bottom line is that although you have a big influence on your child, ultimately, she alone is responsible for the adult she becomes. You may have a lot to teach, but that doesn't mean your child is ready to learn.

Coping with the Loss of Your Own Father

If you're thirty-five or younger, there's a good chance that your life is going pretty well (and if you're over thirty-five, you probably look back at the years between eighteen and thirty-five as among the best of your life). You're in peak physical and mental form, and you're building your career and your family. Sadly, about one in five men in their mid-thirties or younger get a shock that's hard to recover from: the death of their father. Losing one's father is almost always a shock, but at this age it's particularly devastating, for several reasons. First, so many men are still dependent on their father for guidance, finances, even emotional support, and they haven't had a chance to fully move away from the father's influence to fully establish themselves, says Neil Chethik, author of *Fatherloss*. Second, because the loss of the father is usually unexpected, most of the sons have unfinished business—the "I love you's" that were never said (by either side), unexpressed resentments, and so on.

One of the major themes in your relationship with your father is competition —his desire to remain strong and virile vs. your desire to equal or better his accomplishments. (This dynamic starts very early, and you may have noticed a little competition cropping up between you and your child—especially if you have a boy. We'll talk about that in more detail a little later on.) According to Chethik, the death of a father during the son's early adulthood can disrupt the process of the son becoming his father's equal. The result can last a lifetime. In the first month after their loss, 21 percent of the sons in Chethik's study who had lost their father between eighteen and thirty-two used alcohol or nonprescription drugs to help cope—that was more than three times the rate for men who were over thirty-two when their father died. In the longer term, it's not surprising that so many men who are young when they lose their father suffer from depression, withdraw socially, and have constant self-esteem problems, the result of never having been able to "prove" themselves by "beating" Dad, or never having been accepted by Dad for the things they did.

You and Your Child

Why Be Involved with Your Eight-Year-Old?

- By being available to your eight-year-old and making her a part of every aspect of your life, you're teaching valuable lessons about perseverance, achievement, and motivation. Having the opportunity to see you and imitate you builds children's—especially boys'—problem-solving abilities, according to fatherhood researcher Henry Biller.
- When fathers are warm and involved, and work with their third-graders, children feel more confident in their abilities to solve problems—whether or not those problems are actually solvable—according to researchers Barry Wagner and Deborah Phillips.
- Boys who have positive relationships with their father have a more clearly developed sense of right and wrong.
- Boys and girls with involved dads behave more responsibly and are more likely to accept responsibility when they don't. They're less likely to blame others or "bad luck," according to Biller.
- Being loved by her father is just as important to a child as being loved by her mother. In some cases, it's even more important, according to Ronald Rohner and Robert Veneziano, who analyzed about one hundred studies on parent-child relationships. Specifically, Rohner and Veneziano found that having a loving and nurturing father was as important for a child's happiness

and well-being as having a loving mother; that father's love is sometimes a better predictor than a mother's love for delinquency and conduct problems, substance abuse, and overall mental health and well-being; and that the father's love was the sole significant predictor for certain outcomes, such as psychological adjustment problems, conduct problems, and substance abuse.

♦ You're showing what it means to be a man in our society. Boys are learning how men walk, talk, behave, handle stress and frustration, manage their emotions, deal with problems, and treat others in their lives. Girls are learning the same, as well as about the kind of behavior they should expect from other men in their lives.

Friendships in the School Years

Starting at about six, kids become much more sophisticated in their friendships. Relationships between school-age children are far less about simply being together (although that's still extremely important) and more about exchanges—sharing, taking turns, and helping each other. Kids are now becoming very aware of cliques. And according to educational psychologist Steven Asher, "One of the central challenges for kids this age is to avoid rejection and be accepted by friends."

By seven or eight, a child also starts thinking about—and respecting—her friends' likes and dislikes and has begun to develop some specific expectations of what she wants from a friend. "If I want to do something and Laura doesn't, she usually lets me do it even though she doesn't want to," said one seven-year-old I spoke with. "And when she's sad, or if she fell down and scraped her knee, then I would help her by hugging and patting her." The all-important concept of reciprocity is beginning to sink in.

Friendships at this stage still rarely cross gender lines. Girls are generally establishing fewer but more intense friendships, while boys may have a larger but less intense circle of friends.

Some children have a talent for making friends and always seem to be at the center of things. Others may have only a few friends. As we've discussed before, what children need most of is quality, not quantity (unless the quantity is zero). Here's how you can help promote friendships at this age:

♦ **Be a good role model.** Be kind, expressing your genuine concern for the feelings of others; treat the people you come in contact with in the way you'd like to be treated; and demonstrate proper ways to respect people you disagree with. This will give your kids a great model for their own behavior.

♦ **Talk about the important skills of friendship.** See the sidebar "Recipe for a Great Friendship" on page 169 for more on this.

RECIPE FOR A GREAT FRIENDSHIP

Although it comes naturally to some, for others, making friends is very difficult. Here are seven characteristics that researchers believe (and common sense confirms) are critical to the formation of long-lasting, healthy friendships:

- Friends share—anything from toys to secrets.
- Friends help each other. This might range from helping a fellow preschooler look for a lost doll to helping a fellow twelve-year-old deal with the death of a parent.
- Friends forgive. This is easy enough for a toddler, a little harder for school-age kids, and pretty tough for preadolescents.
- Friends manage their conflicts. Everyone has fights once in a while, but friends are willing to spend the time it takes to work things out.
- Friends are active participants in maintaining the relationship and don't just wait for the others to call.
- Friends want the chance to be open and frank with someone who is open and frank with them.
- Friends keep each other's confidences and stick up for each other.

- **Respect your child's style.** If she can't stand large groups, don't think you can help her overcome her fears by forcing her to face them. Help her by setting up play dates with one or two friends. When (if) she feels completely comfortable in small settings, she may be ready to gradually increase the size of the group.

- **Encourage younger grade-schoolers to have lots of one-on-one playtime with their agemates.** This will minimize the possibility of one child being rejected. At this age two really is company, and three too often results in tears.

- **If your child is often excluded, it's important to acknowledge her feelings.** Help her talk through the emotions she's feeling by using specific words, such as *jealousy, anger,* and *sadness.* The more she's able to understand her own emotions, the more she'll be able to understand the emotions of others.

- **Make sure your child gets plenty of chances to develop the skills that are valued by her peers.** Learning to play a variety of sports and games, for example, gives both boys and girls a great way to interact with others their own age.

Computer Games and Other Tech Toys for Six to Eight

When my oldest daughter was little, she and I used to spend a lot of time at our local library. One day we were heading down the stairs on our way to the bathroom when we heard a lot of clicking and clacking coming from a room down the hall. I recognized the sound right away, but my daughter was curious, so we poked our heads in. We stood there for a few minutes, watching a bunch of office workers banging away at their IBM Selectrics. My daughter asked me what they were doing. I explained that those machines were typewriters, and that the keyboards were just like the one on her computer at home. She thought about that for a minute, then turned to me and asked, "But there's no screen. How do they see what they're writing?"

It was right then that I realized that my children were growing up in a very different world than mine. To me, computers and other tech gadgets and games were very cool, tremendous advances over what we had when I was little. But to my kids, who'd been surrounded by technology their entire lives, computers and all things digital were as natural as breathing. Computer expert Marc Prensky calls today's children (and anyone born after about 1980) "digital natives." And their parents? "Digital immigrants": people who— no matter how techie they become—always remember the old country and the way things used to be.

By the time your child has reached these middle years of childhood, she'll be incredibly technologically sophisticated. Her superb manual dexterity makes dragging, dropping, and other mouse skills a charm. She uses a computer at school and at home and is almost certainly playing with her older sibling's game console. She can probably help you with some annoying Windows glitches, and she's a whiz at graphics. She's also pretty darn adept at surfing the Web, and chances are, she knows more than you do about IM (instant messaging), TM (text messaging), blogs, file sharing, YouTube, My Space, and chat rooms.

Okay, Now's When You Can Start Worrying

The Internet and all its cousins are amazing tools, giving us nearly instant access to resources and information that make our lives a lot easier. But there are also some significant risks:

♦ **Pedophiles.** Despite the stereotypes, pedophiles are not always creepy-looking guys driving around trying to lure children with a bag of candy. Rob Nickel, a former police officer and the author of *Staying Safe in a Wired World*, says there's no single profile. Over the course of his years working undercover, he's arrested doctors, dentists, lawyers, teachers, principals, journalists, businessmen, pizza delivery guys, and many others. One thing Internet pedophiles *do* have in common, says Nickel, is that they "are very good at what they do. . . . They show affection for their targets, listen to their problems, give them the sympathy they crave, and are a shoulder to cry on. They even go so far as to send gifts to their targets to show they care."

♦ **Phishers and other nasty individuals.** Not every unpleasant person lurking on the Internet wants to get into your child's pants. Many would be content to just get into their bank accounts (and yours too). At least ten or twenty times per week I get very realistic-looking spam e-mail claiming to be sent by my bank, asking me to verify something by entering my password. I'm sure you get the same thing. Plenty of adults are tricked by this kind of "phishing," so you can imagine how many kids—who are generally less suspicious than grown-ups—are fooled too. Other crooks want to

Go ask your search engine.

hack into your computer to get access to passwords and other personal information, destroy your data, or use your e-mail to send out viruses to everyone in your address book.

♦ **Undesirable content.** The Internet is almost completely unregulated, which means that if you don't have some kind of filtering software (see pages 173–74), your child can access porn, or sites that can teach her how to refine Sudafed decongestant tablets into crystal meth or build an A-bomb.

♦ **Cyberbullies.** When we were growing up, bullies spent most of their time in schools, tormenting other kids. But now they can do their bullying from the comfort of their own home. Cyberbullies come in all sorts of flavors. Some send obscene, hurtful, threatening e-mails or text messages to others. They may also leave threatening or obscene voice-mail messages on the victim's phone. Some post pictures (like a nude locker-room shot captured by camera phone) on Web sites, in an attempt to humiliate or embarrass the victim. Some pose as a friend in a chat room, get the victim to reveal a secret, and then spread it all over the place. Children who are bullied online can suffer from tension, depression, nightmares, and a drop in self-esteem and confidence. Being bullied can also make a child afraid to go to school and can result in poor grades, an inability to concentrate, and more. If your child is being cyberbullied, do these four things immediately:

◊ **Print out as many examples of the bullying as you can.** Save any voice-mail messages and capture as much information about the bully as possible.

◊ **Report the incidents to your child's teachers and school administrators.**

◊ **Report the incidents to your Internet service provider (ISP).**

◊ **Report the incidents to the police.** Many departments have officers who deal only with cybercrimes. One of my kids was the victim of a cyberbully, and I was pleasantly surprised by how seriously the police took the issue, and how quickly they tracked down the little creep who was doing it.

Keeping Your Child Safe Online

Even though your child is careening toward double digits, the most important word to remember when it comes to computers is *supervision*. The following steps can't guarantee that your child will be 100 percent safe online—nothing can. But you can significantly reduce the risks.

♦ **Keep any Internet-connected computer in a public place, not behind your child's closed door.** You're the parent. You have a right—and an obligation—to know what your kids are doing online.

♦ **Teach her *never* to give out any kind of personal information online.** That means address, phone number, gender, photographs, bank account information, passwords, and so on. She should also *never* accept gifts from someone she hasn't met in person.

♦ **Forbid her from meeting anyone she met online alone.** You or your partner chaperone, or the meeting doesn't happen.

♦ **Talk to her about why you're concerned, and why you're doing what you're doing.** And remind her that there's no way to be absolutely sure that the person she's talking with online is who he or she claims to be. You're likely to get a lot of eye rolling and "I knooooooow, Daddy, I'm not stupid" from this and the previous two bullets. But don't let that keep you from reminding your child every once in a while.

♦ **Be very suspicious.** If you walk up behind your child and all of a sudden the screen display changes, consider that a red flag.

♦ **Install some parental control software.** Ideally, you should never leave your child unattended while she's online. But of course there are going to be all sorts of situations where that's just not going to be possible, which is why I highly recommend installing some filtering or blocking software. Some antivirus programs, like Norton and McAfee, will allow you to restrict certain types of Internet sites for certain users. Other similar programs include Cybersitter (cybersitter.com), Net Nanny (netnanny.com), and Content Protect (contentwatch.com). Make sure you install these programs using your Administrator settings and that your child doesn't know your password.

♦ **Monitor them (also sometimes known as spying).** All Internet browsers allow you to see a history of all the sites that have been visited by users of a given computer. If you're not sure what the site is, check it out. Understand, though, that there are plenty of ways to clear this history, and your child may know them. If you try to check the history and the file is empty, or if you want to probe even deeper, you'll need to get one of the many programs out there that can help you track Internet chats, IMs, and just about every keystroke. Some of the ones suggested by Rob Nickel include: Spector (spectorsoft.com), Invisible Keylogger (invisiblekeylogger.com), and I Am Big Brother (iambigbrother.com). All of these programs run in the background, and it's completely up to you whether you tell your child that she's under surveillance or not. My suggestion is to let your child know that you're monitoring her—not because you don't trust her, but because of the potential dangers. That way you avoid having to deal with your child feeling betrayed if she finds about it later.

♦ **Whether you're spying or not, read the glossary of terms in the "Talking the Talk" sidebar on the opposite page.** If you see any of these abbreviations, it could be a red flag.

Are Video Games *Good* for Children?

It's one thing to acknowledge that computer games, video games, handholds, and other tech toys may not be as bad as they're made out to be. But could they actually be *good* for kids? Absolutely!

Various studies show that children who play tech games have better hand-eye coordination, better visualization skills, and faster reaction times than kids who don't. Game-playing children are also more confident and think more creatively than those who don't play games.

Part of the issue here has to do with the way digital natives learn. In most schools today you have digital immigrants teaching the way they always have, using lectures, worksheets, flashcards, and textbooks. But digital natives don't

TALKING THE TALK

Kids these days . . . you can hardly understand them. And nowhere is their language harder to decipher than on the Internet, where they're so busy that they don't have time to type out entire words. There are literally hundreds of abbreviations that are used in e-mail, chat rooms, IMs, and text messages. Whether you're snooping over your child's shoulder or reviewing some of the information captured by a monitoring program, here are some of the potentially problematic ones that you might see.

A3	anytime, anywhere, anyplace
ASL	age, sex, location
ASLMH	age, sex, location, music, hobbies
ASLP	age, sex, location, picture
BF	boyfriend
BIOYN	blow it out your nose
DYFM	dude, you fascinate me
EMA	what is your e-mail address?
F2F	face to face
GF	girlfriend
IAD8	it's a date
IHAIM	I have another instant message
ILU	I love you
IPN	I'm posting naked
KOC	kiss on cheek
KOL	kiss on lips
L8R	later
LY	love you
LYWAMH	love you with all my heart
MOOS	member of the opposite sex
NP	nosy parents
P911	my parents are coming
PANB	parents are nearby
RPG	role-playing games
RUMF	are you male or female
SHCOON	shoot hot coffee out of nose
TAW	teachers are watching
WTGP	want to go private?
WYCM	will you call me?

respond well to that kind of teaching. Everything in their lives moves quickly, and they're used to nearly instant feedback (that's why so much of their communication takes place via IM or text messaging—e-mail just isn't fast enough anymore). You can complain about this all you want, but attempting to fight technology is a complete waste of time. We'll all be far better off if we can use technology to our advantage, which is exactly what tech games do.

One of the features that make tech games so attractive and potentially such important educational resources is that they give the digital natives the kind of instant feedback they need. They also require creative thinking and put players into situations where the decisions they make have significant consequences. For example, in Roller Coaster Tycoon, players must create a successful theme park from scratch, on a limited budget. They have to hire a staff, construct and maintain rides and infrastructure, and charge admission. If ticket prices are too high, no one will come. If they're low, a lot of customers will show up, but if the lines are long or there aren't enough restaurants or bathrooms, no one will come back.

Other games put children into historical situations where their decisions affect the outcome. If you were George Washington, what would happen if you decided not to cross the Delaware? Still other games teach reading, math, chemistry, and many more subjects. As Marc Prensky puts it, "Kids learn more positive, useful things for their future from their video games than they learn in school."

Tech games are so good at honing skills that the U.S. Military does a lot of its training in video-game format. And Dr. James Rosser, who runs the Advanced Medical Technology Institute at Beth Israel Hospital in New York City, found that surgeons who played video games for three or more hours per week in the past made 37 percent fewer errors than surgeons who had never played video games. They were also 27 percent faster than those that didn't play games. Rosser now has his surgeons warm up before surgery by playing video games for thirty minutes.

There's also some indication that digital games have physical benefits as well. If you want to see that theory in action, head down to a local arcade or bowling alley, or anyplace where there are a lot of video games. You're sure to see kids jumping and stomping and spinning—and sweating up a storm—on an extremely popular game called Dance Dance Revolution. There are also home versions of the game for Nintendo's PlayStation and DS platforms, and I can tell you from my own experience that they're exhausting.

Now, in the interests of fairness, I should mention that playing video games has been associated with childhood obesity and smoking. But that in no way makes me any less of a game supporter. The operative words here are *participation* and *moderation*.

♦ **Participation.** Read up on games, platforms, advances, and the latest studies, and use games to augment your child's interests. Get involved in the game-selection process. Ask your child what she likes about her favorite games and what she's learning. Then, after she's gone to bed, log on and teach yourself how to play. Sit with your child while she plays, and if you feel confident, ask if you can join in.

♦ **Moderation.** Never use video games as a babysitter, and make sure your child has some flesh-and-blood friends in addition to her virtual ones. As we talked about in Chapter 2 (pages 67–71), interactive media should be just one component of your child's education, and just one pastime. Enforce breaks, and make sure your child has plenty of opportunities to play outside.

When evaluating games and other resources, opt for the ones that provide the most imaginative experience, that fill your child with the joy of "I did it!" And don't focus too much on the learning component. As with preschoolers, your child will learn more and have a lot more fun playing games that are "accidentally educational." Below are some games your school-age child will love. You can find more reviews and suggestions at gamespot.com, games2train.com, childrenssoftware.com, commonsensemedia.com, or superkids.com.

LOGICAL JOURNEY OF THE ZOOMBINIS
Platform: Mac and PC
Players help rescue the adorable Zoombinis from the enemies who've taken over Zombini Isle. This wonderful game features logic, math, hypothesis testing, and organizational skills in an incredibly engaging format.

CARMEN SAN DIEGO (there are many titles in this series)
Platform: Mac and PC
Help world detective Carmen San Diego fights a ring of thieves, tricksters, and charlatans.

CLUE FINDERS 3RD GRADE (but not the others in the Clue Finders series)
Platform: Mac and PC
Your child joins a team of kid detectives who have to discover why jungle animals are disappearing. Encourages math, logic, and thinking skills, and continually adapts to your child's level to provide just the right level of challenge.

WWW.ANSWERS.COM
Platform: Web site
Billing itself as one of the leading information sites on the Internet, Answers.com is a collection of over three million answers drawn from over sixty titles from brand-name publishers, as well as original content created by their own editorial team. The site offers useful info in categories like business, health, travel, technology, science, entertainment, arts, history, and many more. It's terrific for homework help and researching almost any question your child will throw at you.

COREFX THREE LEVEL
Platform: PC
A powerful graphics program with which your child can make anything from crayon drawings to animated graphics to doctored digital. *Children's Software Review* called this "the best consumer level drawing program on the market, for both children and adults."

ELECTROPLANKTON
Platform: Nintendo DS
Art and music collide in Electroplankton, which features the striking visual style of Japanese interactive media artist Toshio Iwai. When the player comes in contact with any of the ten species of electroplankton or elements of their environment, the microscopic merrymakers give off a unique sound. This game offers a fun and amazingly creative way for your child to actually put herself inside the game. She is the conductor, and a new world of musical composition has opened up for her to explore.

HARVEST MOON: ANOTHER WONDERFUL LIFE
Platform: GameCube
The lead character of this game is female, still relatively unusual in the gaming world. Harvest Moon allows children to start a farm from scratch, including caring for many farm animals and growing crops. In addition, players can charm a husband and start a family. Even though the game requires a large amount of reading, it's great, addictive fun.

RETRO ATARI
Platform: Nintendo DS
Your child may have to hide this one from you, since it's loaded with games that you grew up with. You can show your child how to play everything from

Asteroids to Pong, and regale her with stories of the olden days of arcade games and pinball.

Other good choices:

EXPLORER GLOBE
Platform: LeapFrog
Teaches kids everything they could possibly want to know about geography.

TALKING MAT MATH CHALLENGE (Learning Resources)
A floor math-quiz game where players step on the right answer.

MATH SHARK (Educational Insights)
Platform: Handheld
Combines the best of multi-level, skill-building math activities with a basic calculator.

MR. PENCIL'S LEARN TO DRAW AND WRITE
Platform: Leapster
Activities include a coloring book, traceable pictures, mazes, or step-by-step lessons in animation. There are a total of 150 lessons that illustrate how to draw favorite animals, objects, and characters as well as upper- and lowercase letters and numbers.

FLY THROUGH MATH and FLY THROUGH SPELLING
Application: FLY pentop computer (LeapFrog)
Defies definition. A pen-based system that can give real-time feedback on spelling, math, and other subjects.

What Are Daddies Made Of? PART 3

Still more ways to be a strong father:
- **Eat meals together.** It's nearly impossible these days to get Mom, Dad, and the kids all in the same place at the same time. But some recent research might give you a little incentive to make family meals a priority. According to the National Center on Addiction and Substance Abuse, children who eat with their family at least five times per week do better in school, are less stressed and anxious, and have better relationships with

YOU AND YOUR DAUGHTER:
TALKING ABOUT PUBERTY

It's reasonably safe to assume that your partner (or ex, if you're now a single parent), will be talking to your daughter about puberty and menstruation. Even if she does, it's a good idea for you to prepare yourself to deal with these issues anyway. Women's bodies have always been something of a mystery to most men; it's perfectly normal to be confused, embarrassed, or even somewhat put off by your daughter's physical changes.

First of all, take some time to learn a little about girls' puberty. The book *What's Happening to My Body for Girls* by Linda Maderas is a terrific resource. That way, if your daughter has questions or you need to talk to her, you'll be more knowledgeable.

Somewhere between the ages of eight and fourteen, the process will start. Your daughter will start to develop breasts and start growing hair on her genitals and under her arms. Much to her chagrin, her skin may start breaking out, and eventually she'll start menstruating. The whole process usually takes from eighteen months to as long as seven or eight years to complete. If your daughter seems to be starting puberty at the very early end of the age range or hasn't started by the end of the range, talk with her pediatrician.

Ask your daughter whether she has any questions about what's going on and let her know that she can ask you anything, anytime she wants to talk. She'll probably be far too embarrassed to discuss those intimate details

their parents. Kids who *don't* share as many family meals are more likely to smoke, drink, and do drugs.

Five family meals per week might seem like an impossible goal, particularly if you and your partner are both holding down jobs and you've got more than one child. But start small; one dinner together every week is better than none. And you can build from there.

Family meals don't have to be elaborate feasts, with five courses; they don't even need to happen at home. They just have to be good enough that people won't spend the whole meal complaining about the food. No time to cook? Stock your freezer with frozen pizzas and other easy-to-warm meals. If you can afford it, hire someone to do some cooking for you. My wife and I did that for a few months, and it was great. Just make sure the person you hire is able to make kid-friendly meals; there's no sense paying someone to

with a guy (which may come as a relief to you), but having made the offer will let her know that you care, and that's what's truly important. The next best thing you can do is help your partner practice her birds-and-bees speech.

If you sense that your daughter isn't getting the information she needs from your partner, offer to put her in touch with an adult female friend or relative she might feel more comfortable talking to.

It's very likely that your daughter may feel fat, embarrassed, and uncomfortable in her new body. She may constantly compare her rate of development to that of her girlfriends, and if she's started early, she may have to deal with some increased attention, both good and bad, from boys.

In addition, as strange as it sounds, your daughter's puberty is going to affect you, too. She may, for example, start flirting with you just like she did when she was a toddler, which can be a little disconcerting. And while you may have loved having her sit on your lap when she was two or three, it might make you a little uncomfortable to be in such close proximity to her newly feminine body. Unfortunately, a lot of guys get scared and end up backing away, as if to keep their daughters from harm. Don't do that. Just like when she was three, she needs to experiment with all sorts of different behaviors to see what kind of reactions she'll get from people. She also needs to know that what she's going through is normal and that you, the most important male figure in her life, love her. If you push her away, no matter how good your intentions, she's going to feel rejected and bad about herself.

prepare meals that your kids will refuse to touch. And ask your chef-for-hire to double or triple the recipes so you can freeze the rest.

As far as ground rules, the simpler the better. Everyone must attend, no television anywhere near the table, no answering the phone or checking e-mail before the meal is over, and everyone has to listen and speak respectfully to each other.

♦ **Get out your dictionary and look up the word** *fair.* In most kids' minds, the word *fair* is a synonym for *the same.* Younger ones will always complain that the older ones get more privileges, and the older ones will always complain that the younger ones have fewer obligations. If you have two or more kids, you may be perpetuating the problem by bringing back identical toys for each child from a business trip, or trying to do the exact same activities with each one. Karl Marx isn't a guy generally looked at as a parenting expert, but he did have one great line that parents should keep in mind: "From each according to his abilities, to each according to his needs." If you can get your children to understand that deceptively simple message, their childhood will be enjoyable for everyone concerned. In a few years, when they're heading off to college, they can decide for themselves whether they like anything else Marx had to say.

♦ **Recognize good behavior.** It's very easy to focus on what your child doesn't do and ignore what she does. What happens is that we decide in our minds that whatever she's doing right is what she's *supposed* to be doing, and therefore not particularly notable. But as my grandmother always said, "You catch more flies with sugar than with vinegar." So if your preschooler gets dressed by herself or says "Please," tell her how proud you are. If your six-year-old cleans her room up well enough that you can actually see the floor, tell her how great her room looks. If your eight-year-old takes the garbage out without being asked, thank her. In some ways this is a glass-half-empty-versus-half-full kind of thing, but it goes a step further by recognizing incremental improvement. For example, if your child got an F in a class last term and raised the grade to a D this term, you can either criticize and complain that she's still doing miserably, or you can take her out for ice cream to celebrate the fantastic progress she made. If you're interested in seeing that D go up any higher, you'll have a better shot with the second option than with the first.

♦ **Schedule dates with each child.** Try to get in some one-on-one time every day, or at least a few times a week. It doesn't have to be a huge block of time, and it doesn't matter what you do, as long as the time is special. (As the old saying goes, How do kids spell *love*? T-I-M-E.) The object is for you and your child to get to know each other better. Going for a walk around the neighborhood, cleaning out the garage together, going to the grocery store, playing gin rummy, or even having her help you with a project around the house are all fine. Try to schedule your private dates at times when it's good for your child, rather than when it's convenient for you. And let your child pick the activity.

♦ **Enough about them . . .** How much do your kids know about you, what your childhood was like, what you loved and hated? Tell them about your life, especially the things you did to get into trouble. Telling them about yourself helps them understand themselves better and lets them know that you value them and their company. It also helps connect them with their history. If any of their grandparents or older relatives are still alive, encourage your children to talk with them about *their* life. You might want to do

I think oral sex is when they only just talk about it.

the same thing yourself. Chances are you don't know nearly as much about your own father as you should or could.

Another great way to help your children get to know you better is to take them to work with you. It doesn't matter what you do—your child will be thrilled to be a part of it. I still remember very clearly a time when I was about nine and my dad took me to work with him. He was an assistant district attorney and the two of us went to the county jail, where I got fingerprinted and spent about a minute locked up in a cell. Then we went to the courtroom, where I got to watch him try a couple of cases. I'm sure I had no idea what was going on, and it didn't matter. All I cared about was that I was there with Dad, and he was a pretty cool guy.

♦ **Discipline, but don't punish.** It's your job to create firm limits and enforce them. It's your child's job to test them. Children need consistent boundaries and discipline—that teaches them self-control and gives them comfort and confidence that you really care about them. Being inconsistent or too much of a pushover (how many times have you given your child sixteen "last warnings" and threatened to take away all her privileges until she's thirty-five?) may make your child fear independence. Know when to compromise—and when not to (health and safety issues top this list).

Above all, make sure you understand your child. Trying to discipline her without understanding why she's doing what she's doing is a little like taking cough syrup for emphysema: the thing that's bugging you goes away for a while, but the underlying problem remains—and keeps getting worse with time. The most direct way to solve this is to simply ask your child what's going on and why she's acting the way she is; in many cases, she'll tell you. If she won't, or doesn't have the vocabulary to do so, make an educated guess and ask ("Are you writing on the walls because you want me to spend more time with you?").

Finally, don't let yourself slip—or get pushed—into the role of "wait-till-your-father-comes-home" disciplinarian. You and your partner should both be responsible for discipline, and the two of you should present a united front as much as possible.

♦ **Safety first.** Even though your child is well on her way to adulthood, you still need to make sure the house is childproofed. Periodically check that knives, fertilizers, paints, poisons, and so on are locked safely away. And always insist on proper safety gear when biking, roller-blading, or doing any other sport. If you've got a little one around the house, crawl around and check for loose wires, choking hazards, bookshelves that might fall or get pulled over, ungated stairways, and other tempting dangers the baby will want to explore. If you find any hazards, get out your toolbox and fix them. Also, ask your older child(ren) to help with the childproofing by keeping anything with small pieces or sharp edges secured. Check the Consumer Products Safety Commission's Web site (cpsc.gov) regularly to make sure you've got the most recent recommendations and regulations for car and booster seats, and that you're aware of any product recalls.

Hey, Where Did I Come From?
More About Adoption and
Assistive Reproductive Technology (ART)

Adoption

A lot of adoption experts feel that the early school years are the perfect time to tell your child about her adoption. Besides your child being able to understand the concept, there are three other good reasons:

♦ By the time she's six or seven, she'll probably be feeling secure enough in your family not to be shattered at the thought that she was adopted, according to Dr. Steven Nickman.

But are you my birth mother?

- There's a pretty good chance that your child is going to have a unit in school on biology or genetics, and the issue of hereditary traits and blood relatives will probably come up.
- Waiting until your child is a teenager could hurt her. "Disclosure at that time can be devastating to children's self-esteem and to their faith in their parents," writes Dr. Nickman.

On the other hand, there are a few minor hitches to talking about adoption and assistive reproductive technology (ART) at this age:

- In the early school years kids live in a black-and-white world, and your child may have some strong ideas about how life is supposed to work, including how children are supposed to come into the world. Being adopted may not meet the standard.
- During these years, when being accepted and fitting in are becoming more and more important, the idea of having been given away—no matter how well you explain it—can feel like rejection to some kids. They may take it personally, thinking that they were put up for adoption because they were bad or flawed in some way.

♦ In keeping with the general black-and-white world she lives in, a seven-to-eight-year-old may still believe that she was either adopted or "born," one or the other, as if being adopted didn't have birth as a prerequisite. For that reason, the National Adoption Information Clearinghouse (childwelfare.gov) suggests that when telling your child about her adoption, you help her understand that she was *born* first, and that "all children, adopted or not—are conceived and born in the same way. The birth came first, then the adoption."

♦ Your child may go through a grieving period for her biological parents. This will be similar to the grief a lot of adoptive parents have over the "loss" of the biological child they'll never have.

♦ Later on, if your child ever decides to try to find her birth parents, she may worry that doing so will hurt your feelings.

Some kids who find out they're adopted are incredibly curious and ply their parents with thousands of questions. If so, try to answer them—but don't give any more information than they're asking for. It's tempting to respond to a question like "Where did I come from?" with a long explanation about sperm and eggs, gene splicing, and adoption law, when all that was necessary "Norfolk, Virginia" would have been a fine answer. Other kids seem completely uninterested. Still others might actually be dying to ask but may worry that their questions will offend you. No matter how your child responds, it's critical to speak openly and honestly and let her know that you'll be available to answer questions any time she has them. If she's more on the silent end, revisit the issue from time to time. Don't push, but asking whether she has any questions every once in a while can really help. It could take several years of occasional discussions before your child really and truly understands.

If your child is interested, introduce her to some other adoptees, including adults. She might find it helpful to know that being adopted doesn't have to have any impact on how successful you can be in life. But make sure you leave the option of whom to tell about the adoption up to her. She'll appreciate that you trust her to manage that information.

Assistive Reproductive Technology

Deciding if, when, and how to talk to a child who was conceived by ART is a more complicated matter. The general consensus is that seven to ten is about the right age. But before you make your final decision and start writing your script, psychologist Diane Ehrensaft, author of *Mommies, Daddies, Donors, Surrogates*, suggests that you ask yourself the following questions:

♦ What will be the benefits of my child's knowing?

♦ What would be the benefits of shielding my child from the information?

♦ Do I think any harm would come to my child by knowing that she was born with the aid of a surrogate or donor?

♦ Would harm come from her not knowing? (For example, the child might be concerned that she's at risk of inheriting a condition you or your partner have, even though that's a biological impossibility.)

♦ Would my relationship with my child be strengthened, threatened, or unchanged if she knew?

♦ How will the family react to the news?

♦ How would the community react if they knew?

♦ What will it be like if other people know but my child doesn't?

♦ What will it be like if my child knows but others don't?

There are, as you might expect, no easy answers to these questions. Here are a few reasons you might be hemming and hawing:

♦ You may still secretly (or not so secretly) wish that the child was your "real" child—and after all these years, you may have almost come to believe that she is. Having the discussion will mean facing an unpleasant reality.

♦ You might be worried that the information will upset your child.

♦ If you're not the biological father, you may be worried that your child might reject you.

♦ You might be ashamed or embarrassed about your infertility, or worry that people will think you weren't "man enough" to become a father the "right" way. Interestingly, this isn't as big an issue for women, possibly because they can still carry and give birth to a baby who isn't biologically theirs.

What's especially important is that if you choose to raise the ART issue with your child, you do it in the most upbeat, positive way possible, and that you get past whatever second-guessing you're still doing. If you seem uncomfortable or wary, your child will get the idea that there's something wrong.

Good News, Better News

A lot of people wonder whether children conceived with the help of ART differ from those conceived the "regular" way. The answer is a pretty definitive "No." A number of studies have shown that there aren't any significant differences between ART and non-ART kids in terms of behavior, self-esteem, intelligence, or anything else.

People also wonder about differences between the *parents* of both types of children. Contrary to what you might think, parents of ART children actually report less parenting-related stress than other parents, according to Chun-Shin Hahn, a researcher at Johns Hopkins University. Parents in Hahn's study also reported "more positive mother- and father-child relationships" than parents of naturally conceived children. Other researchers have found that ART parents may be warmer and more emotionally involved with their children. Part of the issue is that ART parents really, really want a child, and they've thought a lot more about what it means to be a parent than those of us for whom conceiving wasn't much trouble. They've also spent a lot of money trying to have a baby, and they're going to do whatever they can to protect their investment.

You and Your Partner

The Building Blocks of a Good
Stepfather-Stepchild Relationship

As we discussed earlier, forging a relationship with your stepchildren isn't going to be easy. But independent studies by researchers Kay Pasley, Lou Everett, William MacDonald, Alfred DeMaris, and Mark Rosin have identified a number of factors that can make the difference between feeling satisfied as a stepfather and feeling frustrated:

- Having talked over your role *before* you formally became a stepfather.
- The amount of time you spend with your stepchildren—the more the better.
- A loving relationship between you and your partner.
- The support you get from your new partner for your involvement in the discipline of the stepchildren.
- "Claiming" the children, meaning thinking about them as "ours" rather than as "hers."
- Being a parent, *not* a friend, to your stepchild.
- Your willingness to take things easy. Jumping in and demanding conformity right away leads to bitterness on both sides.

Here are some other very important steps you can take to make stepfathering a more enjoyable experience for everyone:

- **Have realistic expectations.** The idea that her kids and you are going to fall instantly in love with one another is a fantasy. Relying on it too much will only set you up for failure. Taking a stepparenting class can help you keep your expectations reasonable.

THE LANGUAGE OF STEPFATHERHOOD

Sometimes the littlest things can make a huge difference—for example, introducing the stepchildren as "my children" instead of "my stepchildren" or saying, "We have three children" instead of "She has two, and we have one together." Comments like those strengthen the connection between you and your stepchildren.

The word *dad* is a very powerful one in positive and negative ways. If your stepchildren call you "Dad," it will feel great and will bring you closer together. But it could make their biological father furious (you'd feel the same way too if your kids were calling some other guy "Dad"). So never ask them to call you Dad or Daddy or anything other than your first name. On the other hand, if you're new to fatherhood, "Dad" or Daddy" could be extremely scary to you. The word in this context carries responsibilities (drive me here, give me money) but allows for few rights, including discipline.

- **Relocate.** If you can afford to move to a new home, you won't have to worry about some people in the new family feeling like they have a home field advantage and others like they're always visitors.

- **Don't try to get attached too fast.** Doing so makes you vulnerable to rejection, which you're going to be getting a lot of for quite a while anyway. It's especially good if you can spend some one-on-one time with each stepchild, engaged in an activity you both enjoy. Or take turns teaching each other something the other doesn't know how to do.

- **Don't let the stepkids get to you, or at least don't let them see that they did.** It will make them use the same hurtful tactics over and over. In particular, expect to hear a lot of "You're not my father, so I don't have to listen to you."

- **Be a grown-up.** If they hurt your feelings, don't try to get even by rejecting them.

- **Be flexible.** The kids will love you one day and hate you the next. You may feel the same about them.

- **Support their biological father (or their new stepfather).** Don't be offended if your stepchildren want to spend a lot of time with their biological dad. There's going to be some natural competitiveness between the two of you, especially if your partner tells you he isn't a particularly nice guy. But you absolutely must support the kids' relationship with their father. (If the situation is reversed, try to help your new wife understand that your kids are going to want to spend a lot of time with their mother and that she

Good evening. I am Martha's son by a previous marriage.

should try as hard as she can to support that relationship.) Just thinking about it may make you nauseous, but do it anyway. And never, ever bad-mouth anyone (this includes your ex, her new beau, your current partner, her ex, and his new partner. Whew). If your stepchildren's father died, you may find yourself competing with an idealized image of him.

♦ **Support and encourage your stepchildren's relationship with their mother.** When they have her undivided attention they'll be less likely to resent you for stealing her away from them.

♦ **Defer.** Each of you should feel free to make comments and suggestions, but neither should ever argue (in front of the kids) with a position the biological parent has taken. Ultimately, the biological parent should have 51 percent of the votes.

♦ **Establish some new family traditions.** Rituals and customs help families bond. You have some from your family, your partner has some from hers. Neither is better or worse, they're just different. Coming up with new traditions that can make all of you feel that you're working together to create something special.

♦ **Keep your relationship with your partner healthy.** This is the foundation of your new family. Talk with her, discuss the role she expects you to take in her children's life, or that you expect her to take in your kids' life. Don't be naive and think that everything will work itself out—it won't. Over half of remarried women and about two-thirds of remarried men get divorced again. Major problems include conflicts over child rearing, the children's behavior, and the relationship between the stepparent and stepchildren. So don't be afraid to get some couples therapy if you need it.

♦ **Cut Mom some slack.** If you're the bio dad and your partner is the stepmother, or you're both stepparenting each other's children, help her out. Being a stepmother is even tougher than being a stepfather. Less than a third of children who have a stepmother consider her a "real" parent and are happy that Dad remarried, according to Constance Ahrons, a family researcher at the Radcliffe Institute for Advanced Study. On the other hand, almost half of kids with stepfathers see them as "real" parents and are happy Mom remarried. Ahrons also found that two-thirds of kids felt close to their stepfathers but less than half felt that way about their stepmother.

♦ **Pay attention to how the kids react.** If you and your new partner both have kids from previous relationships, don't underestimate the magnitude of the changes they're going to experience: new routines, a new house, new customs, new bedrooms—they may even have to share a room—and possibly a new birth order. A child who was once the oldest, and had all the privileges that went along with that, might resent being bumped by an older child. The same might happen with a child who gets displaced as the baby of the family. Don't make the mistake of expecting that everyone's going to live in one big, happy family. Give the kids plenty of time to get used to each other and to their new stepparents. It's not going to be easy on any of you.

Just Like a Real Person, Only Shorter

What's Going On with Your Child

Physically

- Your baby is approaching double digits and looking more and more like an adult. By ten, girls are getting softer around the edges (some may even start to develop breasts and menstruate), while boys are packing on muscle and getting firmer.
- Your nine-year-old, regardless of gender, is proud of his physical strength, agility, and stamina and loves to show them off. Like eight-year-olds, nine-year-olds are still moving pretty quickly. But with the increase in coordination and muscle control that comes this year, life in general seems calmer.
- Girls will start their pre-puberty growth spurt early this year. Boys will start toward the end of the year. But both may complain of growing pains, mostly in the legs and mostly at night.
- Remember that trip to the orthodontist last year? It's time to go back. By the end of his ninth year, he may be ready for braces. But braces or not, he'll still need to be reminded to brush his teeth.
- Now that he's using the computer and doing a lot more reading for school, watch out for eyestrain. And while you've got your insurance card handy, a trip to the optometrist may be in order.

Intellectually

- Mathematical concepts are making more sense. He now understands about odd and even, larger and smaller, and groups (Ford, Chevy, and Lexus are all cars). He'll make endless lists of everyone he knows, organized by hair color or height.

♦ He uses reference books (dictionaries, encyclopedias) with increasing ease. With supervision, this is a fine time for him to begin exploring the Internet as a research tool in connection with school projects.

♦ He defines himself in terms of what he can do (I can tap-dance, I can torture my brother, I can lift my daddy off the floor).

♦ His stubbornness blossoms into perseverance, and he begins working on skills repeatedly until he masters them.

♦ He's got a good attention span and can return to a task after an interruption. Occasionally, he thinks of the future, though mostly in terms of doing the same things that Dad or Mom have done in their lives.

♦ He may show couch-potato tendencies, enjoying TV, DVDs, and video games so much that he'll often pass up a chance to play outside in favor of sitting passively in front of a screen.

♦ His sense of fairness is growing beyond himself, and he is developing his own standards of right and wrong.

♦ He's reading magazines and comic books. Boys may become fascinated with horror stories and tales of gore, while girls will gravitate more towards drama, like *The Diary of Anne Frank*. Girls may also start showing an interest in gossip magazines like *Teen People*, *YM*, and *US Weekly*.

Emotionally/Socially

♦ He's more responsible, independent, and self-motivated. He's the one planning his play dates now, and, if you agree, he often takes outings—hikes, bicycle rides—with his friends without adult supervision. This is the perfect time to give him his own house key on a new key ring.

♦ He's developed a conscience. Your nine-year-old will tell you when he's done something wrong and will accept the consequences as long as he thinks they're fair.

♦ He worries about the unknown—death, divorce, abandonment, high school, not being popular, growing up. Girls are starting to get very interested in fashion and will spend an amazing amount of time in front of a mirror.

♦ He's self-conscious and worried that everyone is looking at him all the time. In spite of this, he always wants to be first in line and first to be called on. Perfectly ordinary things become embarrassing. You, for example.

♦ Guess what? He craves recognition from his peers more than from you. He's becoming more of a social creature and finding it easier and more natural to make friends. He and his buddies frequently resolve their problems by judging each other without parental intervention.

- Last year he might have quit a hobby because he wasn't as good at it as a friend. This year he'll be motivated to do whatever it takes to improve.
- While your eight-year-old rarely finished a project, at nine he'll start many and finish them all. You may wake up in the middle of the night to find your child feverishly working on a set of Styrofoam igloos for a school project or snuggled up in bed with a book he just has to finish that night.
- Sibling rivalry issues are pretty much a thing of the past. Your nine-year-old will now protect and defend a younger sib and brag worshipfully about an older one.

What's Going On with You

The Good Enough Dad

Raising a family in today's world is a high-pressure job, and we parents need all the help we can get. Or maybe not. We're bombarded from all sides with information on everything from throwing the best birthday parties and teaching manners to picking the perfect extracurricular activities and protecting our children from strangers. No aspect of parenting is overlooked, and the distinct impression one gets is that *not* following someone's six or eight or twelve sure-fire steps will have dire consequences for the children and will brand us as terrible parents.

The fallout from all this fearmongering is that we don't trust ourselves. Is my child eating enough vegetables? Is his self-esteem high enough? Is she bored? Does he always say "please" and "thank you"? Did she learn to walk or talk early enough? Was he toilet trained at the right age? Does she have enough friends? Could he be victimized at school by a bully? Are her grades good enough? Will he ever be able to get a job? Will she show up one day on the back of a Harley, with a tongue piercing and a tattoo? It's enough to drive you nuts.

We worry that the world is a dangerous place—far more dangerous than the one we grew up in—and we're so afraid of making mistakes that we sometimes end up smothering our children with attention and protection. We stuff them full of the "right" foods, sign them up for five extracurricular activities every day so they won't get "bored," and buy all sorts of fancy gadgets that are guaranteed to make them smarter. And we *don't* let them cross the street by themselves, ride their bike to a friend's house a few blocks away, stay at home alone

I bet you're glad you got out of politics
to spend more time with your family.

until they're over twelve, play in the backyard unsupervised for a few minutes, or do a lot of the things we did as kids.

Worse than that, we worry that we have to be perfect. The reality, though, is that most of the things that keep us up at night simply aren't worth the trouble. Let me give you just one example.

How many children do you think disappear in the United States every year? Fifty thousand? Five hundred thousand? A million? All of those numbers (and some that are even higher) come up frequently in the media. Parents hear those stats, and they imagine that their children are in constant danger of being kidnapped, molested, and murdered.

Fortunately, that's nowhere near true. The reality is that the overwhelming majority of those "missing" children were runaway teens, three-quarters of whom were back home within twenty-four hours. The next biggest category is kids who are abducted by family members, usually in the midst of a custody battle. All the way at the bottom of the list is the "stereotypical kidnapping," the one we all fear. In the 1990s, there were an average of two to three hundred stranger abductions per year. In 2001, those numbers dropped to about one hundred per year. In about fifty of those cases, the child was killed.

Now, I'm not pooh-poohing the number of true child abductions and murders; every single one is a tragedy most of us will, thankfully, never have to live through. But realistically, the chances that your child will be kidnapped by a stranger are less than one in a million. And the fifty abducted and murdered children constitute only 5 percent of all children murdered in the United States (most of the rest are killed by parents). A child actually is more likely to choke to death on food than be murdered by a stranger.

There's no question that it's a good idea to be cautious and teach your children what to do if they're approached by a stranger. But are we really helping things by exaggerating the problem and whipping ourselves and everyone else into a frenzy of suspicion and paranoia? Not in my view.

Not long ago I received this e-mail that brought home the absurdity of our parenting paranoia and obsession with worrying:

To: Armin Brott
Subject: If you were born in the 50s, 60s, 70s, or 80s . . .

♦ We survived being born to mothers who smoked and/or drank while pregnant. They took aspirin, ate blue cheese dressing, and didn't get tested for diabetes.

♦ After that trauma, our baby cribs were covered with bright-colored lead-based paint. We had no childproof lids on medicine bottles, doors, or cabinets, and when we rode our bikes, we had no helmets. Not to mention the risks we took hitchhiking.

♦ As children, we rode in cars without seat belts or air bags. Riding in the back of a pickup on a warm day was always a special treat.

♦ We drank water from the garden hose and not from a bottle.

♦ We shared one soft drink with four friends, drinking from one bottle, and no one actually died from this.

♦ We ate cupcakes, bread and butter, and drank soda pop with sugar in it, but we weren't overweight because we were always outside playing.

♦ We would leave home in the morning and could play all day, as long we were back when the streetlights came on. No one was able to reach us all day.

♦ We would spend hours building our go-carts out of scraps and then ride down a hill, only to find out we forgot the brakes. After running into the bushes a few times, we learned to solve the problem.

♦ We did not have PlayStations or Nintendo DX, no 99 channels on cable, videotape movies, surround sound, cell phones, personal computers, or Internet chat rooms. We had friends! We went outside and found them.

♦ We fell out of trees, got cut, broke bones and teeth, and there were no lawsuits from these accidents.

- We made up games with sticks and tennis balls and ate worms, and although we were told it would happen, we did not put out very many eyes, nor did the worms live in us forever.
- We were given BB guns for our tenth birthdays.
- We rode bikes to a friend's house, knocked on the door or rang the bell, or just walked over and yelled for them.
- The idea of a parent bailing us out if we broke the law was unheard of. They actually sided with the law.
- This generation produced some of the best risk-takers and problem-solvers and inventors ever. The past fifty years have been an explosion of innovation and new ideas.
- We had freedom, failure, success and responsibility, and we learned how to deal with it all!

So here's the message: Lower your expectations, give yourself a break, and stop worrying so much. If every meal your child eats isn't perfectly balanced, or if he has a candy bar now and then, he'll survive. If he gets a B in school, gets into fights with his siblings, doesn't play the Beethoven violin concerto or pitch a perfect game before he gets to middle school, he'll survive. If *you* lose your temper and say something you really shouldn't have said, your kids will survive. If Saturday morning comes and you haven't planned a single activity for the weekend, or if you park your child in front of a video one evening while you take a nap, chances are he'll still turn out to be a relatively well adjusted, tax-paying member of society. If he doesn't, you can always take all the money out of his college savings fund and open up a therapy fund instead.

You don't have to be perfect. All you have to be is good enough. As far as I'm concerned, if everyone in the family is alive and fed at the end of the day, you've done a great job.

What's Going On with Your Child, PART 1

Why Be Involved with Your Nine-Year-Old?
- Girls who have warm relationships with their fathers and feel accepted by them "are more likely to feel comfortable and confident when relating to the opposite sex," according to psychologist Richard Warshak.
- Being involved with your daughter could delay the onset of puberty and sexual maturity. Girls who have close, positive relationships with their fathers during their first five years, and whose fathers were active caregivers and had

good relationships with the mothers, enter puberty later in life, according to Bruce Ellis, a researcher at the University of Canterbury in New Zealand. "We've learned that girls who grow up without fathers tend to become sexually active at earlier ages, that girls without fathers tend to look for male approval in intimate relationships before they're emotionally ready."

♦ For boys and girls, the greater the father's involvement with his children, the greater the children's intellectual and critical thinking skills, and creativity when facing problems.

♦ When you're involved with your children, they have healthier relationships with their siblings, have less tension in their interactions with other children, and solve conflicts at school by themselves rather than seeking the teacher's assistance, according to German researchers Gerhard Suess, Klaus Grossman, and Alan Sroufe.

♦ Having regular meals with your family reduces the risks that your children will smoke, drink, use drugs, have suicidal thoughts or other mental health issues, and have problems at school.

♦ Successful, high-performing, creative, independent women are more likely than less successful women to have enjoyed close, supportive relationships with their father, according to researcher Michael Lamb.

Education

Hey, Quit Dys'n My Kid;
or, What to Do If Your Child Has a Learning Disability

On average, 5 to 10 percent of children three and older have some kind of learning disability, or LD. Boys are far more likely than girls to be diagnosed. Okay, now that we've got the statistics out of the way, the big question is, What *is* a learning disability?

Generally speaking, learning disabilities are problems relating to processing written, oral, or visual information. For some reason, they almost always start with *dys*. Some people can have one, others more than one. Often, there's a little ADD/ADHD (attention deficit/hyperactivity disorder) thrown in to complicate the issue. Here are some of the most common ones:

♦ **Dyslexia** (trouble with reading and spelling).

♦ **Dyscalculia** (trouble understanding basic number concepts, trouble making change, adding, subtracting, carrying, borrowing).

♦ **Dysgraphia** (trouble writing, mixing up upper- and lowercase letters, printing and cursive, painfully slow writing).

TURNING A BLIND EYE TO BLUBBER

Today, 60 percent of adults in this country are overweight or obese. More than 30 percent of American children age six to eleven are overweight. Fifteen percent are classified as obese, including 10 percent of kids age two to five. Those numbers are *four times higher* than they were when you were growing up.

Obesity is linked with asthma, diabetes, high blood pressure, sleep apnea (when you stop breathing in your sleep), and bone damage (most commonly the legs bowing under all the extra weight). It can also make other conditions, such as depression, worse. About a third of obese preschoolers and half of obese school-age children will remain obese as adults.

Why am I telling you all this? Because the only way your child will be able to control his weight is with your help. But you can't help if you don't see the problem—and chances are, you won't. Seventy-five to 90 percent of parents misjudge their children's weight—and all of them underestimate it. Mothers are a little more accurate than dads, and overweight dads have the worst vision when it comes to assessing their children. Interestingly, moms and dads are both more likely to say that a daughter is overweight than a son, even though more boys than girls are.

The only truly effective way to lose weight permanently is to reduce the number of calories your child eats and help him get more exercise. And both have to be patient: it takes about the same amount of time to lose the weight as it did to gain it, which is about one or two pounds per week. Losing weight faster than that isn't healthy, and won't last.

One pound of fat is about 3,500 calories. So if every day you can cut 250 calories out of your child's diet (the equivalent of one candy bar) and burn another 250 (by doing as little as twenty to thirty minutes of walking), he'll lose a pound a week. Keep that up for six months, and he'll have lost twenty-five pounds!

As long as you're focusing on your child's weight, you and your partner should hop on the scale too. Oddly enough, for every child a couple has, Mom's risk of being obese goes up 7 percent. Yours goes up 4 percent.

♦ **Dyspraxia** (trouble with small motor skills).
♦ **Dysphasia** (problems with speech, pronouncing certain words, producing certain sounds, or processing what people say).
♦ **Dysorganization** (trouble putting together thoughts, or general trouble getting life organized. And yes, I know it's supposed to be D-*I*-S, but the *Y* makes the list look more consistent).

EAT WELL AND PROSPER

Maintaining a healthy weight doesn't require a lot of effort. Below you'll find a number of ways that will help. The more you can follow, the easier it will be.

- Limit your family's fat intake to no more than 30 percent of the calories you eat every day. Have baked potatoes instead of French fries, get your salad dressing on the side and don't use all of it, and skip the cheese on your burger.
- Eat slowly, pay attention to how you feel, and have your child do the same. Despite what your mother may have said, you do not always need to finish everything on your plate.
- During meals, ask your child every once in a while whether he's *really* hungry.
- Don't skip breakfast. People who eat a healthy breakfast tend to eat less during the day, and are able to concentrate better at school and at home.
- Eat out less often. Home-cooked meals tend to be lower in calories and fat than restaurant-cooked foods.
- Get everyone in your family into the habit of reading the ingredients panel on food packages. Avoid high-calorie, high-fat, high-sodium snack foods or fast foods.
- Avoid any food that contains partially hydrogenated oils (aka *trans fats*), which are unhealthy. Also watch out for the phrase "fully hydrogenated." These oils, also called *interesterified fats* are being billed as a healthy alternative to trans fats. But recent research is suggesting that they aren't any better, Instead, look for the actual name of the oil (corn, canola, olive, and so on).
- Avoid any ingredient that has a number in its name (FD&C Red No. 3, Blue No. 5, and so on).
- Drink at least eight glasses of water every day.
- Eat more fresh fruits and vegetables.

No one knows for sure what causes LDs, but the current best guess is that they're brain development issues. The trouble could be random, genetic, or caused by some kind of toxin that the child was exposed to before birth (such as Mom smoking or using drugs or alcohol when she was pregnant) or after (for example, food additives or exposure to secondhand smoke).

If you can, try to think of the *D* in LD as "difference" instead of "disability." "Learning disabled" is *not* the same as "developmentally delayed" or "developmentally disabled." Those terms generally refer to severe physical or mental problems, such as Down syndrome, cerebral palsy, or mental retardation. In fact, many children with LDs are of above-average intelligence.

As we've discussed throughout this book, your role in your child's life is critical. As the father of a child with an LD, you're even more important now than ever. Here's how you can help your child, your partner, and the rest of your family cope:

+ **Learn about your child's LD.** The first time you hear about it will probably be from his school. So talk to his teacher to find out exactly what the issues are and what resources there are available to help. The more you understand it, the less out-of-control you'll feel. A good knowledge of the LD will also help you better explain it to your child. It will also assist you to be a strong advocate for your child, making sure that he gets the services he needs.

+ **Talk with your child.** He already knows that he's having trouble in certain areas, and without an explanation, he may imagine the worst, that he's stupid or that there's something wrong with him. Telling him about others who have LDs may make him feel a little less like a freak. Some famous people with LDs he may have heard of include Walt Disney, actor Orlando Bloom (who starred in the *Lord of the Rings* and *Pirates of the Carribean* movies), singer Jewel, musician Stephan Jenkins (from Third Eye Blind), and children's book author and illustrator Patricia Polacco. (See page 235 in the Resources section for more.) When you have this conversation, make sure you do it at a time when neither of you has to rush off. You want to allow plenty of time for him to respond. And be prepared to have the talk more than once. He probably won't absorb all the information the first time and will undoubtedly think of some important questions later.

+ **Be sympathetic.** Hearing that he has a learning disability can be confusing and frightening for a child. Over the course of a few weeks he'll probably do all of the following:
  ◊ Lash out at you for suggesting that there's a problem.
  ◊ Blame the problem on the school or the teacher or come up with some kind of creative way of explaining away the problem.
  ◊ Lash out at himself, saying things like, "I can't do anything right."
  ◊ Withdraw. He may not want to go to school.

It's important that you listen carefully to what he says, and that you *not* fight back or defend his school or teacher. That's the quickest way to settle the discussion. Instead, try to draw him out by asking a lot of open-ended questions.

- **Hide your disappointment.** With fathers, more than mothers, feeling that he's not living up to your expectations can hurt a child more than your anger. Anger is usually a flash in the pan, but disappointment can leave permanent scars.
- **Be demonstrative.** Your child needs to be reminded—a lot—that you love him and that you'll always be there for him. Don't assume that he knows.
- **Praise the little things and focus on what your child *can* do instead of what he *can't*.** Did he get a homework assignment turned in on time? Improve his score on a reading test? Showing how proud you are of those small steps will help make bigger ones possible as time goes on. And encourage him to develop other skills. Having an LD in one area shouldn't get in the way of excelling in another.
- **Don't forget about your other children.** When one person has an LD, the rest of the family does too. You and your partner are going to be spending a disproportionate amount of time and energy (and probably money) on the child with the LD, and your other children may feel jealous and/or resentful. So bring them into the loop. Tell them exactly what the issues are, help them understand that their sibling isn't damaged goods, and be sure to schedule some special, one-on-one time with them.
- **Have some fun.** Working with your child to overcome an LD can take a lot of time. But don't let that be the only way you spend your time together. Interestingly, dads of children with LDs generally spend as much time with their children as other dads. The difference is that they spend more of it indoors, perhaps because they feel that they're being scrutinized.
- **Don't compare your child to anyone else.** Being competitive is a natural part of being a dad, and it's easy to slip into the mode of trying to rate how our kids stack up relative to others the same age, to friends' children, or to other children with a similar LD. Don't do it.
- **Stand up for yourself.** The Foundation for People with Learning Disabilities recently conducted a study of issues faced by fathers of children with LDs. They found that "when a baby is born with a learning disability, support is often focused on the mother. Fathers can subsequently feel sidelined and excluded from decisions affecting their child." So if you want to know what's going on, you're going to have to take the initiative. You can download a summary of their report at www.learningdisabilities.org.uk/ or on my Web site, at mrdad.com/links/Ldreport.
- **Get some support.** Most dads of children with LDs are incredibly supportive of their child and their partner. Unfortunately, they generally forget all about themselves. While taking care of everyone else is very chivalrous,

TAKING THE NEWS

Hearing the diagnosis that your child has an LD—even if you suspected as much—can be especially hard on dads. We're supposed to be the provider-protector, the guy with all the answers. We also tend to focus a little more than moms on helping our kids become independent and self-sufficient in the real world (moms are somewhat more concerned about the child's emotional life). But most experts believe that there's no cure for learning disabilities. As a result, some fathers feel useless, less than masculine, as though they've somehow failed.

Most don't take the news about the LD particularly well, but they generally recover nicely. Christine Towers, who did a study for the Foundation for People with Learning Disabilities, found that while for some fathers it's a struggle to have a child with an LD, quite a few say that it brought them and their child closer together. Fathers in her study also said that having a child with an LD made them better fathers (in part because they now spend more time together as a family); forced them to seriously reevaluate their values and what's truly most important in their lives; made them more patient, tolerant, and assertive in advocating for their child; helped them appreciate how important they are in their child's life; and even improved their relationship with their partner.

not taking care of your own needs can take a pretty heavy toll. Your relationship with your partner can suffer, as can friendships. It's hard, but dads who reach out to others find it helpful and have an easier time coping than those who try to go it alone. You'll have to do some searching, though. Most of the resources out there are aimed at moms. I've put together a few dad-friendly starting points in the Resources section, on page 235.

♦ **Be a little self-indulgent.** As the provider-protector, your first inclination is going to be to make sure that your child is well taken care of. Next, you'll make sure that your partner is getting the support she needs. Last on your list—if you get there at all—is taking care of yourself. It's hard, but try to carve out some time for yourself, even if it's just a few minutes here and there. If you're anxious, stressed out, and tense, you can't possibly be the kind of supportive parent your child needs you to be.

♦ **Remain calm.** Sometimes people can be incredible jerks, and you're going to overhear someone saying that your child is lazy or stupid or shouldn't be allowed in school or something equally infuriating. Resist the urge to punch them out.

♦ **Be involved in your child's education.** Make sure you have regular contact with your child's teachers and any specialists or special ed people who work with her. And get involved in putting together your child's IEP (Individualized Education Program). As with children who don't have LDs, the more involved you are in your child's education, the better he'll do.

♦ **Nurture your relationship with your partner.** Having a child with an LD can strain your relationship. But if the two of you support each other and work together, you'll both be a lot happier.

♦ **Talk to your accountant.** Having a child with an LD isn't cheap. There's testing, tutoring, therapy, special teachers, and more. If he goes to a public school, many—but not all—of these expenses will be picked up by the school district. In some cases the district covers a portion of the expenses for kids in private schools. It's even possible that your health insurance will pay for some expenses, such as psychological assessments. But regardless of your insurance or the kind of school he goes to, you'll probably have to finance some of it. That's the bad news. The good news is that you may be able to get help from other sources. You may, for example, be able to collect SSI on behalf of your child and use that money to pay some of the bills. There's also a chance that you're eligible for some federal and/or state tax credits (sometimes even retroactively), or that you'll be able to deduct some of the special schooling, teachers, or programs.

What's Going On with Your Child, PART 2

Reading to Your Nine-and-Older Child

Reading aloud to your child is just as important as it ever was. Actually, now it may be even *more* important. More than 40 percent of children ages five to eight are high-frequency readers, meaning they read for fun every day. But that percentage drops to 29 at age nine, and continues to slide until age seventeen, (according to the *Kids and Family Reading Report* conducted by Yankelovich and Scholastic). It's no coincidence that this dramatic shift happens at the exact time when most parents stop reading to their children: right around the end of the fourth grade.

I suggest that you continue to read to your child until he shoves you out the door, which will probably happen in a year or two. Besides all the great benefits we've discussed in earlier chapters, reading to your almost-preadolescent can keep your relationship with him strong. The storyline or illustrations can spark all sorts of interesting discussions. You may be reminded of a story

It's dawn, Dad. Want to knock off for breakfast?

about something that happened to you years before. Or your child may decide to tell you about something that's going on with him. Some nights you may end up spending more time talking about life than reading the words on the page. And your evening read-aloud sessions may gradually turn into read-*with* sessions. As long as the two of you are able to keep those lines of communication open, and as long as your child remains interested in reading, that's all okay. Here are some steps you can take to ensure that happens.

- **Let your children see you and your partner read on your own.** According to the *Kids and Family Reading Report*, when both parents are frequent readers, their children read more. And children of high-frequency-reading parents are more likely than other children to read for fun.
- **Keep suggesting books.** Although he's getting suggestions from teachers, librarians, friends, and many other sources, you're the one whose recommendations matter most.
- **Encourage your child to go beyond books, magazines, and newspapers.** Graphic novels (aka comic books) and what he reads online should count too.
- **Spice up his reading experience by giving him something a little out of the ordinary once.** Try this paragraph I came across recently:

Aoccdrnig to a rscheearer at Cmabrigde Uinervtisy, it deosn't mttaer in waht oredr the ltteers in a wrod are, the olny iprmoetnt tihng is taht the frist and lsat ltteer be at the rghit pclae. The rset can be a total mses and you can sitll raed it wouthit porbelm. Tihs is bcuseae the huamn mnid deos not raed ervey lteter by istlef, but the wrod as a wlohe.

At this age, your child shouldn't have had much trouble deciphering that paragraph. In case he (or you) did, here it is in English.

According to a researcher at Cambridge University, it doesn't matter in what order the letters in a word are, the only important thing is that the first and last letter be at the right place. The rest can be a total mess and you can still read it without problem. This is because the human mind does not read every letter by itself but the word as a whole.

Kids in the *Kids and Family Reading Report* said that the number-one reason why they don't read more is that they can't find books they like to read. Hopefully, with all the titles we've listed in this book, that won't be an issue for your child. And speaking of lists, here's one listing of books that is sure to engage kids nine and up.

GENERAL
Al Capone Does My Shirts, Gennifer Choldenko
Anne Frank, Josephine Poole
The Birchbark House, Louise Ehrdrich
The Buffalo and the Indians: A Shared Destiny, Dorothy Hinshaw
  Patent
Captain Raptor and the Moon Mystery, Kevin O'Malley
The Complete Wreck: A Series of Unfortunate Events, Lemony Snicket
Fairest, Gail Levine Carson
From the Mixed-Up Files of Mrs. Basil E. Frankweiler, E. L. Konigsburg
Harry Potter and the Sorcerer's Stone (and others in the Harry Potter series),
  J. K. Rowling
His Dark Materials Trilogy, Philip Pullman
How to Eat Fried Worms, Thomas Rockwell
*The Journey That Saved Curious George: The True Wartime Escape of
  Margret and H. A. Rey,* Louise Borden
Kamishibai Man, Allen Say
A Kick in the Head: An Every Day Guide to Poetic Forms, Paul B. Janeczko
Kibitzers and Fools: Tales My Zayda Told Me, Simms Taback

Klondike Gold, Alice Provensen

Poetry Speaks to Children, Elisa Paschen and Dominique Raccah, editors

The Prairie Builders: Reconstructing America's Lost Grassland, Sneed B.
   Collard

Sarah, Plain and Tall, Patricia MacLachlan

Sweetgrass Basket, Marlene Carvell

Tales of a Fourth Grade Nothing, Judy Blume

Tuck Everlasting, Natalie Babbitt

The Watsons Go to Birmingham—1963, Christopher Paul Curtis

SCHOOL

If You're Not Here, Please Raise Your Hand: Poems about School, Kalli Dakos

The Kid in the Red Jacket, Barbara Park

My Name is Maria Isabel, Alma Flor Ada

Other Activities to Do with Your Nine-Year-Old

Your nine-year-old is in an interesting and bittersweet place: he knows he's still a kid but longs for the independence of adolescence, which is, thankfully (from your perspective), a few years out. He's losing interest in activities he considers "kid stuff," he wants to spend his free time with his friends or by himself, and he sometimes resents that he needs you so much. At the same time, he still loves to play, he may dread the responsibilities that go along with being a teenager, and he isn't quite ready to leave childhood behind.

As a result of all of this, it may be a little harder than it was just a year or two ago to find fun ways of spending time together. But it can be done. One big difference, though, is that now you may be doing some activities silently, side by side instead of face to face. It's important to understand that intimacy and connection don't always require speaking. Here are some great ways of staying connected with your nine-year old with and without words.

- **Start a father-child book club.** If possible, the kids should be the same gender. You and your child can read the same book, then analyze it at the club meeting. If your child isn't a club kind of kid, the two of you can start your own private group.
- **Make a movie.** Decent video cameras are remarkably inexpensive. Have your child write a script, cast, direct, and film.
- **Build something.** A while ago you were the one who picked the project, put together the shopping list, and supervised the construction. Now it's your child's turn to take the lead. Of course, you'll help him if he asks, but let him do as much of the planning and preparation as he can.

- **Hit the road.** Take a long hike or, if you're feeling more adventurous, jointly plan a trip just for the two of you.

- **Discover his world.** Have him tell you about his favorite bands, and listen to some of their CDs. Then ask him to go online and find out whether any of them will be in town. He picks the show date, you buy the tickets.

- **Get fit.** But in keeping with your child's more brooding personality, occasionally do a sport that allows you to focus on the game, that you can play together without feeling obliged to carry on a conversation. Tennis, playing catch with a baseball or football, skiing, and martial arts are great. Something like golf isn't as good because there's so much down time between holes.

- **Make music.** If both of you play instruments, look for some duets you can do together. A wonderful way to connect without words.

- **Talk.** But with a twist. A lot of children (especially boys) find it hard to have face-to-face conversations with their parents. So instead of talking over dinner, where misinterpreted facial expressions or body language are conversation killers, hop in the car. Just like psychiatrists who have their patients lie out the couch, you may be able to have some great talks with your child while you're both looking out the window. Another great way to connect in a roundabout way is through movies. One of my favorites for this is Alfred Hitchcock's "I Confess," in which a priest hears the confession of a murderer who then tries to frame the priest for the murder. Because the priest isn't allowed to break the confidentiality of the confession, he's unable to defend himself against the accusations. My kids and I literally spent hours discussing this movie. How far should someone go to keep a secret? When is it okay to break a promise? Would you put yourself in danger to protect a friend who's done something wrong?

- **Take a class together.** Could be cooking, welding, gardening, photography, sculpture, or anything else. The object is to develop a common interest.

- **Play word games.** My kids and I have had great fun with some books by Richard Lederer, such as *The Play of Words*. For example, come up with as many expressions as you can that include colors (white elephant, red herring, once in a blue moon, looking at the world through rose-colored glasses, golden oldies, and so on). Or phrases that involve weather (brainstorming, cloudy memories, frozen assets, tempest in a teapot, icebreakers, greased lightening, stealing someone's thunder, and so on). The possibilities are endless.

- **Write together.** Most people wouldn't put writing at the top of their list of interactivities, but it can be rewarding. Get the whole family together and

We're really bonding now, aren't we, Dad?

have everyone jot down three words or phrases (a person, a place, a thing, and so on) on strips of paper. Drop all the strips into a bag mix 'em up and pull out five. Then set a timer for 10 minutes and everyone writes a story that incorporates all of the chosen words. Then, of course, each person reads his or her story to the group.

Dads and Boys, Dads and Girls

Most fathers claim they'd treat their sons and daughters the same way. But in reality, that's rarely the case. The truth is that fathers (and mothers too) treat boys and girls very differently. We've talked about this a little in previous

GOT GIRL?

HOW HAVING A GIRL MAY CHANGE YOUR LIFE

Throughout this book we've talked about some of the ways fatherhood changes us. We expand our emotional repertoire, become more tolerant and more involved in our community, and reconsider our values. But could having children—specifically girls—change our politics or influence how long our marriages last? Oddly enough, it's yes on both counts. Some fascinating research shows that compared to fathers of boys, fathers of girls are:

- **More likely to be politically to the left.** British researchers Andrew Oswald and Nattavudh Powdthavee discovered that for every daughter a man has, he's 2 percent more likely to vote to the left. In Germany, that number was 2.5 percent. Fathers with three daughters and no sons were almost twice as likely to vote left than guys with three sons and no daughters. Oswald and Powdthavee also studied people who switched parties. Those with more daughters were more likely to switch from right to left than vice versa.

- **More likely to try for another child.** American economists Gordon Dahl and Enrico Moretti did an exhaustive analysis of U.S. Census and population data and found that "in families with at least two children, the probability of having another child is higher for all-girl families than all-boy families." In other words, couples with two girls are more likely to keep trying to conceive a boy, but couples with two boys are more likely to stop right there.

- **More likely to get divorced.** Dahl and Moretti also found that parents with one daughter are about 5 percent more likely to divorce than parents of one son, and the odds go up with each additional daughter.

chapters, but some of it bears repeating here. For example, parents tend to encourage boys' independence more than girls', and they're more protective of girls than boys. (As a friend who has sons once said, "It's easier raising a boy because you only have one penis to worry about.") Academically, parents—again, mothers as well as fathers—are more likely to push their sons than their daughters. Dads in particular are usually more physically playful with their sons than their daughters. There are, of course, plenty of exceptions. But generally speaking, that's the way it plays out.

This means that your relationship with your daughter is going to be very different from the one you have with your son. One interesting thing that hap-

Parents of three girls are about 10 percent more likely to divorce than parents of three boys. The prospect of becoming the father to a daughter is sometimes enough to keep men from getting married in the first place. "Among women who have taken an ultrasound test during pregnancy, and therefore probabilistically know the gender of their child in advance, we find that mothers who have a girl are less likely to be married *at delivery* than mothers who have a boy," write Dahl and Moretti.

♦ **More likely to get prostate cancer.** This is about as weird as it gets. In 2007, a team of Israeli researchers found that compared to men with at least one son, those who fathered three daughters were 40 percent more likely to develop prostate cancer. However, this may be one of those studies where correlation doesn't mean causation. In other words, although fathers with a lot of daughters may be more likely to get prostate cancer, the girls themselves aren't the cause of the increase in risk. Instead, the researchers believe that the issue could be a genetic quirk on the Y chromosome that both increases the risk of cancer *and* the chances of fathering a daughter.

In addition to all this, men seem to be less interested in becoming stepfathers of daughters. Dahl and Moretti found that remarried women with daughters are more likely to divorce again if they have girls than if they have boys.

No one is quite clear what any of this means. We've all heard the stories about how parents in China and India and other countries have a strong preference for boys. But the same thing—to a smaller degree—is happening here. American women express a slight preference for a girl, but men are 250 percent more likely to express a preference for a boy than a girl.

pens to the father-son relationship during the school years is the development of competition. Sounds silly, I know. A grown man competing with a fourth-grader? A fourth-grader competing with his dad?

From the father's sometimes way-too-mortal perspective, the son is a threat, living proof of the father's mortality, the one who will soon take the father's place in the world of men. The boy is healthy, has his whole life ahead of him, and the father, though far from being on the way out, is probably noticing a few aches and pains that didn't use to be there. The result is, as we talked about in previous chapters, that a lot of dads start exercising more, eating healthier, and generally taking better care of themselves, in an attempt to keep up with their

Summer's coming. How does pre-med camp sound?

kids, especially their sons—and it only gets more intense as the sons (and the dads) get older.

Some of a son's competitiveness with his father is oedipal (fantastic news if you're a Freud fan), which is just a fancy way of saying that deep down inside, he loves his mother, wants to keep her for himself, and feels that he has to overcome his father to win her love. The human mind is a very warped thing, isn't it? Another part of the son's competition has to do with how the males in our society (and most others as well) generally interact with each other: constantly sizing one another up, seeing where they fit in, and trying to be stronger, richer, better-looking, and more powerful than everyone else. There's much to dispute as to whether that competitive drive is the result of socialization or genetic wiring. My vote says it's mostly hardwiring.

Part of the father's role is to guide his son through this oedipal phase by helping him separate from his mother and from the world of women. No, this isn't some kind of misogynistic rant. Boys need to model themselves after men in order to develop a healthy gender identity; women simply can't provide that kind of direction. It's a lot harder for boys to learn what it means to be mascu-

YOU AND YOUR SON: TALKING ABOUT PUBERTY

Isn't it amazing how polliwogs change into frogs and caterpillars into butterflies? Well, the changes that the human body goes through during puberty are just as amazing. And you know what all those changes are about, right? Hormones raging through your son's body, preparing it to reproduce—what a horrifying thought.

Puberty usually starts at age eleven or twelve, although the range is roughly from nine to fourteen, and can take four to eight years to complete. Your son's penis and scrotum will get bigger, he'll start sprouting pubic and underarm hair, his voice will change, and his skin may start breaking out. If he's started at the very early end of the age range or hasn't started by the time he's fourteen, have a talk with his pediatrician.

With all the mystery surrounding girls' puberty, people somehow assume that the whole process is a breeze for boys. Ha! At some point early on he'll have his first wet dreams, which he may find anything from annoying to confusing to scary as hell. He may think he's wet the bed or that something is drastically wrong with him. He may become obsessed with comparing his pubertal progress to that of his friends—and may feel horribly inadequate if he's not keeping up. Locker rooms are a terrible place to be for a boy who's developing a little on the slow side. And then, of course, there are those spontaneous erections that seem to happen at the most inopportune moments, like on the bus or in the middle of math class or anytime the wind blows. Since you've been there, done that, you're the best person for him to talk to about these things.

While your son's puberty is going to be tough on him, it may not be that easy for you either. You and your partner may experience all sorts of conflicting emotions. Both of you may have fond—or horrible—memories of going through puberty yourself. You may remember comparing pubic hair counts in the bathroom with your friends. You may also be incredibly proud that your son is becoming a man, or, as we discussed above, you may suddenly find yourself feeling competitive with—or even a little threatened by—him.

For the moment, it's important to focus on your son. What he needs most of all from you is information, patience, and reassurance that what he's going through is normal. By the time girls reach puberty, they've been exposed to all sorts of magazine articles and books that have prepared them—at least a little—for what they're going through. But there's

(continued on page 214)

TALKING ABOUT PUBERTY *(continued from page 213)*
precious little out there for boys. Pick up a copy of Linda Maderas's *What's Happening to My Body for Boys* and read it. This book contains lot of good information, so you'll be ready when your son asks you questions. Be sure to let him know that he can ask you anything, although, as with girls, he may be too embarrassed to do so. Don't feel rejected: it may sting a little, but he's behaving like a normal adolescent.

line than for girls to learn what it is to be feminine. Most teachers are female, and so are most babysitters and day-care workers, which means that girls have constant access to female role models, and boys don't have anyone to look to.

In addition, "The messages from adults are not consistent," says gender-role expert Carole Beal. "Mothers and teachers would like boys to behave one way—masculine, yes, but also neat, well-mannered, and considerate—while fathers and male peers encourage other types of behavior, including rough physical play and independence." The result is a lot of boys who are confused about what it means to be a man. Fortunately, you can do something about that. "Fathers' warm, close, guiding support encourages their sons' acceptance of them as their primary models," says John Snarey. "Fathers' broad support of their sons' physical-athletic, intellectual, and social-emotional development promotes this transition and the continuation of their boys' sense of basic trust and autonomy."

As odd as it sounds, fathers also play a very important role in helping their daughters develop a healthy gender identity. A girl's primary identification will be (and should be) with her mother. At the same time, a healthy physical-athletic dad-daughter relationship will help her "avoid an extremely traditional sex-role identification," according to Snarey. In addition, a girl looks to her father—the very first man in her life—to demonstrate how she can expect to be treated as she grows up. Challenging her, supporting her, having high expectations, and making her feel loved, respected, and important are critical, especially as she approaches puberty. "The girl who receives the least amount of male attention at home is the one to seek it most aggressively outside the home—namely at school," writes Nicky Marone in *How to Father a Successful Daughter.* "Any girl who has doubts about her worth can find encouragement by capitalizing on her helplessness, flaunting her youthful sex appeal, and abandoning (in many cases permanently) achievement-oriented behavior." Not to put pressure on you or anything . . .

You and Your Partner

The Relationship Workout

The most important thing to remember about your relationship with your partner is that it—like the two of you—is constantly changing. Rachel Egan, author of *Life after "I Do!"* likens relationships to the letter W. Right after the wedding, when everything is marvelous, your relationship is at the top left of the W. In the first few years, you find yourself on a downward slope. You're getting to really know your partner and your in-laws, figuring out what it means to live with another person, feuding over chores. And then, when the kids start showing up, no sleep, no sex, no time for yourself, worrying about everything. Conflicts—particularly having to do with raising the kids—increase. That lands you at the bottom.

Life, and the W, start picking up again when the kids are in the preschool and school years. You've got the whole parenting thing pretty well figured out, the kids love you, think you know everything, and want to be with you. That takes you back up to the center of the W. As you might expect, things take a turn for the worse when the kids hit adolescence and you start worrying about drugs, alcohol, dating, sex, and more. It's tough on you, on the kids, and on the marriage. Tune into the next book in this series for all the gruesome details. Then, as the kids head off to college, you, your partner, and your relationship claw your way back up to the far right end of the W. Exhausting, isn't it?

Taking care of your relationship is like taking care of your body. You can't just have one good day at the gym and expect to stay in shape for very long. You might feel good for a while, but soon you'll start getting flabby. With at least half of marriages—and a larger percentage of non-marriage relationships—breaking up prematurely, it's important that you make a commitment to keeping your relationship firm and toned. Here's how:

- ♦ **Make the marriage a priority.** Care for it as if it were another child living in the home.
- ♦ **Fight a little.** Among the top sources of marital spats are money, division of labor issues, and differences in parenting styles. As counterintuitive as it sounds, having a good fight now and then could be good for both of you. In fact, you may be far better off letting off some steam in her direction (in a reasonable way) than in suppressing it. "In trying to avoid conflict, we may create even more," says psychologist Brad Sachs. "Internalized anger causes emotional and physical symptoms like depression, alienation, ulcers, fatigue, backaches, and high blood pressure. Also, we have to remember that if we don't express it directly, it will come out anyway, but sideways, in

a way we can't control. The phone message that we forgot to deliver to our partner, the medicine we forget to give to the baby, the check we forget to deposit, can all be passive aggressions directed against our spouse when we're afraid of what we're feeling."

Even more counterintuitive, fighting in front of your kids—within reason—could be good for them too. Naturally, you should avoid having *huge* fights in front of your children. (Kids are scared and confused when their parents yell at each other, and researchers have found that the angrier the parents, the more distressed the children.) But this doesn't mean that whenever the kids are around, you and your partner always have to see eye to eye (or at least seem to). In fact, just the opposite is true. Watching you and Mom fight, apologize, forgive each other, and make up teaches your children skills they'll be able to use to handle disagreements with friends and, later on, with life partners. So let your child see you and your partner squabble about easily resolvable things and schedule weekly or, if necessary, daily meetings *away from the kids* to discuss the bigger issues.

Big or small, if you do ever have a disagreement in front of your child, pay close attention to how you make up afterward. "It is probably useful for young children to observe how adults re-negotiate their relationship following a squabble or moments of hostility," says childbirth educator Lilian Katz. "These observations can reassure the child that when distance and anger come between him and members of the family, the relationship is not over but can be resumed to be enjoyed again."

♦ **Run it like a business.** People in business often talk about how a partnership is like a marriage. Well, it works the other way too. If you don't have a commitment from all the shareholders to keep the business running smoothly, you'll be bankrupt soon. At the risk of beating this analogy to death, schedule regular shareholder meetings. You and your partner need to set aside some time to talk about the family, what's going on with the kids, how each of you can help the other be a better parent, and so on.

This is also the time to discuss issues you don't want to talk about in front of the kids. These meetings don't have to be incredibly formal—you could chat while you're getting dressed for work in the morning. But they should be regular. Daily is ideal, but try for at least once a week. The point is to keep the communication open and to talk about problems before they get too big. Find some common ground on smaller issues and work on bigger ones over time.

Be sure to allocate plenty of time to parenting strategies. Thirteen percent of fathers say that raising children causes the most disagreements in their marriages.

♦ **Make time for each other.** As a parent, you have the best of intentions, and you want to make sure you have lots of time for your children. But that time has to come from somewhere, and the likeliest prospect is to sacrifice time you might otherwise have spent on yourself or your relationship. The result is that you can easily lose track of the interests, passions, hobbies, philosophies, and other things that made you who you are and brought you and your partner together in the first place.

Perhaps the best solution to this problem is to schedule some dates. Yep, just like the good old days, before you had kids. The basic idea is the same: the two of you go out and spend a few hours together staring into each other's eyes and getting to know each other. A few of the ground rules have changed, though:

◊ **Don't try to make up for lost time.** Packing too many things into a single evening can put a lot of pressure on both of you.

◊ **Make it clear that there are no strings attached.** Either of you may be suspicious that the "date" will be used as a way of getting the other in the sack.

◊ **If lack of sex has been an issue for you, however, you may want to schedule a date to do nothing but that.** See below for more.

◊ **Don't talk about the children.** Let's be realistic: your kids are the ones you and your partner are trying to get away from, the ones who have consumed so much of your time that the two of you have neglected each other. So, unlike the shareholder meetings above, no talk of homework, carpools, standardized testing, or anything else having to do with the kids. Setting aside as little as fifteen minutes every day for non-kid conversations will do wonders for your relationship.

◊ **Make it a regular thing.** Consider getting a sitter and putting him or her on retainer for one evening every week. If you can't do that, maybe you can have lunch or go see a movie together during the week. If that doesn't work, use your DVD player as a babysitter. (I'm *not* suggesting that you do this a lot. But your child will be just fine if you plop him in front of a video for an hour a week while you and your partner have some quality time together.)

♦ **Learn each other's language.** Men tend to express their love by doing things, but women don't always get the message. They often need tangible "proof" and have to hear the words. So working hard at your job, fixing the car, painting the house, and driving the kids to school might not say, "I love you," as much as a dozen roses and a romantic dinner.

♦ **Try to relax.** Fighting with your partner could kill you. Relationship stress over a long period of time can cause heart damage, says Tim Smith, a researcher at the University of Utah. But what hurts women is very different from what hurts men. For women, the issue is hostility—her own or being on the receiving end of yours. But for men, it's the feeling of losing control of the relationship.

♦ **Figure out what "involved father" means to you and your partner.** Your definition is almost guaranteed to be different from hers, but most couples I've spoken with have never actually had this very important discussion. The problem is that if you're not on the same page or even in the same book, you can't possibly support each other. Even more important, she can't be your advocate.

♦ **Try to come up with a united front.** You and your partner are on the same team. Don't override each other; if you disagree on something, talk about it after the kids have gone to bed. And don't let the kids play you off each other ("but Daddy said . . .").

♦ **Praise your partner.** Telling her to her face that you think she's doing a great job is wonderful. Telling someone else—especially if your partner is within earshot—may be even better.

Library Books, Okay. But Can Fathers Be Renewed?

Well, according to sociologists, the answer is yes. The term *renewed fathers* refers to men in their forties or older who have grown kids from a previous relationship, but got remarried to younger women who want kids of their own. There are a lot of differences between renewed fathers and their nonrenewed brothers. First, the renewed dads tend to be more financially secure and less interested in career advancement. They also have more interest in spending time—and have more time to spend—with their young children. Overall, the older the father, the more relaxed, caring, flexible, and supportive he is, according to my colleague Ross Parke. Parke has found that men and women age differently. Women get more task- and goal-oriented as they get older, while men get more nurturing: "Witness the man who was a stern parent turn into an old softy around his grandkids."

On the downside, renewed fathers—like older fathers in general—don't usually spend as much time playing with their kids as younger dads who haven't turned themselves in for the deposit yet. "But his intellectual level is still high enough to more than make up for the difference," says Parke.

Some of the issues that recycled fathers and their partners have to deal with are similar to those faced by biological dad-stepmom couples (we talked about this extensively on pages 130–33 and 191). But unlike a blended family, where you and your new partner each bring children into the relationship, when you add in a new baby—who has the same biological relationship to you as your older children do, things get even more complicated—for your kids, your new partner, and you. Most older children feel somewhat abandoned and jealous when a younger half-sibling comes along. If they aren't living with you full-time, these feelings may get kicked to an even higher level when you start a new family. They may feel that your loyalty and your love (and sometimes your money) will be spent on your new baby, the one who's with you all the time, and they may resent having to share those things with anyone. They may also see how much more involved you are with their new half-sibling and resent that you weren't that way with them. (This may or may not reflect reality, but your kids' feelings are just as real either way.)

At the same time, your new family may disrupt your older children's loyalties. On the one hand, they'll continue (as they should) to feel deeply loyal to their mother. On the other hand, they'll feel a naturally growing allegiance to their half-sibling and to their stepmother. But as those newer relationships deepen, the children may feel guilty that they're abandoning their mother—as if allowing themselves to be part of a new family means they have to stop loving her. This can sometimes make them lash out at you, the baby, and/or your partner.

As tough as your renewed fatherhood status is for your children and your partner, it's no less difficult for you. The nice, linear progression of your development as a father has been derailed. Usually you get married, have kids, the kids grow up and get married, they have kids of their own and make you a grandfather. But if you're a renewed dad, you're literally in two places at the same time. You're still on your original track with your older children, but you're also starting the process all over again with your new family.

Sometimes it's easy—and fun—to be on both tracks. Having been through it before will probably make the early stages of fatherhood less stressful and more relaxing. Other times, though, you'll feel as though your two tracks are on a collision course with each other. Your new partner may interpret your laid-back attitude as a lack of interest or excitement. But the more time you spend with your new family, the more abandoned and resentful your older kids may feel, jealous of the things they never got. You might feel guilty too, about not having been a better dad the first time around. But the more time you spend with your older children, the more your new family will feel excluded.

All in all, you're in a tough spot, and you'll have to figure out a way to juggle the often conflicting needs of your two families in a way that works for everyone —including you. But whatever you do, don't give in to pressure or temptation to sever—or even loosen—ties with your older children. They need you, and you need them, even if you don't get to see each other as often as you'd like.

Your challenge is to create a new family unit, one that integrates your older children, your new child, and your partner. Notice that I'm *not* saying to make the older kids part of your new family or to make the new family part of the old one. Either of those approaches will make one group or the other feel second best. Instead, both groups have to understand that they're part of something bigger and that your loyalties are not divided but are spread out evenly.

Conclusion

Can you remember the way your life was back when your child was three? Chances are, the past seven years are all pretty much a blur. Over that time, your child went from a dependent little soul to an independent one, from a wide-eyed little kid to a somewhat self-conscious, gulp, pre-adolescent. And what about you? If you're like most dads, being a father is one of your defining features. There probably isn't a single aspect of your life that hasn't been shaped, at least in some small way, by having had children: where you live, who your friends are, your hobbies and interests, your health, your relationship with your partner, your bank accounts, and maybe even your career.

Of course, even though I'm a pro-father kind of guy, I'm the first to acknowledge that not all the changes fatherhood brings are positive or even welcome. There have been plenty of times I seriously wondered why I'd ever had kids in the first place. And in the thousands of interviews I've done, I've never met anyone who hadn't had feelings like those. But at the end of the day (or, in this case, the end of the book), it's been a pretty remarkable journey hasn't it? One you probably wouldn't trade for anything.

You and your children exist in a kind of symbiotic relationship, each influencing and adapting to the other, each growing and changing, struggling to find their bearings in a constantly shifting landscape. It's a never-ending developmental process for both of you; it started when you were still an expectant father and won't stop until your heart does. There'll be ups and downs along the way, but in a few years you'll look back—as you're doing now—and you'll be amazed at how far you've come and at how much more lies ahead.

Selected Bibliography

Books

Allen, W., and M. Connor. "An African American Perspective on Generative Fathering." In Generative Fathering: Beyond Deficit Perspectives, ed. A. J. Hawkins and D. C. Dollahite, pp. 52–70. Newbury Park, Calif.: Sage, 1997.

Anthony, E. James, and Therese Benedek. *Parenthood: Its Psychology and Psychopathology.* Boston: Little, Brown, 1970.

Baker, David P., and Gerald K. Letendre. *National Differences, Global Similarities: World Culture and the Future of Schooling.* Stanford, Calif.: Stanford University Press, 2005.

Berkenkamp, Lauri. *Kid Disasters and How to Fix Them.* Chicago: Nomad Press, 2002.

Bernstein, Jeffrey. *Ten Days to a Less Defiant Child.* New York: Marlowe & Company, 2006.

Bianchi, Suzanne, John Robinson, and Melissa Milkie. *Changing Rhythms of American Family Life.* New York: Russell Sage Foundation, 2006.

Biller, Henry. *Fathers and Families.* Westport, Conn.: Auburn House, 1993.

Biller, Henry, and Robert Trotter. *Father Factor: What You Need to Know to Make a Difference.* New York: Pocket Books, 1994

Bleidner, Larry. *Mack Daddy.* New York: Citadel Press, 2006

Brenner, Mark. *Pacifiers, Blankets, Bottles and Thumbs: What Every Parent Should Know about Starting and Stopping.* New York: Fireside, 2004.

Brodzinsky, D., and Schechter, M., eds. *The Psychology of Adoption.* New York: Oxford University Press, 1990.

Bee-Gates, Donna. *I Want It Now.* New York: Palgrave Macmillan, 2006.

Brott, Armin. *Fathering Your Toddler.* New York: Abbeville Press, 2005.

———. *The Single Father: A Dad's Guide to Parenting without a Partner.* New York: Abbeville Press, 1999.

Carnoy, Martin, and David Carnoy. *Fathers of a Certain Age: The Joys and Problems of Middle-aged Fatherhood.* Minneapolis: Fairview Press, 1997.

Chadwick, Charles. *It's All Right Now.* New York: HarperCollins, 2005.

Chethik, Neil. *Fatherloss: How Sons of All Ages Come to Terms with the Deaths of Their Dads.* New York: Hyperion, 2001.

Chethik, Neil. *VoiceMale*. New York: Simon & Schuster, 2006.

Christakis, Dimitri. *The Elephant in the Living Room*. Emmaus, Pa.: Rodale, 2006.

Coleman, J. *Imperfect Harmony: How to Stay Married for the Sake of Your Children and Still Be Happy*. New York: St. Martin's Press, 2003.

Cox, Adam. *Boys of Few Words: Raising Our Sons to Communicate and Connect*. New York: Guilford Press, 2006.

Craker, Lorilee. *The Wide Eyed Wonder Years*. Grand Rapids, Mich.: Revel Press, 2006.

Day, Randal, and Michael Lamb, eds. *Conceptualizing and Measuring Father Involvement*. Mahwah, N.J.: Lawrence Erlbaum Associates, 2004.

Egan, Rachel. *Life after "I Do!"* Philadelphia: Xlibris, 2004.

Ehrensaft, Diane. *Mommies, Daddies, Donors, Surrogates: Answering Tough Questions and Building Strong Families*. New York: Guilford Press, 2005.

Eisen, Andrew, and Linda Engler. *Helping Your Child Overcome Separation Anxiety or School Refusal*. Oakland, Calif.: New Harbinger, 2006

Flynn, Denis. "The Adoptive Father." In *The Importance of Fathers: A Psychoanalytic Re-evaluation*, edited by Judith Trowell and Alicia Etchegoyen, pp. 203–21. New York: Brunner-Routledge, 2002.

Furedi, Frank. *Paranoid Parenting: Why Ignoring the Experts May Be Best for Your Child*. Chicago: Chicago Review Press, 2002.

Gardner, Howard. *Multiple Intelligences for the 21st Century*. New York: Basic Books, 2000.

Garland, Trudi Hammel, and Charity Vaughan Kahn. *Math and Music*. Palo Alto, Calif.: Dale Seymour, 1995.

Goleman, Daniel. *Emotional Intelligence*. New York: Bantam, 1997.

Haug, Werner, Paul Compton, and Youssef Courbage. *The Demographic Characteristics of National Minorities in Certain European States*, vol. 2. Population Studies no. 31. Strasbourg, France: Council of Europe Publishing, 2000.

Healy, Christopher. *Pop Culture: The Sane Man's Guide to the Insane World of New Fatherhood*. New York: Penguin, 2006.

Hetherington, Mavis, and J. Kelly. *For Better or for Worse: Divorce Reconsidered*. New York: W. W. Norton, 2002.

Hillman, Mayer, J. Adams, and J. Witlegg. *One False Move . . . : A Study of Children's Independent Mobility*. London: Policy Institute, 1990.

Kaplowitz, Paul and Jeffrey Baron. *The Short Child: A Parent's Guide to the Causes, Consequences, and Treatment of Growth Problems*. New York: Warner Wellness, 2006.

Koball, H. L., and D. Principe. *Do Nonresident Fathers Who Pay Child Support Visit Their Children More?* Washington, D.C.: Urban Institute, 2002.

Kohn, Alfie. *The Homework Myth: Why Our Kids Get Too Much of a Bad Thing*. Cambridge, Mass.: Da Capo Press, 2006.

Lamb, M. E. "Infant-Father Attachments and Their Impact on Child Development." In *Handbook of Father Involvement: Multidisciplinary Perspectives*, edited by C. S. Tamis-LeMonda and N. Cabrera, pp. 93–118. Mahwah, N.J.: Erlbaum, 2002.

Last, Cynthia. *Help for Worried Kids: How Your Child Can Conquer Anxiety and Fear*. New York: Guilford Press, 2006.

Lederer, Richard. *The Play of Words: Fun and Games for Language Lovers.* New York: Pocket Books, 1990.

Lee, Jeffrey. *Catch a Fish, Throw a Ball, Fly a Kite: Twenty-one Timeless Skills Every Child Should Know and Any Parent Can Teach.* New York: Three Rivers, 2004.

Lekovic, Jill. *Diaper-Free before Three.* New York: Three Rivers Press, 2006.

Lloyd, T. *Reading for the Future: Boys' and Fathers' Views on Reading.* London: Save the Children, 1999.

Louv, Richard. *Last Child in the Woods: Saving Our Children from Nature-Deficit Disorder.* Chapel Hill, N.C.: Algonquin Books, 2005

McNeal, James. *The Kids' Market: Myths and Realities.* Ithaca, N.Y.: Paramount Market, 1999.

Nord, C. W., D. A. Brimholl, and J. West. *Fathers' Involvement in Their Children's School.* Washington, D.C.: U.S. Department of Education, National Center for Education Statistics, 1997.

O'Shea, Kevin, and James Windell. *The Fatherstyle Advantage.* New York: Stewart, Tabori, and Chang, 2006.

Palkovitz, Rob. "Involved Fathering and Child Development: Advancing Our Understanding of Good Fathering." In *Handbook of Father Involvement: Multidisciplinary Perspectives,* edited by C. S. Tamis-LeMonda and N. Cabrera, pp. 119–40. Mahwah, N.J.: Erlbaum, 2002.

———. *Involved Fathering and Men's Adult Development: Provisional Balances.* Mahwah, N.J.: Erlbaum, 2002.

Parke, Ross, D. J. McDowell, M. Kim, C, Killian, J. Dennis, and M. L. Flyr. "Fathers' Contributions to Children's Peer Relationships." In *Handbook of Father Involvement: Multidisciplinary Perspectives,* edited by C. S. Tamis-LeMonda and N. Cabrera, pp. 141–67. Mahwah, N.J.: Erlbaum, 2002.

Pasley, Kay et al. "Remarriage and Stepfamilies: Making Progress in Understanding." In *Stepparenting: Issues in Theory, Research, and Practice,* edited by Kay Pasley and Marilyn Ihinger-Tallman. Westport, Conn.: Greenwood Press, 1994.

Pelar, Colleen. *Living with Kids and Dogs . . . without Losing Your Mind.* Woodbridge, Va.: C & R, 2005.

Phelan, Thomas W. *1-2-3 Magic: Effective Discipline for Children 2–12.* 3d ed. Glen Ellyn, Ill.: ParentMatic, 2003.

Pickhardt, Carl. *The Everything Parent's Guide to Positive Discipline.* Avon, Mass.: Adams Media, 2004.

Piette, Linda. *Just Two More Bites: Helping Picky Eaters Say Yes to Food.* New York: Three Rivers Press, 2006.

Pollack, Neal. *Alternadad.* New York: Pantheon, 2007.

Poulter, Stephan. *The Father Factor.* Amherst, N.Y.: Prometheus Books, 2006.

Prensky, Marc. *Don't Bother Me Mom—I'm Learning!* New York: Paragon House, 2006.

Pruett, Kyle. *Fatherneed: Why Father Care Is as Essential as Mother Care for Your Child.* New York: Free Press, 2000.

Ricker, Audrey. *How Happy Families Happen.* Center City, Minn.: Hazelden, 2006.

Robinson, Bryan E., and Robert L. Barret. *The Developing Father: Emerging Roles in Contemporary Society*. New York: Guilford Press, 1986.

Rosenberg, Jeffrey, and W. Bradford Wilcox. *The Importance of Fathers in the Healthy Development of Children*. Washington, D.C.: U.S. Department of Health and Human Services, Administration for Children and Families, Office on Child Abuse and Neglect, 2006.

Sax, Leonard. *Why Gender Matters*. New York: Broadway, 2005.

Smutny, Joan Franklin. *Stand Up for Your Gifted Child*. Minneapolis: Free Spirit, 2001

Snarey, John. *How Fathers Care for the Next Generation: A Four-Decade Study*. Cambridge, Mass.: Harvard University Press, 1993.

Steinberg, Laurence. *The 10 Basic Principles of Good Parenting*. New York: Simon & Schuster, 2004.

Strasburger, Victor C., and Barbara J. Wilson. *Children, Adolescents and the Media*. Thousand Oaks, Calif.: Sage, 2002.

Towers, Christine, and Paul Swift. *Recognising Fathers: Understanding the Issues Faced by Fathers of Children with a Learning Disability*. London: Foundation for People with Learning Disabilities, 2006.

Turner, Jessica Barron. *Your Musical Child*. New York: String Letter, 2004.

Warshak, Richard. *Divorce Poison: Protecting the Parent-Child Bond from a Vindictive Ex*. New York: Regan Books, 2003.

Welsh, E., A. Buchanan, E. Flouri, and J. Lewis. *"Involved" Fathering and Child Well-Being: Fathers' Involvement with Secondary School Age Children*. York, England: Joseph Rowntree Foundation, 2004.

Wolkoff, Sandra Radzanower. "School Readiness: It May Not Be What You Think." In *Raising Young Children Well*, edited by Sandra Radzanower Wolkoff, Neala Schwartzberg, and Jane Meckwood-Yazdpour. New York: Other Press, 2006.

Journals

Allen, S. M., and A. J. Hawkins. "Maternal Gatekeeping: Mothers' Beliefs and Behaviors That Inhibit Greater Father Involvement in Family Work." *Journal of Marriage and the Family* 61, no. 1 (1999): 199–212.

Anderson, David, and Mykol Hamilton. "Gender Role Stereotyping of parents in children's picture books : The Invisible Father." *Sex Roles* 52, nos. 3–4 (2005): 145–51.

Anderson, Gabrielle, Shane Jimerson, and Angela Whipple. "Children's Ratings of Stressful Experiences at Home and School: Loss of a Parent and Grade Retention as Superlative Stressors." *Journal of Applied School Psychology* 21, no. 1 (2002).

Ang, Rebecca P. "Fathers Do Matter: Evidence from an Asian School-Based Aggressive Sample." *American Journal of Family Therapy* 34, no. 1 (2006).

Bouchard, Geneviève, and Catherine M. Lee. "The Marital Context for Father Involvement with Their Preschool Children: The Role of Partner Support." *Journal of Prevention and Intervention in the Community* 20, no. 1/2 (2000).

Brown, B., E. Michelsen, T. Halle, and K. Moore. *Fathers' Activities with Their Kids.* Washington, D.C.: Child Trends, 2001.

Cabrera, Natasha J. "In Their Own Voices: How Men Become Fathers." *Human Development* 46, no. 4 (2003): 250–58.

Carson, James L., and Ross D. Parke. "Reciprocal Negative Affect in Parent-Child Interactions and Children's Peer Competency." *Child Development* 67, no. 5 (1996): 2217–26.

Civitas: The Institute for the Study of the Civilized Society. "How Do Fathers Fit In?" December 2001. Online at www.civitas.org.uk/hwu/FatherFactsheet.pdf.

Colarusso, Calvin A. "The Evolution of Paternal Identity in Late Adulthood." *Journal of the American Psychoanalytic Association* 53, no. 1 (2005): 51–81.

Committee on Communications, American Academy of Pediatrics. "Children, Adolescents, and Advertising." *Pediatrics* 118, no. 6 (December 2006): 2563–69.

Cooper, Harris, Jorgianne Civey Robinson, and Erika A. Patall. "Does Homework Improve Academic Achievement: A Synthesis of Research, 1987–2003." *Review of Educational Research* 76 (2006): 1–62.

Crain, William. "How Nature Helps Children Develop." *Montessori Life*, Summer 2001.

Crow, James F. "The High Spontaneous Mutation Rate: Is It a Health Risk?" *Proceedings of the National Academy of Sciences of the United States of America* 94, no. 16 (1997): 8380–86.

Dahl, Gordon B., and Enrico Moretti. "The Demand for Sons: Evidence from Divorce, Fertility, and Shotgun Marriage." NBER Working Paper No. W10281, National Bureau of Economic Research, January 2004.

De Luccie, Mary. "Predictors of Paternal Involvement and Satisfaction." *Psychological Reports* 79, no. 3, pt. 2 (1996): 1351–59.

Denton, D. "Finding Alternatives to Failure: Can States End Social Promotion and Reduce Retention Rates?" January 2001. Online at www.sreb.org/programs/srr/pubs/alternatives/AlternativesToFailure.pdf.

Drenovsky, Cynthia K., and Melissa Meshyock. "Young Adults' Perception of Their Relationship with Parents: An Exploration into the Effects of Late Birthtiming." *International Social Science Review* 75, nos. 3–4 (2000): 15–22.

Dubowitz, H., M. M. Black, C. E. Cox, M. A. Kerr, A. J. Litrownik, A. Radhakrishna, D. J. English, M. W. Schneider, and D. K. Runyan. "Father Involvement and Children's Functioning at Age 6 Years: A Multisite Study." *Child Maltreatment* 6, no. 4 (2001): 300–309.

Easterbrooks, M. Ann., and Wendy Goldberg. "Toddler Development in the Family: Impact of Father Involvement and Parenting Characteristics" *Child Development* 53 (1984): 740–52.

"The Effects of Father Involvement: A Summary of the Research Evidence." *Newsletter of the Father Involvement Initiative Ontario Network*, Fall 2002. Online at www.webapps.ccs.uoguelph.ca/cfww/fira.

Ellis, Bruce. "Timing of Pubertal Maturation in Girls: An Integrated Life History Approach." *Psychological Bulletin* 130 (2004): 920–58.

Ellis, Bruce J., John E. Bates, Kenneth A. Dodge, David M. Fergusson, L. John Horwood, Gregory S. Pettit, and Lianne Woodward. "Does Father Absence Place Daughters at Special Risk for Early Sexual Activity and Teenage Pregnancy?" *Child Development* 74, no. 3 (2003): 801–21.

"Engaging Fathers: Involving Parents, Raising Achievement." London: DfES, 2004. Online at www.teachernet.gov.uk.

Essex, Elizabeth Lehr. "Mothers and Fathers of Adults with Mental Retardation: Feelings of Intergenerational Closeness." *Family Relations: Interdisciplinary Journal of Applied Family Studies* 51, no. 2 (2002): 156–65.

Etelson, D., D. Brand, P. Patrick, et al. "Childhood Obesity: Do Parents Recognize This Health Risk?" *Obesity Research* 11 (November 2003): 1362–68.

Everett, Lou Whichard. "Factors That Contribute to Satisfaction or Dissatisfaction in Stepfather-Stepchild Relationships." *Perspectives in Psychiatric Care*, April–June 1998.

Feldman, S. S. , and K. R. Wentzel. "Relations among Family Interaction Patterns, Classroom Self-Restraint and Academic Achievement in Preadolescent Boys." *Journal of Educational Psychology* 82 (1990): 813–19.

Filppu, Len. "Finally Ready to Be a Dad." *Newsweek*, August 3, 2006.

Fisman, Lianne. "Child's Play: An Empirical Study of the Relationship between the Physical Form of Schoolyards and Children's Behavior." 2001; accessed online January 21, 2007, from www.yale.edu/hixon/research/pdf/LFisman_Playgrounds.pdf.

Flouri, E., and A. Buchanan. "Early Father's and Mother's Involvement and Child's Later Educational Outcomes." *British Journal of Educational Psychology* 74 (2004): 141–53.

———. "The Role of Father Involvement in Children's Later Mental Health." *Journal of Adolescence* 26 (2003): 63–78.

Flynn, Denis. "The Adoptive Father." In *The Importance of Fathers: A Psychoanalytic Re-evaluation*, edited by Judith Trowell and Alicia Etchegoyen, pp. 203–21. New York: Brunner-Routledge, 2002.

Franz, Carol, David McClelland, and Joel Weinberger, "Childhood Antecedents of Conventional Social Accomplishments in Midlife Adults: A 36-Year Prospective Study," *Journal of Personality and Social Psychology* 60 (1991): 586–95.

Gadsden, Virginia, and A. Ray. "Fathers' Role in Children's Academic Achievement and Early Literacy." *Eric Digest*, November 2003. This research digest is electronically available from ceep.crc.uiuc.edu.

Goel, Namni, Hyungsoo Kim, and Raymund P Lao. "An olfactory stimulus modifies nighttime sleep in young men and women. " *Chronobiology International*, 2005; 22 (5): 889–904

Gorman, Elizabeth H. "Bringing Home the Bacon: Marital Allocation of Income-Earning Responsibility, Job Shifts, and Men's Wages." *Journal of Marriage and the Family* 61, no. 1 (1999): 110–22.

Grolnick, Wendy, and Maria Slowiaczek. "Parents' Involvement in Children's Schooling: A Multidimensional Conceptualization and Motivational Model." *Child Development* 65 (1994): 237–52.

Grossmann, Karin, Klaus E. Grossmann, Elisabeth Fremmer-Bombik, Heinz Kindler, Hermann Scheuerer-Englisch, and Peter Zimmermann. "The Uniqueness of the Child/Father Attachment Relationship: Fathers' Sensitive and Challenging Play as a Pivotal Variable in a 16-Year Longitudinal Study." *Social Development* 11, no. 3 (2002): 307–31.

Green, S. "Involving Fathers in Family Literacy: Outcomes and Insights from the Fathers Reading Every Day Program." *Family Literacy Forum and Literacy Harvest*, Fall 2003, pp. 34–40. Online at www.lacnyc.org.

Hahn, Chun-Shin. "Review: Psychosocial Well-Being of Parents and Their Children Born After Assisted Reproduction." *Journal of Pediatric Psychology* 26, no. 8 (2001): 525–38.

Hartshorne, Joshua, and Michael Ullman. "Why Girls Say 'Holded' More Than Boys." *Developmental Science* 9, no. 1 (2006): 21.

Heath, D. T., and P. C. McKenry. "Adult Family Life of Men Who Fathered as Adolescents." *Families in Society: The Journal of Contemporary Human Services* 74, no.1 (1993): 36–45.

Heath, Terri. (1994). "The Impact of Delayed Fatherhood on the Father-Child Relationship." *Journal of Genetic Psychology* 155, no. 4 (1994): 511–30.

Hirsh-Pasek, Kathy, Marion Hyson, and Leslie Rescorla. "Academic Environments in Preschool: Do They Pressure or Challenge Young Children?" *Early Education and Development*, 1, no. 6 (1990): 401–23.

Hofferth, Sandra, and K. G. Anderson. "Are All Dads Equal? Biology versus Marriage as Basis for Paternal Investment." *Journal of Marriage and Family* 65 (2003): 213–32.

Hofferth, Sandra, and John F. Sandberg. "How American Children Spend Their Time." *Journal of Marriage and Family* 63 (2001): 295–308.

Horwitz, A. V., and H. R. White. "The Relationship of Cohabitation and Mental Health: A Study of a Young Adult Cohort." *Journal of Marriage and the Family* 60 (1998): 505–14.

Hovey, Judith K. "The Needs of Fathers Parenting Children with Chronic Conditions." *Journal of Pediatric Oncology Nursing* 20, no. 5 (2003): 245–51.

Hughes, Claire, Kirby Deater-Deckard, and Alexandra Cutting. " 'Speak Roughly to Your Little Boy'? Sex Differences in the Relations between Parenting and Pre-schoolers' Understanding of Mine." *Social Development* 8, no. 2 (1999): 143–60.

Hyson, Marion C., Kathy Hirsh-Pasek, and Leslie Rescorla. "The Classroom Practices Inventory: An Observation Instrument Based on NAEYC's Guidelines for Developmentally Appropriate Practices for 4- and 5-Year-Old Children." *Early Childhood Research Quarterly* 5, no. 4 (1990): 475–94.

Ishii-Kuntz, M. "Paternal Involvement and Perception toward Fathers' Roles. In *Fatherhood: Contemporary Theory, Research, and Social Policy*, edited by W. Marsiglio, pp. 102–18. Thousand Oaks, Calif.: Sage, 1994.

Jacobson, Linda. "Playtime Is Over." *Teacher*, May 2004, 13–14.

Jeffrey, Allison, Linda Voss, B. S. Brad Metcalf, Sandra Alba, and Terence Wilkin. "Parents' Awareness of Overweight in Themselves and Their Children: Cross Sectional Study within a Cohort." *EarlyBird* 21 (November 2004).

Jimerson, Shane, Gabrielle Anderson, and Angela Whipple. "Winning the Battle and Losing the War: Examining the Relation between Grade Retention and Dropping Out of High School." *Psychology in the Schools* 39 (2002): 441–57.

Kawecki, Ireneusz. "Gender Differences in Young Children's Artwork." *British Educational Research Journal* 20 (1994): 485–90.

Kelly, Joe, and Stacy Smith. "G Movies Give Boys a D: Portraying Males as Dominant, Disconnected and Dangerous." Research brief for the See Jane Program and Annenberg School for Communication, USC, Los Angeles. Duluth, Minn.: Dads and Daughters, 2006. Online at www.seejane.org.

The Kids and Family Reading Report. Yankelovich and Scholastic, June 2006. Online at www.scholastic.com/readingreport.

Klitzing, Kai, Kimberly Kelsay, et al. "Gender-Specific Characteristics of 5-Year-Olds' Play Narratives and Associations with Behavior Ratings." *Journal of the American Academy of Child and Adolescent Psychiatry* 39 (2000): 1017–23.

Koestner, Carol Franz, and Joel Weinberger, "The Family of Origins of Empathic Concern: A 26-Year Longitudinal Study." *Journal of Personality and Social Psychology* 58, no. 4 (1990): 709–17.

Linver, Miriam, Jeanne Brooks-Gunn, and Jodie L. Roth. "Children's Homework Time—Do Parents' Investments Make a Difference?" Paper presented for Teachers College, Columbia University, at the CDS II Early Results Workshop, Ann Arbor, Michigan, June 2005.

MacDonald, William L., and Alfred DeMaris. "Stepfather-Stepchild Relationship Quality: The Stepfather's Demand for Conformity and the Biological Father's Involvement." *Journal of Family Issues* 23, no. 1 (2002): 121–37.

Mantzicopoulos, Panayota Y., Stacy Neuharth-Pritchett, and J. B. Morelock. "Academic Competence, Social Skills, and Behavior among Disadvantaged Children in Developmentally Appropriate and Inappropriate Classrooms." Paper presented at the annual meeting of the American Educational Research Association, New Orleans, April 1994.

Margalit, M. "Perception of Parents' Behavior, Familial Satisfaction, and Sense of Coherence in Hyperactive Children." *Journal of School Psychology* 23 (1985): 355–64.

Marshall, H. "Opportunity Deferred or Opportunity Taken? An Updated Look at Delaying Kindergarten Entry." *Young Children* 58, no. 5 (2003): 84–93.

Marsiglio, William. "When Stepfathers Claim Stepchildren: A Conceptual Analysis. *Journal of Marriage and Family* 66, no. 1 (2004): 22–39.

McGrath, Emily P., and Rena L. Repetti. "Mothers' and Fathers' Attitudes toward Their Children's Academic Performance and Children's Perceptions of Their Academic Competence." *Journal of Youth and Adolescence* 29, no. 6 (2000).

McGrath, Helen. "To Repeat or Not to Repeat?" *WORDS: Journal of the Association of Western Australian Primary Principals,* July 2006.

McKeown, M.G., I. L. Beck, R. C. Omanson, and M. T. Pople. In *The Psychology of Word Meanings,* edited by P. Schwanenflugel. Hillsdale, N.Y.; Lawrence Erlbaum Associates, 1985.

Morrongiello, Barbara. "Children's Perspectives on Injury and Close-call Experiences: Sex Differences in Injury-Outcome Processes." *Journal of Pediatric Psychology* 22, no. 4 (1997): 499–512.

Oswald, Andrew J., and Nattavudh Powdthavee. "Daughters and Left-Wing." IZA Discussion Paper No. 2103, Institute for the Study of Labor (IZA), Bonn, Switzerland, April 2006.

Palm, Glen. "Involved Fatherhood: A Second Chance." *Journal of Men's Studies,* November 1993.

Peretz, Isabelle. "Brain Specialization for Music." *Neuroscientist* 8, no. 4 (2002): 372–80.

Quinlivan, Julie A., and John Condon. "Anxiety and Depression in Fathers in Teenage Pregnancy." *Australian and New Zealand Journal of Psychiatry* 39, no. 10 (2005): 915.

Radin, Norma.The Influence of Fathers upon Sons and Daughters and Implications for School Social Work." *Social Work in Education* 8 (1986): 77–91.

Rohner, Ronald P., and Robert A. Veneziano. "The Importance of Father Love: History and Contemporary Evidence." *Review of General Psychology* 5, no. 4 (2001): 382–405.

Sadeh, Avi, Amiram Raviv, and Reut Gruber. "Sleep Patterns and Sleep Disruptions in School-Age Children." *Developmental Psychology* 36, no. 3 (2000): 291–301.

Stahl, Steven A. "How Words Are Learned Incrementally over Multiple Exposures." *American Educator*, Spring 2003. Online at www.aft.org/pubs-reports/american_educator/issues/index.htm.

Stipek, D. "At What Age Should Children Enter Kindergarten? A Question for Policy Makers and Parents." *Society for Research in Child Development Social Policy Report* 16, no. 2 (2002): 3–16. Online at www.srcd.org/sprv16n2.pdf

Suess, G., K. Grossman, and L. A. Sroufe. "Effects of Infant Attachment to Mother and Father on Quality of Adaptation in Preschool." *International Journal of Behavioral Development* 15 (1992): 43–65.

Sun, Yuelian, et al. "Paternal Age and Apgar Scores of Newborn Infants." *Epidemiology* 17, no. 4 (2006): 473–74.

Taylor, Andrea Faber, Frances Kuo, and William C. Sullivan. "Coping with ADD: The Surprising Connection to Green Play Settings." *Environment and Behavior* 33, no. 1 (2001): 54–77.

Taylor, Brent, R. Giarrusso, and H. Wang. "Paternal Involvement Over the Life Course: Effects of Paternal Involvement on Fathers' Psychological Well-Being." Paper presented at a conference of the Gerontological Society of America, Cincinnati, 1997.

Taylor, Brent, R. Giarrusso, and V. Bengtson. "Cohort Continuities and Changes: Paternal Involvement in 1971 and 1997." Paper presented at a conference of the American Sociological Association, 2001.

Telama, Risto, Xiaolin Yang, Jorma Viikari, et al. "Physical Activity from Childhood to Adulthood: A 21-Year Tracking Study." *American Journal of Preventive Medicine* 28, no. 3 (2005): 267–73.

Tuman, Donna. "Sing a Song of Sixpence: An Examination of Sex Differences in the Subject Preference of Children's Drawings." *Visual Arts Research* 25 (1999) 51–62.

U.S. Department of Education, National Center for Education Statistics. "Students Do Better When Their Fathers Are Involved in School." Issues brief, April 1998. Online at nces.ed.gov/pubsearch/pubsinfo.asp?pubid=98121.

———. "How Involved Are Fathers in Their Children's Schools?" Issues brief, 1998. Online at nces.ed.gov/pubsearch/pubsinfo.asp?pubid=98120.

———. "NAEP 2004 Trends in Academic Progress." 2005. Online at nces.ed.gov/nationsreportcard/pdf/main2005/2005464_3.pdf

Vadasy, P., R. R. Fewell, D. J. Meyer, and M. T. Greenberg. "Supporting Fathers of Handicapped Children: Preliminary Findings of Program Effects." *Analysis and Intervention in Developmental Disabilities* 5 (1985): 151–64.

Volling, Brenda L., and Jay Belsky. "The Contribution of Mother/Child and Father/Child Relationships to the Quality of Sibling Interaction: A Longitudinal Study." *Child Development* 63, no. 5 (1992): 1209–22.

Wagner, B. M, and D. A. Phillips. "Beyond Belief: Parent and Child Behaviors and Children's Perceived Academic Competence." *Developmental Psychology* 63 (1992): 1380–91.

Wells, Nancy M., and Gary W. Evans. "Nearby Nature: A Buffer of Life Stress among Rural Children." *Environment and Behavior* 35, no. 3 (2003): 311–30.

Weng, Haoling H., Lori Bastian, et al. "Number of Children Associated with Obesity in Middle-Aged Women and Men: Results from the Health and Retirement Study." *Journal of Women's Health* 13, no. 1 (2004): 85–91.

Wentzel, K. R., and S. S. Feldman. "Parental Predictors of Boys' Self-Restraint and Motivation to Achieve at School: A Longitudinal Study." *Journal of Early Adolescence* 14 (1993): 268–91.

"What Do Fathers Contribute to Children's Well-Being?" Child Trends research brief. Online at www.childtrends.org.

Woolley, J. D., and J. Van Reet. "Effects of Context on Judgments Concerning the Reality Status of Novel Entities." *Child Development* 77, no. 6 (2006).

"Work-Life Issues: An EAP's Perspective." *WarrenShepell Research Group Report* 3, issue 4 (2004).

Yeung, W. J. 2004. "Fathers: An Overlooked Resource for Children's Educational Success." In *After the Bell: Family Background, Public Policy, and Educational Success,* edited by D. Conley and K. Albright, pp. 145–69. London: Routledge Press, 2004.

Yeung, W. J., G. J. Duncan, and M. S. Hill. "Putting Fathers Back in the Picture: Parental Activities and Children's Attainment." *Journal of Marriage and Family Review* 29, nos. 2/3 and 4 (2000): 97–114. Reprinted in *Fatherhood: Research, Interventions and Policies,* edited by H. E. Peters, G. W. Peterson, S. Steinmetz, and R. D. Day (Binghamton, N.Y.: Haworth Press, 2000).

Resources

Adoption

ADOPTIVE FAMILIES MAGAZINE is chock full of resources for families before, during, and after adoption. adoptivefamilies.com

THE NATIONAL ADOPTION CENTER offers a great list of questions to ask adoption agencies; addresses tax, single parent, and legal issues; and provides photos of kids waiting to be adopted, book reviews, lists of state and local contacts, and links to other adoption-related organizations.
www.adopt.org
e-mail: nac@adopt.org
Tel.: (800) TO-ADOPT

CHILD WELFARE INFORMATION GATEWAY includes state-by-state contact information for a variety of adoption-related organizations and services including public and licensed private adoption agencies, support groups, information on foster parenting and more.
www.childwelfare.gov/nad/index.cfm

Advice, General

PARENTING MAGAZINE presents a comprehensive Web site, with articles, links, and advice on everything from activities to eating to child behavior.
www.parenting.com

PARENTS.COM is another Web site that covers the waterfront in terms of parenting advice.
www.parents.com

PARENTS-TALK.COM is an all-inclusive site, with advice from experts, parent message boards, recipes, games, and more.
www.parents-talk.com

At-Home Dads

SLOWLANE.COM is the most comprehensive resource for stay-at-home dads and primary caregiving dads. They have news, articles, advice, and a fantastic list of dads' groups across the country.
www.slowlane.com
e-mail: liaison@slowlane.com
1216 East Lee St.
Pensacola, FL 32503
Tel.: (850) 434-2626
Fax: (850) 434-7937

Blogs and Online Communities

DAD IN PROGRESS is run by Michael McNally, a manager at Lego, a very nice blog subtitled "Musings on the ups and downs of figuring out how to best use what little free time I have to be a great dad."
Dadinprogress.com

REBELDAD is a relatively new online community and blog for stay-at-home dads. Links to many other Dad blogs, stay-at-home dad groups, playgroups, forums, statistics, articles, and other resources make this site a must.
www.rebeldad.com
e-mail: rebeldad@rebeldad.com

Childcare and Preschool

THE NATIONAL ASSOCIATION FOR THE EDUCATION OF YOUNG CHILDREN has a searchable database, by zip code, where you can find quality preschools for your post-toddler.
www.naeyc.org
e-mail: naeyc@naeyc.org
Tel.: (800) 424-2460

THE NATIONAL RESOURCE CENTER FOR HEALTH AND SAFETY IN CHILDCARE is a wonderful general resource. Plus, it has a listing of childcare regulations for all 50 states.
nrc.uchsc.edu
e-mail: natl.child.res.ctr@uchsc.edu
Tel.: (800) 598-KIDS (5437)

THE NATIONAL ASSOCIATION FOR FAMILY CHILDCARE has a searchable national database for accredited family childcare.
www.nafcc.org/include/parents.asp

Child Development, Emotional and Physical

THE CENTERS FOR DISEASE CONTROL AND PREVENTION have a terrific site that covers all aspects of your child's development, both physical and mental, as well as many links to other resources and "positive parenting tips."
www.cdc.gov/ncbddd/child

BRAIN CONNECTION is a fascinating site that examines the development of your child's brain.
www.brainconnection.com/library/
?main=genhome/child-development

WEBMD allows you to search under a myriad of topics, including your child's development by age. Highly recommended.
www.webmd.com

PEDIATRIC HEALTH ON LINE contains news, quizzes, videos, and more, all covering child development from birth to adolescent development.
pediatric.healthcentersonline.com/growth development/?WT.srch=1&kw=Child%20 Development

Computer Safety

CYBER-SAFETY is a Web site dedicated to helping children online. Developed by Rob Nickel, a fourteen-year veteran of the Ontario Provincial Department who worked for seven years undercover online, this site offers tips for kids and adults on Internet safety.
www.cyber-safety.com

GET NET WISE is a public service sponsored by Internet industry corporations and public interest organizations to help ensure that Internet users have safe, constructive, and educational or entertaining online experiences. Good links.
www.getnetwise.com

WIRED KIDS is a nonprofit organization dedicated to protecting Internet users, especially children, from cybercrime and abuse. It teaches children and adults how to protect their privacy and security on line, as well as responsible Internet use.

Death and Grief

THE NATIONAL ASSOCIATION OF SCHOOL PSYCHOLOGISTS offers a site that explains children's reactions to death and tragedy, as well as concrete actions parents can take to help children cope.
www.nasponline.org/NEAT/grief.html

CONNECT FOR KIDS has a terrific, age-specific section on loss, grief, and fear. Loaded with links covering death to terrorism, this site is invaluable.
www.connectforkids.org/node/392

THE NATIONAL MENTAL HEALTH ASSOCIATION has a plethora of links, information, and tips for helping children cope with loss.
www.nmha.org/reassurance/childcoping.cfm

Discipline

KEEP KIDS HEALTHY is a wonderful resource for parents, loaded with great information and many good links. Much of the site is organized by age.
www.keepkidshealthy.com/parenting_tips/discipline/index.html

KIDSOURCE ON LINE, drawing heavily on the National Committee to Prevent Child Abuse, is a graphically simple site filled with articles and links promoting a no-spanking approach to discipline while offering sensible alternatives.
www.kidsource.com/kidsource/content/discipline.3.19.html

ABOUT OUR KIDS, from NYU's Child Study Center at the NYU School of Medicine, offers smart, commonsense approaches to disciplining your child. This site is rich with links and resources.
www.aboutourkids.org/aboutour/articles/discipline.html

Education

THE NATIONAL EDUCATION ASSOCIATION (NEA)'s comprehensive Web site helps parents get involved and stay involved in their child's education. Loaded with links and sound advice for parents.
www.nea.org/parents/index.html

THE WEB SITE OF THE NATIONAL PTA is a wellspring of resources for parents of all school-age kids. Every parent should bookmark this page.
www.pta.org

On GREAT SCHOOLS.COM, you can see how well your school measures up. Check and compare test scores for all public and many private schools, as well as find handy tips for everything from easing the kindergarten jitters to when, or if, to get your child a cell phone.
www.greatschools.net

THREE FOR ME. The mission of Three for Me is to improve the well-being of children by inspiring and equipping parents/families to be effectively involved in their children's education.
www.three4me.com

NATIONAL ASSOCIATION FOR SINGLE-SEX PUBLIC EDUCATION
www.singlesexschools.org

THE BOYS PROJECT
www.boysproject.net

Family Activities, Rituals, and Traditions

FAMILY TLC is filled with suggestions for family activities. It has a searchable index by age, from babyhood to eighteen-plus (optimistic!).
www.familytlc.net

ABOUT.COM covers everything and then some, but this link offers some solid information on why to establish family rituals.
mentalhealth.about.com/cs/familyresources/a/rituals.htm

FAMILIES WITH PURPOSE is dedicated to helping busy families find and plan activities and make the most of their family life. Links abound, and an entire section is devoted to establishing the family ritual of giving to charity and community service.
www.familieswithpurpose.com

Fatherhood, General

INTERACTIVE DAD MAGAZINE is an online parenting magazine designed specifically for fathers. Updated daily, it offers a wealth of content, bulletin boards, special sections on men's health, family finances, safety alerts, to name a few. It is well-worth bookmarking and checking daily.
www.interactivedadmagazine.com/

DADS AND DAUGHTERS is a nonprofit membership organization for fathers with daughters.
www.dadsanddaughters.org/

THE FAMILIES AND WORK INSTITUTE is a nonprofit research organization focusing on work-family issues.
www.familiesandwork.org

FATHERVILLE.COM has many articles by dads for dads, as well as a good links page.
www.fatherville.com

MR DAD.COM. My Web site, which has many of my articles and columns on all aspects of fatherhood, as well as video and audio.
www.mrdad.com

THE NATIONAL CENTER ON FATHERS AND FAMILIES is a great source of research and data on fathers and father involvement, as well as a terrific links page.
Home page: www.ncoff.gse.upenn.edu
Links page:
fatherfamilylink.gse.upenn.edu

THE DADS AT A DISTANCE Web site, presented by the National Long Distance Relationship Building Institute, is designed for fathers who have to be away from their children for any reason, be it military service or business travel, truckers or noncustodial fathers. Its purpose is to help these fathers maintain and strengthen the relationships they have with their children. Good articles, newsletter, and links.
www.daads.com

Fathering Special Needs Children

THE FATHER'S NETWORK provides up-to-date information and resources for fathers, family members, and caregivers. Fathers share their very personal stories and experiences. The advice is solid; the sense of community is much-needed for fathers of disabled children.
www.fathersnetwork.org

CHILDHOOD LEARNING DISABILITIES provides a ton of useful information on learning disabilities and coping strategies for everyone in the family.
www.learning-disabilities.org/index.html

THE FOUNDATION FOR PEOPLE WITH LEARNING DISABILITIES has information, resources, and support for parents of children with learning disabilities. They also have some terrific reports specifically for fathers.
www.learningdisabilities.org.uk

Between these three Web sites you'll find hundreds of well-known people who have (or had) learning disabilities:
www.schwablearning.org/articles.asp?
r=258
www.childdevelopmentinfo.com/disorders
/famous.shtml
www.happydyslexic.com/node/4

Fathers, Divorced or Single

THE AMERICAN COALITION OF FATHERS AND CHILDREN is dedicated to promoting equal rights of all parties affected by divorce or the breakup of a family. Chapters nationwide:
www.acfc.org
e-mail: info@acfc.org
Tel.: (800) 978-3237

CHILDREN'S RIGHTS COUNCIL (CRC) is a national nonprofit organization that works to assure children meaningful and continuing contact with both their parents and their extended family regardless of the parents' marital status.
www.childrens-rights.org
Tel.: (301) 559-3120

MAKING LEMONADE is an online resource community for single parents. Find support, information, referrals to experts, and a good laugh.
www.makinglemonade.com

HELPGUIDE asks and answers all the questions you may have about how your divorce might affect your children, and then some. Content rich and comforting.
www.helpguide.org/mental/children_divorce.htm

THE NATIONAL FAMILY RESILIENCY CENTER (formerly Children of Separation and Divorce Center) covers all aspects of separation, divorce, and remarriage, and how they affect children. Links to support groups, articles, and much more make this site a comprehensive helper for families going through this transition.
www.divorceabc.com

FAMILIES CHANGE is a kids' guide to separation and divorce. Although the legal section is Canadian and does not apply in the United States, we include this site because it is an extremely valuable tool for children and their parents.
www.familieschange.ca/

Fathers, Military

MILITARY ONESOURCE. Run by the Department of Defense, Military OneSource has many valuable resources for deployed dads, dads whose wives are deployed, and their families.
www.militaryonesource.com

MILITARY HOMEFRONT. Another Department of Defense site with great resources for deployed dads and their families.
www.militaryhomefront.dod.mil

MARINE PARENTS. Great resources for Marines and their families.
www.marinedads.org

CINCHOUSE. A community of military wives and women in uniform.
www.cinchouse.com

THE TREASURE OF STAYING CONNECTED FOR MILITARY COUPLES, by Janel Lange. Written to help military couples to go beyond merely surviving deployments to truly nurturing their relationship.

SURVIVING DEPLOYMENT: A GUIDE FOR MILITARY FAMILIES, by Karen M. Pavlicin. Explains the deployment process, how to cope with separation, and reunions.

Fathers, Older

THE BABY CENTER'S BULLETIN BOARD FOR OLDER FATHERS is a great place to get—and give—advice.
boards.babycenter.com/n/pfx/forum.aspx?webtag=bcus6694

Grandparents

THE GRANDPARENTS' WEB consists of links, articles of interest to grandparents, and much more.
www.cyberparent.com/gran

THE AARP has much useful information on their Grandparenting page.
www.aarp.org/families/grandparents

Healthy Living

GREEN LIVING is an online magazine that offers articles on how to make your life greener. The content is updated daily, and it has lots of practical information.
www.ecomall.com/greenshopping

THE GREEN GUIDE is a wonderful Web site filled with tips for green living, with a particular focus on children.
www.thegreenguide.com

GREENHOME. The green superstore—environmentally friendly, reasonably priced alternatives to all the products you currently use.

Men, General

MEN'S HEALTH NETWORK is a national organization that recognizes men's health as a specific social concern. It is committed to improving the health and wellness of men through education campaigns, partnerships with retailers and other private entities, workplace health programs, data collection, and work with health-care providers to provide better programs and funding for men's health needs.
www.menshealthnetwork.org

MENSTUFF bills itself as the national men's resource, and indeed it is. This site is brimming with resources on men, men's health, fatherhood, parenting, relationships, and more.
www.menstuff.org/frameindex.html

GUYVILLE.COM is a light-hearted site where "men can be guys." It's loaded with articles about everything from how to make toast to health tips for men. There's an advice column, and some good links.
www.guyville.com

Money and Finances

PARENTHOOD.COM's Family Finance Center has useful information on everything from life insurance to allowances. Also great links to other sites that help explain money to children.
parenthood.com/categorydisplay.html?IDENTIFIER=76&segment=home

OUR FAMILY PLACE has a practical guide for the average family on how to create a budget and stick to it.
http://www.ourfamilyplace.com/budget.html

Music

Both the companies whose Web sites are given below offer music and movement programs for children and their parents. Classes are offered throughout the United States. Class listings are available on these Web sites.

www.kindermusik.com

www.musictogether.com

Nutrition and Fitness

MEDLINE PLUS is a comprehensive site from the National Institute of Health offering solid information and great links for everything having to do with children's nutrition and physical fitness. Highly recommended.
www.nlm.nih.gov/medlineplus/childnutrition.html

HEALTH A TO Z is a comprehensive, well-integrated health and medical resource developed by health-care professionals. They aim to improve health care by empowering consumers with the online health programs, information, and technology that help them make healthy lifestyle changes for themselves and their families.
www.healthatoz.com/healthatoz/Atoz/default.jsp

THE MAYO CLINIC has a page devoted to children's fitness and nutrition, with links to articles, how to calculate your child's BMI (body mass index), and an "ask the expert" feature. There is also a link to their Children's Health Center, which is well worth exploring.
www.mayoclinic.com/health/childrens-health/CC00049

Reading

THE NEA has a wonderful parents' guide for helping your children learn to read. Many useful links, too.
www.nea.org/parents/learntoread.html

THE AMERICAN LIBRARY ASSOCIATION has reviews of children's books and lists winners of many awards, including the prestigious Caldecott and Newbury Awards for excellence in children's literature and illustration.
www.ala.org

CHILDREN'S LITERATURE provides a searchable database of reviews of the latest children's books.
www.childrenslit.com/#

CHILDREN'S LITERATURE WEB GUIDE has a wealth of information on children's books and authors, reviews, and recommendations, as well as links to many other good sites.
www.ucalgary.ca/~dkbrown

CHINABERRY is a children's book catalog filled with wonderful, hand-picked books for readers of all ages.
www.chinaberry.com

THE HORN BOOK has lists of children's classics, award winners, and other resources for parents.
www.hbook.com

PLANET ESME.COM reviews, rates, and recommends books for kids of all ages.
www.planetesme.com

REVIEWERS' CHECKLIST offers information on and reviews of the best in children's literature.
reviewerschecklist.com

Safety

SAFE KIDS WORLDWIDE is a global network of organizations whose mission is to prevent accidental childhood injury, a leading killer of children fourteen and under.
www.safekids.org

BOOSTERSEAT.GOV has the most up-to-date information on booster seats, as well as an online test you can take to see if your child is ready for a booster. Links to a child safety passenger planner and state-by-state booster seat laws, as well as other ways to make sure your child is safe on the road.
www.boosterseat.gov

MCGRUFF.ORG is for both parents and their children. Updated and maintained by the National Crime Prevention Council, this site uses the familiar crime fighting dog McGruff, along with comics, online games, and other kid-friendly activities, to teach children about personal safety. For parents and teachers, it offers straightforward advice on not only how to keep their kids safe but how to teach their children about safety.
www.mcgruff.org

SAFERCHILD.COM is an A-Z resource for anything and everything having to do with a child's safety, with a searchable database and links to expert voices like Gavin DeBecker, Colin Powell, and Rod Paige. It has won several awards, and after browsing the site for a while, it's easy to see why. We highly recommend this site.
www.saferchild.org/index.html

Sex, Talking with your Child About

THE TALK WITH YOUR KIDS . . . Web site, part of the Talking with Kids about Tough Issues Campaign from Children Now and the Kaiser Family Foundation, has a very good, candid section, with links to suggested reading for parents on this, as well as other difficult issues.
www.talkingwithkids.org/sex.html

PLANNED PARENTHOOD offers sensible advice to parents on what children need to know about sex, and when they need to know it. Good links here, too.
www.plannedparenthood.org/educational-resources/for-parents/how-to-talk-to-your-child-about-sex.htm

MENSTUFF.ORG yet again is a good site to look for advice on how to talk with your kids about sex. It has solid information, and promotes the idea that fathers should be the ones to give "the talk."
www.menstuff.org/issues/byissue/talktoyourkids.html

Television and Other Media

THE NATIONAL INSTITUTE ON MEDIA AND THE FAMILY helps families become "MediaWise." It does not censor anything, but does offer a "KidScore" rating of the latest movies, videos games, and DVDs. With articles, fact sheets, and information on advocacy, the Internet, studies, and more, this nonsectarian, nonprofit, and nonpartisan site is a rich resource.
www.mediafamily.org/index.shtml

THE AMERICAN ACADEMY OF PEDIATRICS presents a clear-cut and informative article on children and television.
www.aap.org/family/tv1.htm

A link to the famous study in *Pediatrics,* "Early Television Exposure and Subsequent Attentional Problems in Children," which linked early television viewing to attention deficit problems in seven-year-olds:
pediatrics.aappublications.org/cgi/content/abstract/113/4/708

THE CENTER FOR SCREEN TIME AWARENESS, home of National TV Turnoff Week, offers alternative activities to television watching, studies on how television watching affects our children both physically and emotionally, and links to many kid-friendly organizations.
www.tvturnoff.org

Stepfamilies/Blended Families

This section of HELPGUIDE.ORG answers just about any question you may have about stepfamilies.
www.helpguide.org/mental/blended_families_stepfamilies.htm

ABOUT.COM offers links to many excellent resources for stepfathers and blended families:
fatherhood.about.com/od/stepfathering/Stepfathering.htm

Stepfamilies

THE STEPFAMILY LIFE. A huge collection of articles, resources, musings, and thoughts on every conceivable topic having to do with stepfamily life.
www.thestepfamilylife.com/Links.htm

THE NATIONAL STEPFAMILY RESOURCE CENTER is a clearing-house of information, resources, and support for stepfamily members and the professionals who work with them. It has absorbed the Stepfamily Association of America, in case you were looking for them.
www.stepfamilies.info

Technology, Smart Toys, Etc.

GAMES 2 TRAIN is a great source of information, resources, reviews, and anything else you could possibly want.
games2train.com

CHILDREN'S TECHNOLOGY REVIEW has reviews and ratings of electronic games, smart toys, and more. Fee based.
www.childrenssoftware.com

Temperament

THE PREVENTIVE OUNCE. A nonprofit, preventive mental health organization started by two psychologists who were frustrated by long-standing behavioral problems in children. Preventive Ounce has wonderful on-line resources that can help make sense of even the most bizarre childhood behavior.
preventiveoz.org

Resources: Additional Books

Adoption

FOR THREE- TO FOUR-YEAR-OLDS:

The Day We Met You, Phoebe Koehler
I Love You Like Crazy Cakes, Rose A. Lewis
Let's Talk About It: Adoption, Fred Rogers
Tell Me Again About the Night I Was Born, Jamie Lee Curtis

FOR FIVE- TO SIX-YEAR-OLDS:

Chinese Eyes, Marjorie A. Waybill
The Coffee Can Kid, Jan M. Czech
Felicia's Favorite Story, Leslea Newman
Heart of Mine: A Story of Adoption, Dan Hojer and Lotta Hojer
Through Moon and Stars and Night Skies, Ann Turner

FOR SEVEN- TO EIGHT-YEAR-OLDS:

A Forever Family, Roslyn Banish with Jennifer Jordan-Wong
Lucy's Feet, Stephanie Stein
Over the Moon: An Adoption Tale, Karen Katz
The Sea Chest, Toni Buzzeo
We Wanted You, Liz Rosenberg

FOR NINE YEARS AND OLDER:

Dancing in the Streets of Brooklyn, April Lurie

Charity and Compassion

FOR THREE- TO FOUR-YEAR-OLDS:

The Paper Crane, Molly Bang

FOR FIVE- TO SIX-YEAR-OLDS:

The Giving Tree, Shel Silverstein
Uncle Willie and the Soup Kitchen, Dyanne DiSalvo-Ryan
Wilfred Gordon McDonald Partridge, Mem Fox

FOR SEVEN- TO EIGHT-YEAR-OLDS:

Aram's Choice, Marsha Skrypuch
A Chance to Shine, Steve and Alan Shamblin
Destiny's Gift, Natasha Anastasia Tarpley
Mr. George and the Red Hat, Stephen Heigh
The Gift, Allana Brodmann
Miss Tizzy, Libby Moore Gray

FOR NINE YEARS AND OLDER:

Number the Stars, Lois Lowry
Ryan and Jimmy, And the Well in Africa That Brought Them Together, Herb Shoveller

Divorce, Separation, and Stepfamilies

FOR THREE- TO FOUR-YEAR-OLDS:

It's Not Your Fault, Koko Bear, Vicki Lansky

Dinosaurs Divorce, Marc Brown
Stepdog, Judith Schermer
Stepfamilies, Fred Rogers
*Was It the Chocolate Pudding? A Story
    for Little Kids about Divorce*, Sandra
    Levins

FOR FIVE- TO SIX-YEAR-OLDS:

Boundless Grace, Mary Hoffman
Jessica's Two Families, Lynn Hugo
The Not So Wicked Stepmother, Lizi Boyd
My Mother's Getting Married, Joan
    Drescher
Room for Rabbit, Ronnie Schotter
Two's Company, Amanda Benjamin

FOR SEVEN- TO EIGHT-YEAR-OLDS:

Families, Susan Kuklin
Like Jake and Me, Mavis Jukes
The Memory String, Eve Bunting
Mister and Me, Kimberly Willis Holt
My Wicked Stepmother, Leach
When We Married Gary, Anna
    Grossnickle Hines

FOR NINE YEARS AND OLDER:

*Divorce Happens to the Nicest Kids: A Self-
    Help Book for Kids*, Michael Prokop
How Tia Lola Came to (Visit) Stay, Julia
    Alvarez
The Nose from Jupiter, Richard Scrimger
The Truth Cookie, Fiona Dunbar
Witch Twins, Adele Griffin

Fears and Feelings

FOR THREE- TO FOUR-YEAR-OLDS:

There's a Monster under My Bed, James
    Howe
*When Sophie Gets Angry . . . Really,
    Really Angry*, Molly Bang

FOR FIVE- TO SIX-YEAR-OLDS:

Glad Monster, Sad Monster, Anne
    Miranda
Lizzy's Ups and Downs, Jessica Harper
There's No Such Thing As a Dragon, Jack
    Kent

FOR SEVEN- TO EIGHT-YEAR-OLDS:

The Feelings Book, Lynda Madison
Shiela Rae the Brave, Kevin Henkes
Thunder Cake, Patricia Polacco

FOR NINE YEARS AND OLDER:

*How Artists See Feelings: Joy, Sadness,
    Fear, Love*, Colleen Carroll
The Last Dog on Earth, Daniel Ehrenhaft
*My Own Thoughts and Feelings (for
    Boys): A Young Boy's Workbook About
    Exploring Problems*, Wendy Deaton,

Going to the Doctor or Dentist

FOR THREE- TO FOUR-YEAR-OLDS:

The Crocodile and the Dentist, Taro Gomi
Doctor De Soto, William Steig

Dora, Show Me Your Smile! Christine
   Ricci
Harry and the Dinosaurs Say "Raaah!"
   Ian Whybrow
Nicky Goes to the Doctor (Look, Look),
   Richard Scarry
When You're Sick or in the Hospital, Tom
   McGrath

Friendships

FOR THREE- TO FOUR-YEAR-OLDS:

Be Quiet, Marina, Kirsten Debear
Bear's New Friend, Karma Wilson
Best Best Friends, Margaret Chodos-Irvine
Hunter's Best Friend at School, Laura
   Malone Elliott
Just My Friend & Me, Mercer Mayer
Tobin Learns to Make Friends, Diane
   Murrell

FOR FIVE- TO SIX-YEAR-OLDS:

Best Friends for Frances, Russell Hoban,
Bravo, Mildred and Ed! Karen Wagner
How to Lose All Your Friends, Nancy
   Carlson
May I Bring a Friend?, Beatrice de
   Regniers
Nothing Scares Us, Frieda Wishinsky

FOR SEVEN- TO EIGHT-YEAR-OLDS:

How to Be a Friend, Laurie Krasny Brown
How to Make Friends with a Giant,
   Gennifer Choldenko
Toot & Puddle: The New Friend, Holly
   Hobbie

FOR NINE YEARS AND OLDER:

Holes, Louis Sachar
I Like the Way You Are, Eve Bunting
Worst Enemies/Best, Annie Bryant
*The Quiz Book: Clues to You & Your
   Friends,* Laura Allen
The Friend Factory, Gary Crow

Grief and Death

FOR THREE- TO FOUR-YEAR-OLDS:

Everett Anderson's Good-bye, Lucille
   Clifton
Goodbye Mousie, Robie Harris
I Know I Made It Happen, Lynn Bennett
   Blackburn
Jasper's Day, Marjorie Blain Parker
When Dinosaurs Die, Laurie Krasny
   Brown and Marc Brown
When a Pet Dies, Fred Rogers

FOR FIVE- TO SIX-YEAR-OLDS:

Don't Despair on Thursday, Adolph Moser
Goodbye Lulu, Corinne Demas
Grandpa, John Burningham
Gran-Gran's Best Trick, L. Dwight
   Holden, M.D.
Grandfather Twilight, Barbara Berger
*I Wish I Could Hold Your Hand: A Child's
   Guide to Loss and Grief,* Pat Palmer
Lifetimes, Bryan Mellonie
The Tenth Good Thing about Barney,
   Judith Viorst

FOR SEVEN- TO
EIGHT-YEAR-OLDS:

Arvy Aardvark Finds Hope, Donna
O'Toole
The Bridge to Terebithia, Katherine
Paterson
After Charlotte's Mom Died, Cornelia
Spelman
Dad! Why'd You Leave Me? Dorothy Frost
Help Me Say Goodbye, Janis Silverman
Lost and Found, Ellen Yeomans
Stinky Stern Forever, Michelle Edwards

FOR NINE YEARS
AND OLDER:

A Child Remembers, Enid Samuel
Traisman
After You Lose Someone You Love, Amy,
Allie, and David Dennison
A Keepsake of Special Memories, Laurie
Van-Si and Lynn Powers
The Last Goodbye, Jim and Joan Boulden

Moving

FOR THREE- TO
FOUR-YEAR-OLDS:

Gila Monsters Meet You at the Airport,
Marjorie Weinman Sharmat
Good-bye, House, Frank Asch
Moving, Fred Rogers

FOR FIVE- TO
SIX-YEAR-OLDS:

Janey, Charlotte Zolotow
The Lost and Found Home, Michael
Cadnum
We Are Best Friends, Aliki

FOR SEVEN- TO
EIGHT-YEAR-OLDS:

*Alexander; Who's Not (Do You Hear Me? I
Mean It!) Going to Move*, Judith Viorst
Moving Day, Ralph Fletcher
New Home, New School, Lynne Caloggero

FOR NINE YEARS
AND OLDER:

*Big Ernie's New Home: A Story for Young
Children Who Are Moving*, Teresa
Martin
Who Will Be My Friends? Syd Hoff

Siblings

FOR THREE- TO
FOUR-YEAR-OLDS:

A Baby Sister for Frances, Russell Hoban
Silly Mommy, Silly Daddy, Marie-Louise
Fitzpatrick
Welcome Precious, Nikki Grimes,
illustrated by Bryan Collier

FOR FIVE- TO
SIX-YEAR-OLDS:

Darcy and Gran Don't Like Babies, Jane
Cutler
Elizabeti's Doll, Stephanie Stuve-Bodeen
*She Come Bringing Me That Little Baby
Girl*, Eloise Greenfield

FOR SEVEN- TO
EIGHT-YEAR-OLDS:

Henry's Baby, Mary Hoffman
I Love You the Purplest, Barbara Joosse
Jamaica Tag-Along, Juanita Havill

Special Needs/Disabilities

FOR THREE- TO FOUR-YEAR-OLDS:

My Friend Isabelle, Eliza Woloson, et al.
Susan Laughs, Jeanne Willis

FOR FIVE- TO SIX-YEAR-OLDS:

The Safe Place, Tehila Peterseil
He's My Brother, Joe Laske
Keisha's Doors, Marvie Ellis

FOR SEVEN- TO EIGHT-YEAR-OLDS:

Dancing with Katya, Dori Chaconas
Pippi Goes to School, Astrid Lundgren
The View from Saturday, E.L. Konigsberg

FOR NINE YEARS AND OLDER:

Extraordinary People With Disabilities, Deborah Kent
The Survival Guide for Kids With LD, Gary L. Fisher
Niagara Falls, Or Does It? H. Winkler, et al.

REFERENCE BOOKS

The Book of How, Harry N. Abrams
Children's Miscellany Too: More Useless Information That's Essential to Know, Chronicle Books
DK Illustrated Factopedia, DK Publishing
Kingfisher Illustrated Pocket Thesaurus, Kingfisher
Macmillan Dictionary for Children, Simon & Schuster
My Little Picture Atlas, DK Publishing
Our Universe, National Geographic
World Almanac for Kids, World Almanac

Books with Positive Father Role Models

The Abbeville Anthology of Father and Daughter Tales, Josephine Evetts-Secher
All Those Secrets of the World, Jane Yolen
Always My Dad, Sharon Dennis Wyeth
Animal Dads, Sneed Collard
Are We There Yet, Daddy? Virginia Walters
The Barefoot Book of Father and Son Tales, Josephine Evetts-Sacker
Bea and Mr. Jones, Amy Schwartz
Benny Bakes a Cake, Eve Rice
The Berenstain Bears and the Papa's Day Surprise, Stan and Jan Berenstain
Breakfast with my Father, Ron Roy
Butterfly Kisses: A Narrative Poem Celebrating the Love between Fathers and Daughters, Bob and Brooke Carlisle
Buttons, Brock Cole
At the Crossroads, Rachel Isadora
A Cloak for the Dreamer, Aileen Friedman
Dad and Me, Peter Catalanotto
Daddies Are for Catching Fireflies, Harriet Ziefert
Daddy and Ben Together, Miriam B. Stecher
Daddy, Jeannette Franklin Caines and Ronald Himler Caines
Daddy All Day Long, Francesca Rusackas
Daddy and Me, Catherine Daly-Weir
Daddy and Me, Karen Katz
The Daddy Book, Todd Parr
Daddy Day, Daughter Day, Larry King
Daddy Is a Doodlebug, Bruce Degen
Daddy Makes the Best Spaghetti, Anna Grossnickle Hines:
Daddy's Lulla, Tony Bradman
Dad's Back, Ormerod, Jan
Dad's Dinosaur Day, Diane Dawson Hearn

David's Father, Robert Munsch
The Day I Saw My Father Cry, Bill Cos
The Day the Dog Dressed Like Dad, Tom Amico
Dear Daddy, Phillipe Dupasquier
Else-Marie and Her Seven Little Daddies, Pija Lindenbaum
Emily and Her Daddy, Claire Masurel
Faraway Home, Jane Kurtz
Farm Morning, David McPhail
Father Bear's Special Day, Else Holmelund Minarik
The Father Who Had 10 Children, Benedicte Guetier
Father and Son, Denize Lauture
50 Below Zero, Robert Munsch
Fishing in the Air, Sharon Creech
Fishing with Dad, Shelley Rotner
Friday Night Is Papa Night, Ruth A. Sonneborn
Good bye, Geese, Nancy Carlstrom
Guess How Much I Love You, Sam McBratney
Hop on Pop-up! Dr. Seuss
How Many Stars in the Sky, Lenny Hort
I Already Know I Love You, Billy Crystal
I Love My Daddy, Sebastien Braun
I Love My Daddy Because, Laurel Porter-Gaylord
I Love You, Dad, Iris Hiskey Amo
I Shop With My Daddy, Grace MacCarone
If I Were Your Father, Margaret Park Bridges
I'll See You When the Moon Is Full, Susi Gregg Fowler
In Daddy's Arms I Am Tall: African, Javaka Steptoe
I'm Not Sleepy, Dennis Cazet
Just Like Daddy, Frank Asch
Just Me and My Dad, Mercer Mayer
Just My Dad and Me, Leah Komaiko
Just the Two of Us, Will Smith
Kevin and His Dad, Irene Smalls
Little Nino's Pizzeria, Karen Barbour
Lots of Dads, Shelley Rotner

Me and My Dad, Stuart E. Hample
My Dad, Anthony Browne
My Dad Can Do Anything, Stephen Krensky
My Dad Is Awesome, Nick Butterworth
My Daddy, Susan Paradis
My Daddy Was A Soldier, Ray, Deborah Kogan
My Father Always Embarrasses Me, Meir Shalev
My Father Is in the Navy, Robin McKinley
My Grandpa Is Amazing, Nick Butterworth
My Father's Boat, Sherry Garland
My Man Blue: *Poems*, Nikki Grimes
My Ol' Man, Patricia Polacco
My Dad Is Really Something, Lois Osborn
Octopus Hug, Laurence Pringle
On a Wintry Morning, Dori Chaconas and Stephen T. Johnson
Owl Moon, Jane Yolen
Papa, Please Get the Moon for Me, Eric Carle
Papa Tells Chita a Story, Elizabeth Fitzgerald Howard
A Perfect Father's Day, Eve Bunting
Popcorn at the Palace, Emily Arnild McCully
Posy, Charlotte Pomerantz
Ramona and Her Father, Beverly Cleary
Ramona Quim, Age 8, Beverly Cleary
Sam, Bangs, and Moonshine, Evaline Ness
The Sick Day, Patricia MacLachlan
Someday with My Father, Helen Elizabeth Buckley and Ellen Buckley
The Ten Best Things about My Dad, Christine Loomis
33 Uses for a Dad, Harriet Ziefert
Treed: A Pride of Irate Lions, Nathan Zimelman
What Dads Can't Do, Douglas Wood

What Makes My Daddy Best, Burton Albert

What Mommies Do Best/What Daddies Do Best, Laura Joffe Numeroff

When Daddy Came to School, Julie Brillhart

White Dynamite and Curly Kidd, Bill Martin Jr. and John Archambault

Easy Readers

Frida's Office Day, Thomas P. Lewis

Henry and Mudge and the Forever Sea, Cynthia Rylant

Let Me Help! Louise Vitellaro Tidd

My Day at the Baseball Game, Heather L. Feldman

Father's Day

The Berenstain Bears and the Papa's Day Surprise, Stan Berenstain and Jan Berenstain

Happy Father's Day, Marylin Hafner

Happy Father's Day, Steven Kroll

Hooray for Father's Day, Marjorie Weinman Sharmat

A Perfect Father's Day, Eve Bunting

Great Books Specifically for Fathers of Girls (suggested by Linda Nielsen, author of *Embracing Your Father: How to Build the Relationship You've Always Wanted with Your Dad* [McGraw Hill, 2004])

Two Old Potatoes and Me, John Coy

Give Her the River, Michael Browne

A Twinkle in His Eye, Yvette Burton

Animal Dads, Sneed Collard

The Dance, Richard Paul Evans

Daddy Will Be There, Lois Grambling

Tiny's Hat, Ann Grifalconi

After Charlotte's Mom Died, Cornelia Spelman

Night Shift Daddy, Eileen Spinelli

I Live with Daddy, Judith Vigna

Books for Kids Whose Dads Are, or Will Soon Be, Deployed

Daddy Got His Orders, Kathy Mitchell

Daddy Is a Soldier, Kirsten Hallowell

Daddy, Will You Miss Me? Wendy McCormick

Daddy, You're My Hero (and Mommy, You're My Hero), Michelle Ferguson-Cohen

Daddy's in Iraq, but I Want Him Back, Carmen R. Hoyt

I'm Already Home . . . Again: Keeping Your Family Close While on Assignment or Deployment, Elaine Gray Dumler

To Keep Me SAFE! Sarah R. Jones

While You Are Away, Eileen Spinelli

A Year without Dad, Jodi Brunson

A Yellow Ribbon for Daddy, Anissa Mersiowsky

Films with Positive Portrayals of Fathers

Around the World in 80 Days

Breaking Away

Bye Bye Love

Changing Lanes

Cheaper by the Dozen

Chitty Chitty Bang Bang

Crusade

The Diary of Anne Frank

Mrs. Doubtfire

Father of the Bride

Fern Gully

Fiddler on the Roof

Field of Dreams

Finding Nemo

Fly Away Home

Frequency

Friendly Persuasion

Gladiator

Godfather

Guess Who's Coming to Dinner

Iron Giant

To Kill a Mockingbird

Kramer vs. Kramer

Life Is Beautiful

The Lion King

The Little Princess

Meet Me in St. Louis

Meet the Parents

Mr. Skeffington

Ordinary People

Our Vines Have Tender Grapes

The Patriot

Pursuit of Happyness

The Rookie

Shenandoah

Sins of the Children

Sixteen Candles

A Soldier's Daughter Never Cries

The Sound of Music

Spiderman (technically a positive uncle)

Three Men and a Baby

Watch on the Rhine

It's a Wonderful Life

The World of Henry Orient

The Yearling

You Can't Take It with You

ILLUSTRATION CREDITS

Index

3 TO 9 YEARS:
HEIGHT-FOR-AGE AND WEIGHT-FOR-AGE PERCENTILES

These charts are very similar to the ones used by your child's pediatrician. Please remember that "normal" is something of a sliding scale and use these charts for reference only. As always, if you're worried about your child's growth, be sure to discuss your concerns with his or her doctor.

BOYS

GIRLS

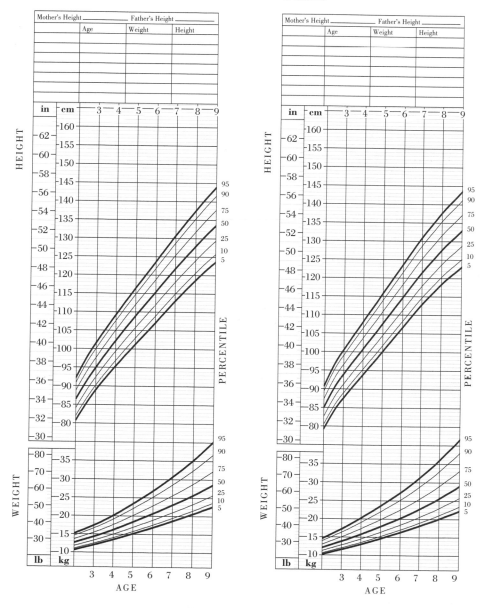

About the Author

A nationally recognized parenting expert, **Armin Brott** is also the author of
*The Expectant Father: Facts, Tips, and Advice for Dads-to-be, Fathering Your
Toddler: A Dad's Guide to the Second and Third Years, The Single Father: A
Dad's Guide to Parenting without a Partner*, and *Father for Life: A Journey of Joy,
Challenge, and Change*. He has written on parenting and fatherhood for *The
New York Times Magazine, The Washington Post, Newsweek*, and dozens of other
periodicals. He also writes a nationally syndicated column, "Ask Mr. Dad," and
hosts "Positive Parenting," a weekly talk show. Armin lives with his family in
Oakland, California. To learn more, please visit his Web site, www.mrdad.com.

ARMIN BROTT: OVER 1,000,000 FATHERHOOD BOOKS IN PRINT!

THE EXPECTANT FATHER
BOXED SET
FATHER KNOWS BEST
ISBN 978-0-7892-0824-8 · $39.95
EXPECTANT FATHER
*Facts, Tips, and Advice for
Dads-to-Be*
NEW FATHER
A Dad's Guide to the First Year
FATHERING YOUR TODDLER
*A Dad's Guide to the Second
and Third Years*

EXPECTANT AND
FIRST-YEAR FATHER
BOXED SET
ISBN 978-0-7892-0840-8 · $27.50
EXPECTANT FATHER
*Facts, Tips, and Advice for
Dads-to-Be*
NEW FATHER
A Dad's Guide to the First Year

THE NEW FATHER SERIES
BOXED SET
ISBN 978-0-7892-0825-5 · $27.50
NEW FATHER
A Dad's Guide to the First Year
FATHERING YOUR TODDLER
*A Dad's Guide to the Second and
Third Years*

THE EXPECTANT FATHER
SECOND EDITION
Facts, Tips, and Advice for Dads-to-Be
By Armin A. Brott and Jennifer Ash
30 black-and-white illustrations
272 pages · 6 x 9"
Paper · 978-0-7892-0538-4 · $11.95
Hardcover · 978-0-7892-0537-7 ·
$16.95

THE NEW FATHER
SECOND EDITION
A Dad's Guide to the First Year
By Armin A. Brott
30 black-and-white illustrations
320 pages · 6 x 9"
Paper · 978-0-7892-0815-6 · $12.95
Hardcover · 978-0-7892-0806-4 ·
$18.95

FATHERING YOUR TODDLER
SECOND EDITION
*A Dad's Guide to the Second and
Third Years*
By Armin A. Brott
20 black-and-white illustrations
288 pages · 6 x 9"
Paper · 978-0-7892-0850-7 · $12.95
Hardcover · 978-0-7892-0849-1 ·
$18.95

*Available from your favorite bookstore, or at www.abbeville.com,
or by calling* 1-800-ARTBOOK